What the reviewers have to say about
The Self-Sufficient Sailor...

"Nothing can keep you cruising longer, safer, and on a lower budget than self-sufficiency, and no one knows more about the subject than Lin and Larry Pardey. They draw on 29 years of cruising to reveal how to handle your boat under sail and at anchor, how to build trust and teamwork in your crew, and how to fortify your boat with backup systems—advice that will keep you sailing onward instead of stuck in port waiting for repair parts."
  Tom Linskey, Senior Editor, *SAIL Magazine*

"When Larry and Lin chose the title for their book they chose well—to go ocean sailing you must be self-sufficient. Yet the same truth applies to all seamanship. Ten miles offshore in any water you must look after yourself...and you must prepare thoroughly while still in port, for there is nobody else to carry the can. That is why we all have something to learn from this book—from authors who have put into practice a principle that applies to us all, but who have done it for longer and farther than most of us will ever do."
  Denny Desoutter, Editor, *Practical Boat Owner*

"*The Self-Sufficient Sailor* is an excellent book full of seakeeping, boatkeeping, and seamanship hints laced with cruising philosophy. If you are going to sea, say the Pardeys, you must learn to operate with little or no outside help...One of the prerequisites is to learn to sail before you go cruising. I couldn't agree more. The Pardeys write that if you learn how to not fall overboard and to keep your boat in good shape, then you very seldom will need safety harnesses. I agree, though many modern sailors do not. Frequently one sees boats that are equipped with all kinds of safety gear...the crews of many of those boats could well need that safety equipment, because the money they spent on equipment should have been spent on making their boats seaworthy. This book should be read by everyone who is doing serious cruising."
  Donald M. Street, Jr., author of *Street's Cruising Guide to the Eastern Caribbean*

"I had the pleasure of reading this book while making a passage from Newport, Rhode Island, to Bermuda on my own cutter, *Frolic*, and wrote this review while anchored in St. Georges Harbor among 15 or 20 other cruising boats. The emphasis that the Pardeys place on simplicity and self-sufficiency makes especially good sense when read at sea; their observations on the drawbacks of cruising large and complicated boats was proven true by the experiences related to me by the sailors here in Bermuda. Just as the Pardeys predict, the small cruisers had uneventful, if not smooth, passages without crew problems—even in rough weather. The larger boats, sailing on the same ocean at the same time, told tales of 'vicious' storms, failed engines, pumps, radios, and electronic equipment, and scared and unhappy crew. Cruising isn't easy, but the Pardeys make excellent recommendations. They offer sound advice on a wide variety of subjects."

Danny Green, *Cruising World*

The
Self-sufficient
Sailor

By the same authors

Cruising in *Seraffyn*
Seraffyn's European Adventure
The Care and Feeding of the Sailing Crew
Serraffyn's Mediterranean Adventure
Serraffyn's Oriental Adventure
The Capable Cruiser
Details of Classic Boat Construction—The Hull
Storm Tactics Handbook
Cost Conscious Cruiser

The
Self-Sufficient
Sailor

Larry and Lin Pardey

Revised Edition

Pardey Books

Visit Lin & Larry at www.paracay.com

Revised Edition—1997
Copyright 1982 and 1997 by Mary Lin and Lawrence F. Pardey
Cover design—Robert C. Johnson
Text design and editorial—Allison Peter
Manufacturing assistance—Mike Schubel
Manufactured in the USA by Thomson Shore Inc.

Grateful acknowledgement is made to Brian Hales, cartoonist, and *Yachting World* for permission to reprint three cartoons from "The Curse of Cruising," by Lin Pardey

Library of Congress Cataloging in Publication Data
Pardey, Larry.
        The self-sufficient sailor.
        Includes index.
        1. Seamanship. 2. Sailing. I. Pardey, Lin.
II. Title.
GV811.5.P37 1982   623.88   81-16951
                                       AACR2

Pardey Books—distributed by Paradise Cay Publishing, P.O. Box 29, Arcata, CA 95518-0029, 800-736-4509

3 4 5 6 7 8 9 0
ISBN 0-9646036-7-5

Contents

Preface

Can there be a yachtsman—or shall I say a "cruising yachtsman"—who has not dreamed of escaping to wide oceans and distant landfalls, of making his boat an almost permanent home from which to view the world? Inspired by a hundred classic writers, from Alain Gerbault to William Robinson, from Harry Pidgeon to Frank Wightman (you can name whom you like), we have all at some time said "if." If we had the money; if we had the time; if we were free of family ties... Too many of us missed our chance in the past, but younger generations are more enterprising, and in the post-war decades a steadily growing number of couples (not always young, I should add) have put their faith, their skill, and their material resources into a 10-tonner and have cast off across the world.

The Pardeys epitomize the modern breed of blue-water sailors. Modest in character and modest in means they quietly set forth in their 24-foot *Seraffyn*. She was certainly not a big boat, nor half so lavishly equipped as many a Saturday afternoon racer which will never see the real sea. It was not in money or mechanical means that the Pardeys put their faith, but in themselves.

As thousands of others have discovered, in the great oceans self-reliance is all that counts. Homewaters sailors are urged, by those who profess to know what others should do, to carry a liferaft, plenty of pyrotechnics, and a VHF radio to call someone else to their assistance. On the wide ocean and far from home, the small boat sailor in need of help must look to himself.

So when Lin and Larry chose the title for their book they chose well—to go ocean sailing you must be self-sufficient. Yet the same truth applies to all seamanship. Ten miles offshore in any water and you must look after yourself...and you must prepare thoroughly while still in port, for there is nobody else to carry the can. That is why we all have something to learn from this book—from authors who have put into practice a principle that applies to us all, but who have done it for longer and farther than most of us will ever do.

Denny Desoutter,
Editor, *Practical Boat Owner*

Poole, Dorset, England

About the Revised Edition and Acknowledgements

It has been 17 years since we wrote the first edition of this book. Things have changed for us during those years. We built and launched *Seraffyn's* bigger sister, *Taleisin,* a 29-foot, 6-inch cutter designed by Lyle Hess. Then we had the pleasure of cruising over 47,000 miles in *Taleisin,* around three of the southern capes of the world, and on to amazing adventures, including horsetreks through the wilds of California and of Northern Tasmania, a seven-month photo safari through four of the southern African countries in a 4-wheel-drive vehicle, a summer of racing with Irish fishermen in their 150-year-old workboats on the bay of Galway. Along with delivering several more boats and adding a solar panel to *Taleisin* so we could make videos, we also began giving seminars for potential cruisers every few years. This not only helps our cruising kitty, but might hopefully work as an antidote to the heavy dose of media pressure that is causing potential cruisers to think "getting out there" costs far too much for any but a few wealthy souls.

For potential cruisers there are changes too. Now there are twice the number of safety items offered "off the shelf," with pressures applied to make sailors feel they might be somehow remiss if they don't buy and carry each and every one. There are far more cruising guides, far more cruising rallies, and probably more cruisers out there to crowd the wonderful places where once people could get off on their own.

Fortunately, as far as cruising goes, change is only superficial. Year after year, the vast majority of cruisers choose to stick to the same routes, visiting the same favorite ports. So for those willing to go only 30 or 40 miles off the beaten track, there are still wonderful, rarely visited places to explore, spots where local people are eager to invite new friends into their lives. Rallies of all types still visit only one or two ports in any country and leave the lovely isolated anchorages for cruisers with more leisurely timetables.

The sea doesn't change, either. It is still a highway to wonderful new adventures—a place where, if you are prepared and willing to be uncomfortable occasionally, you can feel as if you are in control of your own life, your own destiny. But because the sea never changes, the message in this book is doubly important during a time when so many people offer electronic and mechanical devices as answers to all of the potential problems you could encounter out cruising. The key to successful voyaging today is the same as it always has been—self-sufficiency.

That is why we have chosen to update this book and revise it. Everything in it is still valid and important for potential cruisers to consider. In the interests of economy (i.e., to make sure this book doesn't cost you 20% or 30% more), we have not changed the format of the original edition but, instead when possible, have added information at the end of each chapter. In some cases, where space was not available, we have added the update at the end of the book, on pages 313 through 315.

Many people have helped us with this book; some, such as Ron Wall, Gordon Yates, Tony Crispino, Bob Dorris, Eric and Susan Hiscock, Hal Roth, and Lyle Hess, gave us ideas for the original articles. Eric Swenson and Sam Lovel encouraged us when we first wrote this book, as did Spencer Smith. Patience Wales, editor of *SAIL Magazine,* helped us not only with the original project but with this revision as well. Thanks to all of them, plus Tom Linskey, senior editor at *SAIL,* Rob Johnson, and Allison Peter for their help, and Matt Morehouse for his input.

Special appreciation goes to Micky and Randy Short of Oxnard, California, who provided us with a wonderful hideaway on the edge of the bay so we could do this revision.

Our thanks also go to all of the warm, friendly sailors we've met everywhere we've been. It was with them that we discussed the questions about cruising, sailing, and boat maintenance that eventually led to each of these chapters.

Lin and Larry Pardey
On board *Taleisin,* en route to Scotland, summer 1997

Introduction

About a month after we arrived in the Gulf Islands of British Columbia, we met a delightful sailing enthusiast. We'd been enjoying meandering from cove to cove among the hundreds of islands while we recovered from the mental and cultural shock of our forty-nine-day North Pacific crossing. As soon as we dropped our anchor in front of his house, Greg came out to invite us in for a drink of hot chocolate next to his fireplace.

Late the next afternoon, the three of us took a short sail around the island and as the September day drew to a nippy close, Lin went below to warm up the cabin while Greg and I sailed into the bay, set the anchor, and furled *Seraffyn's* sails.

When we climbed below, Lin had hot fresh bread ready along with bowls full of thick French onion soup with gobs of baked cheese on top. The stereo was playing an Andres Segovia tape, one of my favorites. The oil lamps kept the cabin warm and cheerful. I urged Greg to settle back into what I call my lotus position—back against the bulkhead, legs up on the settee, elbow on the table. He relaxed, swung his feet up, and after commenting on the easy way our gravity water system let Lin fill the tea kettle for another round of hot buttered rum, he asked, "I hope you don't mind me being personal, but how do you do it? How have you been able to afford to live like this for the past ten years? How does *Seraffyn* look so organized even though you've gone over 40,000 miles on her?"

Both Lin and I tried to answer at the same time, "We've kept our overhead down by trying to simplify everything." We'd been asked this same question probably five hundred times in thirty-two different countries. We'd been asked through Japanese, Polish, Russian, Spanish, and Finnish translators. We'd tried to answer it in articles for various yachting magazines over the past five years.

After I rowed Greg home, Lin and I spent several hours trying to figure out how to put the answer clearly and concisely on paper. We discussed the fact that *Seraffyn* had never had a gear failure, that in spite of working only three or four months a year we were financially sound, and that we still looked forward to more cruising together. "If you want to sum it up," Lin said, "we've tried every way we can to become a self-sufficient team."

But that's too pat an answer. I suggested thinking about some of the articles we'd written that caused interesting comments from people we met in our wanderings. A common thread seemed to run through the most popular ones: choosing and outfitting your boat to make it simpler and easier to maintain and cruise in. In the end Lin and I decided the best answer to Greg's question and to those of hundreds of good friends *Seraffyn* has helped us make, would be this book, a collection of several of our most popular older articles and some new ones.

This is our answer to the couple or young sailor who earns just an average salary in today's changeable, rushing society. If you want to do more than dream of taking six months, a year, or a whole lifetime off to go wandering, we hope this book gives you some of the clues that help you become a self-sufficient sailor.

GUARANTEE

Not one of the ideas expressed in this book is new, original, or very clever. Each one comes from sailors we've met in one or another of three hundred ports around the northern hemisphere. Each idea has been tested at sea by us and several other sailors. So we know they work.

The
Self-sufficient
Sailor

How Can I Do It?

How can I get the sailing experience to go cruising? How can I earn a living out there? What size boat can I afford and sail easily? Wow, can I really make big money delivering some rich guy's yacht?

The four chapters in Section I answer common financial questions like these that we've been asked by interested would-be cruisers.

1

Hitchhiking across Oceans

It's April and the bulletin boards in Malta are sprouting signs like: "Crew needed this week for passage to Athens"; "Charter boat seeks cordon bleu cook"; "Willing crew available to go anywhere"; "Couple seeking passage toward England." The sailing magazines have whole columns of crew positions in their classified advertising sections. Summer is coming and people want to go sailing. Charter boats need crew. Delivery skippers need crew. Cruising boats without self-steering vanes need crew. Single-handers tired of being alone need crew.

During the past five years there has been a huge increase in the number of large private sailing boats and charter yachts. These vessels aren't staying in one marina anymore. They are making ocean crossings, circumnavigations or year-long meandering cruises. Few of their owners are willing to hire full-time professional crewmembers. At first they are able to fill their crew ranks with friends and relatives who want a few week's holiday. But as the friends and relatives use up their free time or run out of spare funds, more and more good crewing positions become available for would-be wanderers.

We've personally met several hundred people hitchhiking across oceans. It can be a great way to travel and will introduce you to a whole new way of life. It will also give you good practical information for that day when you buy or build your own cruising boat. When we delivered a 50-ton ketch from Palma, Mallorca, to New Orleans, one of our crew was a delightful twenty-three-year-old New Yorker who had just spent six months backpacking in Europe and wanted to save his air fare home. Another friend, Phin, took a crew-woman to cook on his 60-foot schooner for the voyage from Tahiti toward Singapore. Then he married her in Bali five months later and we met them a year after that on their way through the Mediterranean.

How can you find these crew positions? Unfortunately, to locate the best rides you need some money and lots of time. Many people find a spot by reading advertisements in sailing magazines or local yachting newspapers. This is a good way to hitch rides out of places like England, Scandinavia, or New England. But you will find your best chances by actually going to ports in the sunshine belt or places where sailors stop to refit or restock before they set off across oceans.

One of the best places to look is Gibraltar from October to December if you wish to cross the Atlantic, April to June if you want to head eastward into the Mediterranean; Malta, Rhodes, and Piraeus are similar to Gibraltar. For a trip across the Atlantic, look in Tenerife, Canary Islands, from October to January. Antigua, Barbados, St. Thomas, and Puerto Rico abound with open crew spots during October and November. Panama is a good place to look anytime of the year, but for west-bound rides May seems a popular month, and few people head into the Caribbean during the hurricane season. Tahiti is reported to be a good place to look around July 14 each year. Singapore and Honolulu are two other places well worth a try; best months depend on which way you wish to go. Wherever charter boats congregate for the off-season, you might pick up an interesting job: Miami, San Francisco, Long Beach, San Diego. All major ports where crusing people do their final outfitting before heading offshore are worth a try.

You'll need money to find a good crew position. It's unwise and usually difficult to find the position you want without spending two or three weeks looking in each port. In fact the most successful potential crewmembers have the money to move to another country or another port if their quest demands. How much money you need depends on your tastes. In Spain or other Mediterranean countries you'll need about $15 a day to live meagerly and have shelter over your head. Then you'll have expenses once you find a berth. Few people are willing to take on a crewmember and pay all of his/her expenses. You may be asked to share in food costs. You'll definitely need money for drinks or dinners ashore, a new pair of sandals, a few books, or souvenirs. Based on discussions we've had with people crewing on long-distance cruising boats, $400 a month will usually prove sufficient once you have a berth.

But the most important expense anyone becoming a crewmember must plan for is what we call the "Crewmember's Insurance Fund." This is a minimum of $900 that is put aside in such a way that you can't easily spend it. This money is for airfare home from the farthest place you are likely to reach. It is really important and could mean the difference between having a fine adventure and quitting cruising for life. If you have this insurance fund, you won't feel forced to take any berth that comes along just because you are broke. If you happen to choose unwisely and end up as crew on a boat full of problems, you will have the financial security to move on or to say to the skipper, "Hey, let's try to straighten this situation out." Being trapped on an unhappy cruising boat because you are too broke to fly out could be worse than being in prison. (Though at first glance $900 may seem like too little insurance, it is enough because most international airlines give a discount of 25 percent or more on one-way airfares, depending where you fly from, to seaman being repatriated. To qualify for a special seaman's ticket you need to present proof that you are being removed from the crew's list of a vessel that has arrived from a foreign port. For further information on this, contact the business office of the overseas desk, not the reservation desk. One further benefit of flying this way is that returning seaman are given a double luggage allowance.)

One way of extending your funds while you look for a good berth is to offer your services as a varnisher, painter, or general handyman on any large yacht in the harbor, either power or sail. It's rare when you can't find one that needs a hand. Usually you'll be offered a bunk and meals for a few hours labor each day. Not only will this save you money, but it will put you in a ringside seat where you can get first-hand information on which boats are going where. You will also be earning yourself a valuable recommendation. I know we chose the crew we mentioned earlier for that delivery to New Orleans because Malcolm Horsley, the skipper on *Stormvogel*, a 75-footer being refitted in Palma, told us, "Richard has been living with us for two weeks. He's easy to be around, works hard at anything we ask him to do, and cleans up after himself." We picked Richard from among four potential crew on this recommendation.

As you consider the various berths available to you, remember that you will be living with these people twenty-four hours a day—working, eating, sleeping, putting up with bad weather, and playing within 20 or 30 feet of each other for weeks on end. You'll be putting your life in the hands of the skipper. So it pays to learn enough beforehand to judge not only the qualifications of the skipper, but the seaworthiness of his boat. It's worthwhile taking the time to ask around for recommendations. If a crew is leaving, find out why. It may be a simple personality conflict, time for the crew to go home to a job or school, or time for him or her to move on to a more exciting position on another yacht. But there may be more serious reasons. A friend of ours became tired of single-handed sailing and jumped at the berth that was offered to him by a husband and wife sailing with their long-limbed, blue-eyed eighteen-year-old daughter. Bill had met the young Costa Rican that had crewed on this family's 40-foot sloop during the previous three months, but he had never thought to ask Jose why he was leaving. Bill sold his 25-foot Folkboat and sailed off as crew, bound for the Caribbean. Pretty soon he learned the truth. The family was broke. So he loaned them first $500, then another $500, with their reassurances that he would be paid back "as soon as we reach Miami when the whole family will be going back to work." After three months the family owed him $4,000, all the money he'd received for his Folkboat. When he stopped the cash flow the family made life unbearable and finally kicked him off the boat in Colombia, South America. Bill never recovered his money. But as Bill told us later, "I never asked anyone about that family. Jose had the same problem; that's why he left. Not only that, but they bragged to me about all the shipyard bills they'd skipped out on." A bit of quiet investigation at the local chandleries or shipyards and among the cruising fleet could have prevented this awful experience.

I was walking into Corfu, Greece, when I met an Australian who had responded to a newspaper advertisement and joined a 38-foot yacht bound directly for the Mediterranean. "I'd sailed dinghies before," James told me, "but nothing prepared me for the last 10,000 miles. We worked like dogs for a week to get ready. Then we had 31 days at sea. Arrived in Djibouti and spent two weeks repairing the boat. Set off up the Red Sea, 18 days without stopping. One day off in Suez; ten days sailing to Greece. Hell! What's the fun of it all: work, sail, work, sail." I could sympathize with James. He'd made the mistake of hitching a ride on a delivery job. Unless you are in a real hurry to cross an ocean or love ocean passages, it's much more fun to find a berth on a yacht that plans a leisurely cruise along shores with inviting harbors. For the first-time crewman, James's statement really summed it up: "Crewing on an ocean passage before I ever had a chance to learn about casual cruising has turned me off. It's back to dinghy sailing for me."

One way to find a job on a boat that will be doing day-hops and lots of sightseeing is to sign on a charter yacht. In the Mediterranean you might even be offered the standard crew's wages of $10 a day while preparing for charters and $50 a day while the boat is actually on charter. Lots of good positions are available, but crewing on a charter yacht is a full-time, demanding job. Zillah, who worked as stewardess on the luxurious 60-foot wishbone schooner *Carina,* agrees: "It's like working in a hotel that goes to windward. I get up at 0600 when we are on charter and fall asleep exhausted at 2300. If all goes well I get three hours free in the afternoon. Between charters we have to work full-time keeping up the varnish, refueling, buying stores. Some of the people who charter the boat are real pains. One lady actually expected me to hand-wash her undies. But most are fantastic fun. I work as stewardess each summer on *Carina* because I love the boat, like the skipper, and I'd rather be out in the sun and wind at coolies' wages than cooped up in an office in London."

If you want a charter-boat job, start looking at least two months before the charter season starts. Competition is keen, and skippers always need help with the spring refit. Preferential treatment will go to the potential crewmember who has been around to help with some of the dirty work.

"Pierhead Jumpers" are an unpopular breed of potential crew. They search around, promising to crew on four or five different yachts, then make up their minds an hour before departure time. This way the Pierhead Jumper avoids the tedious pre-departure work involved in preparing for any voyage. The PHJ is cheating both himself and his future sailing mates. He doesn't have time to learn about the ship he's sailing on. Since the PHJ hasn't helped buy any provisions and store them away, he is always asking, "Where is the so-and-so? Where do I put such-and-such?" until he is resented by everyone on board. Working and living together on a sailing boat, no matter what its size, requires teamwork and understanding. So spend a week or two with your potential sailing partners—checking over the boat, splicing some new halyards, buying one more set of spare batteries, wrapping another five dozen tomatoes, lashing down one last can of water—to give yourself an idea of the personalities on board.

It is hard to say whether couples looking for crewing positions have as much luck as single people. I know that when we want two crew for a long-distance delivery job, we are reluctant to hire a couple. We figure that if one or the other of the couple doesn't work out, we are liable to lose our whole crew at the next port. On the other hand, a husband and wife on a cruising boat are likely to prefer the social benefits of a couple when it's time to take on crew for an ocean crossing.

Once you've found a berth on a boat bound for adventure, there are a few tips that can help make your life afloat more fun for everyone involved. First and most important, remember that whatever the outward appearance of the boat, whatever its size, every yacht is its owner's pride and joy. You'll only create hurt feelings by saying, "The last 40-foot ketch I sailed on had a better set of winches than this one"; or, "If this was a sloop instead of a schooner we could go to windward like the 38-footer my friend Bill crews on." Yacht owners are particularly sensitive to any possible slight to their boat or seamanship. In fact the main reason people own yachts and go off cruising is to gain the freedom to do things their own way. So it pays to take an interest in how the skipper handles his boat. Notice how he cleats his halyards and jibsheets. Coil lines the way he does and use the same kind of knots to tie off the sail covers, even if your way seems better. If your way is vastly superior, wait until a relaxed private moment and tactfully show the skipper why you use a different method.

If you are new to sailing or are hitching your first rides on long-distance passages, it may be worth your life to take a keen interest in learning to sail the boat and to navigate. Skippers can't help but feel flattered when you ask them to teach you to read a chart or figure a noon sight. Then if an emergency does occur, if the skipper becomes too ill to handle things, the minutes you spent studying will pay off. Larry learned celestial navigation during his first ocean passage, a voyage from Newport Beach, California, to Honolulu and back as pick-up crew on an 85-foot schooner. He also learned some neat rope work from the skipper, Bob Sloan, who was a master rigger. There is only one snag. Don't ask to use another sailor's sextant. Sextants seem to be as personal as lovers. The poor skipper who is too polite to refuse your request will sit and suffer silent agonies as he or she watches you handle the precious sextant and prays you don't slip or fall overboard. If you are offered the use of the sextant, get a leather thong and secure the sextant around your neck.

There is almost nowhere in the world where a sense of humor is more necessary than in the close confines of an ocean passage-making sailboat. We were on a delivery from Miami to Puerto Rico with a new 37-foot motorsailer. This production boat kept surprising us with new breakdowns. The diesel quit because the injection pump was jammed with fiberglass dust left in the bonded-in fuel tanks during construction. We proceeded into the Atlantic toward San Salvador under sail, 40-knot squalls making each watch a wet miserable two hours. Heavy spray flew across the central cockpit. There was no helmsman's seat. Yet one statement by our good-humored pick-up crewman saved our tempers: Rod Pringle slid open the hatch and water streamed down his face as he called, "Rise and sparkle, Lin, time for your two-hour Caribbean sunshine cruise." This ability to make light of discomfort is one of the main reasons we were eager to give Rod a letter of recommendation in case he ever again wanted another job as crew.

If you know you've done a good job on the yacht you are leaving, don't be shy about asking for a recommendation. The fact that you had the foresight to do so could impress future skippers. It will also serve as proof of your experience and sea time if you eventually want to take the examinations for a U.S. Coast Guard 100-ton ticket or Royal Yachting Association yachtmaster's certificate.

Women are joining the offshore crew market in larger numbers each year. They have one extra problem to contend with. I have heard several stories about boat owners who said, "Don't worry; you are just crew, separate cabin, no romantic nonsense." Then 200 miles out these same skippers changed their tune. Before you leave terra firma as the only woman on board, it pays to have lived on board with the crew and skipper and possibly to have made a few short voyages together.

Male or female, anyone joining a yacht as crew, owes it to himself to make sure of the financial, social, and labor details before setting sail. If it's a sharing-expenses arrangement, get down on paper exactly what expenses will be shared. Normally, shared expenses include food and fuel, but not engine repairs or boat upkeep. If your deal is different, make sure it is *clear* beforehand. If you are lucky enough to land a paying job, write out the wages expected and the jobs you'll generally be expected to do. Discuss details such as shipboard entertainment. Find out about who finances nights ashore and if you like an occasional drink, ask permission to bring a few bottles of your own liquor on board. If the owner or captain prefers a dry ship, that's his prerogative. But if cocktail hour is a custom on board, having your own bottle to share will make everyone happier. While you are discussing the conditions of your crew job, find out which bunk you'll have and what gear you'll need besides oilskins and boots of your own. Ask if the ship has spare bedding or if you should bring a sleeping bag. Determine who will pay your fare home if you are on a delivery job and whether that means just air fare or bus fare to the airport also. Go off somewhere and write a list of all these details; then go over the written list with your prospective skipper. Give him a carbon copy of your list of agreements so he can refer to it later if necessary. I know it's hard to talk these affairs out and get them down on paper when you are eager to go off on the new adventure of an ocean passage. But it is harder still to heal the breaches made because you weren't clear on the deal before you signed on as crew.

Whether you just want a free trip home from Europe, a cruise to Tahiti, or the chance to gather experience toward becoming a full-time professional yacht skipper, the sunshine belt is the place to look. Conservatively speaking, I can think of 60 different crew that were available in Malta alone during one winter. And Malta is just one of a dozen fitting-out ports. Do a bit of research; get some money ahead; and join the wonderful world of offshore sailing the least expensive way there is: As a crew on an ocean-going yacht.

Update

Crew positions seem to be even more readily available now than when we first wrote this chapter. On page 19 we list where to look for berths and when. We'd like to add some other ports where you might have a good chance of finding crewing positions. They include San Diego and other Southern California ports in September and October for boats headed toward Mexico; February for boats headed to the South Pacific. La Paz, Baja California, from January to March for boats heading toward the South Pacific. New Zealand, March or April, for boats headed toward all areas of the South Pacific and Australia. Miami, New York, south coast of England, September or October, for boats heading to the Caribbean. In Honolulu in August, boats are delivered back to the U.S. mainland.

Charter companies in remote areas like Raiatea, French Polynesia, and Tonga often asked us if we knew of good crew or cooks we could recommend. They offer only $40 or $50 a day plus room and board, but you can gain invaluable experience working with these charter boats and so could probably pick up a good berth for further voyaging.

2

Go Now, Pay on the Way

Cruising costs money. Stores and maintenance nibble away funds. Entertainment doubles the pleasure of your cruise, but costs money. No one guesses correctly what the expenses of their first extended cruise will be; everyone tends to underestimate.

A simple modest yacht will make cruising more economical. Two people and a self-steering vane can sail a smaller yacht alone, with no crew and less expense. Guests can come and go but you aren't dependent on them.

A boat that sails well in light winds, one with only a single mast and plenty of light air sails, will keep costs down. Less motoring, less fuel, less wear and tear on the engine.

But no matter how one economizes, one still needs money. And getting it and enjoying cruising at the same time is possible.

Peace of mind is having enough money tucked away somewhere to live on for six months should a catastrophe strike. The money should be slightly difficult to get without some careful thinking beforehand so you don't deplete the fund frivolously. We've tried to keep at least $3,000 in this fund at all times. Then we outfit *Seraffyn* completely with as many stores as she'll hold (about three or four month's food). We earn enough money to last six to nine months of normal cruising on top, and sail onward. When we are near the point of where our immediate cruising funds are down to three month's worth, we look for work. After 11 years we've found that if we have three months to look, we usually find something that pays well and is interesting.

What does it cost us to cruise? We live on a very small yacht with no engine and do all of our own repairs and maintenance other than those to our radio receiver and stereo. We drink wine with most dinners and eat very well. We love to travel inland, sometimes by public transport, occasionally in a rented car. From 1977 to 1980 our costs averaged $450 per month including a new camera and two new sails. We seem to be about average for people with boats under 30 feet. (See the following chapter for more information about costs in relation to boat size.) People who plan to cruise for one year or less will spend less because with a new boat and gear they will have lower maintenance costs (see update).

One thing we've learned from our own experiences and those of people all the way around the world is that you can't depend on chartering to finance your voyage. We have never met a cruising boat that paid its way chartering. Some have earned occasional spending money, but never enough to pay for all their cruising.

To charter successfully, your boat must be large enough to sleep at least four plus crew. That means you carry the expense of a large boat when you are cruising and it only pays for itself when you are chartering.

Chartering is seasonal and people generally charter boats by reputation, so you have to be in the area for at least two seasons to get a good following. This means two seasons of cruising gone. You are competing with professional organizations that offer immaculate, well-found yachts designed for chartering—with crew, agents, and advertising paid for out of substantial budgets.

Friends who have chartered complain that they work their tails off—cooking, sailing, cleaning, and making up bunks. Like running a hotel that goes to windward, it's not really fun.

Day chartering does provide extra income with none of the hassles of meals and overnight guests. Roger Olsen on *Xipthias,* a 28-foot cutter, earned extra money to continue his cruise by working for the

Club Mediterrean in Bora Bora, Tahiti, in 1980. His Bristol Channel Cutter has wide side decks with room for six guests, their cameras, and box lunches provided by the hotels, but there is a lot of wear and tear on his boat. Day chartering means remaining in a resort town long enough to become known, and the best chartering season is usually the very best cruising season.

One successful way of earning money in the off-season is by using your boat as your workshop and assisting other less prepared or less skilled yachtsmen in maintaining, repairing or upgrading their yachts. A rigger or sailmaker is in demand everywhere. In the Panama Canal there are over one hundred resident yachts and not one sailmaker or sail-stitching machine to be found. A skilled mechanic with a full complement of tools can be a blessing anywhere. A good electrician is just as much in demand. A refrigeration expert will often find work. But it is carpenters who seem to get the most offers of high-paying jobs, especially right before the charter season starts.

General maintenance and repairs can easily be done with the tools you can carry on a small boat. By arriving in a port that has both cruising boats and charter boats just at fitting-out time, you can almost guarantee yourself lots of work. September in Florida, March in England, October in the Virgin Islands, February throughout the Mediterranean—wherever there is a yachting season starting, painters, varnishers, and repairers are overworked. The secret to getting the jobs is your own boat—your calling card, so to speak. If it is well maintained and well painted, work will soon follow. Power yachts are good targets for seasonal maintenance work since many of these owners pay to get their work done.

Never undercut locals. We charge our normal rates or the same as the locals, whichever is higher. Then we try to work twice as hard. Undercutting only leads to resentment.

The same applies to yacht deliveries. Cruising people occasionally arrive in a port where a yacht is stranded because its owner must get it back home and either doesn't have the time, the crew, or the skill to move it. So he hires a delivery team. This is a great but unpredictable way to earn money. If your own boat looks well cared for, the owner of an elaborate, valuable yacht will have more confidence in your ability to bring his home in good condition. (See Chapter 4 for more about yacht deliveries.)

Seasonal resorts are always short of help. As a waitress, bartender, sailing instructor, tour guide, or cook, any semi-skilled or just plain hard-working person can earn well during a four-month season. Living on your boat will help you save money fast.

Several cruising friends have taken over the management of small resort concerns during the off-season, so the owners could take a good long holiday. Resort life is a complete change from cruising and not only will you reinforce your funds, but very probably your desire to cruise off to a deserted island.

Crew positions are good seasonal work. Cooks are always in demand on charter yachts—difficult work but it often pays well, with tips besides if you work on a luxury yacht.

Getting away from yachts often produces the best results. Technical skills are in demand in every developing country. Electronic specialist friends have had offers of work in Costa Rica, Panama, and Colombia. Doctors, teachers, and farm specialists receive very high wages in developing Latin countries. Write ahead to the board or department that is in charge of positions for your profession and you may find they have a list of available jobs that are perfect for you. Celia Vanderpool wrote the New Zealand School Board and was offered a position teaching physically-handicapped mentally-advanced children if she sent her credentials in ahead of time. She was assured of a high-paying job a year in advance, so cruising through the South Pacific caused fewer financial worries. If you are offered a job in a foreign country, you can usually be sure of getting a visa. No one expects you stay forever. Six months is the average time any person raised in a temperate climate enjoys working in the deep tropics; one year is the usual professional contract limit in British Commonwealth countries.

We've met several doctors and dentists who have closed their own practices and put their names on locum lists maintained by various employment agencies worldwide. These professionals can then take over another physician's practice for two or three months at a very good salary while the resident doctor has a vacation. George Bilsbarrow, a Canadian doctor, cruised all around Europe and the Mediterranean this way. He'd accept temporary jobs in England and Scotland which usually came complete with the doctor's residence and car. He'd work three months, then cruise for six or seven more.

Labor jobs such as construction worker, waitress, fishing boat crew, or plumber's helper can easily be found in the United States, its territories, or most British Commonwealth countries. In some places you will have to sign contracts in order to get proper working visas. Ask around among the cruising fleet for information about getting the proper papers. Sometimes approaching the right office first will make a big difference.

Writing sounds like the perfect way to finance a cruise, and once you are well established and known to editors, it can certainly help take the sting out of expenses. The Hiscocks find they earn enough writing to live modestly but comfortably. But, it took them almost twenty years and five books to reach that point. Competition for limited editorial space can be tough, especially since several yachting magazines have either folded or consolidated during the past three years. Worst yet are the delays caused by overseas mail slow-ups and the time editors take to get to your particular manuscript. An editor at *Sail* magazine said she gets about sixty unsolicited manuscripts a month. So a two-month delay in reading something from an unknown author is not unusual. Add that to the mail hang-ups and it means you may have to wait four to six months to know if you've been successful. On the other hand, writing is a wonderful way to fill those rainy, foggy, or stormy days when you are harbor-bound. It's an extremely portable profession, and if the money from an article you do sell can be counted as a bonus, not a necessity, you may come to really enjoy the challenge.

We've met artists who were able to sell their watercolors and sketches to local shops and other cruising sailors. In fact, a delightful young man who lives on a 26-foot Saint Pierre dory in Canada's Gulf Islands showed us some small sketches he'd made of *Seraffyn* when we sailed into Canoe Cove. We were hooked and ordered a 12-by-18 pen-and-ink sketch from Ron Wall. We saw another enterprising bit of artistry in Antigua where Nick Skeates, who was cruising on his 30-footer, *Wylo*, earned extra money by building replicas of people's boats inside tiny bottles.

Almost all cruising people eventually try trading to supplement their funds. We successfully purchased some beautiful handsewn artwork from the Cuna Indians near Panama and turned an investment of $75 into $600 over the next year. But we had the help of some local experts. We met two ex-Peace Corps volunteers who had studied Indonesian art for four years. They sailed from there towards Israel with close to $2,000 worth of antiques and artwork on their trimaran. In Israel they put on a show for local yacht club members and their friends and netted $6,000 the first evening. To trade successfully you must have knowledge of the items you are buying, then the patience to wait for the right resale market. One unwary yachtsman was sold gems by a reputable dealer in Sri Lanka. It turned out the rubies and opals he bought were no bargain at the time, just fairly priced. But over the next two years there was a tremendous increase in gem prices which would have netted the yachtsman a good profit, if he'd had the money to wait. Instead he sold the gems for no profit and cursed the Sri Lankan dealer. Unless you have excellent knowledge of gems and jewelry, this is one type of trading to avoid.

Trading can be extremely interesting and, once again, it's a good way to make bonus money, not something to depend on.

Be extremely careful of local import laws before you offer to sell things from your boat. Sailors all know they can forfeit their boat and their liberty for selling or even carrying narcotics. But few realize that the sale of one bottle of liquor can lead to the same thing in Saudi Arabia. In Sri Lanka it is illegal to sell anything that is imported without paying 100 percent import duties. So until you check on the local rules, don't start trading.

Shell collecting can add to your cruising funds if you enjoy skin-diving and are visiting areas of the world that have good reefs and warm water. This is a field where knowledge, both of shells and of packaging for shipment, is important. It also pays to find an outlet for your shells before you set sail.

The most exclusive way we saw of financing a cruise was that used by the French owner of a glorious 58-foot Herreshoff ketch. He was the owner of eight large companies, located in eight different countries. He cruised from one to the other, checking them over. But this is a rare case. Cruising and business back home don't usually mix well. We know. We tried it the last year of our cruise, and the constant rush to reach a telephone tainted some of our finest days. We had to forsake out-of-the-way coves to be near post offices to receive and send mail.

One cruising man we met in the bar in the Bayonna Yacht Club in northern Spain was surrounded by packed luggage, though he'd only just sailed in the day before. "I called my office this morning just to see how things were going. Now I have to cancel my voyage across the Atlantic, leave my boat, and fly home. If I hadn't called, they'd probably have handled the problems without me. But now I'd worry too much to enjoy myself." If you want to go cruising and enjoy real freedom, you should probably close your business or sell it and arrange to put the receipts in some sort of investment that does not require constant attention.

Annabell and Gordon Yates voyaged enjoyably for several years on the proceeds from the rental of their fully paid-for house. Once a year, Annabell flew home to check the house over and do their business banking. It provided a good holiday for her and a chance to see the children. But the rest of the year, she and Gordon had no business worries.

However you decide to arrange your income, don't worry too much about finding ways to earn as you go. We've seen no enterprising cruising sailor who couldn't find some way to earn money along the way. Get your reasonably sized cruiser, put some cash in the bank, and go. Waiting until you can afford to live in the style you'd like to become accustomed to is a curse against setting sail for distant horizons.

Update

Surprisingly, cruising costs have not kept up with inflation. Although there is truth in the saying, "Cruising costs as much as you have," we found our 1997 cruising expenses averaged about $900 a month, even in Europe. But we do know of people on boats from 28 to 35 feet in several parts of the world with budgets as low as $500 per month.

Although boat-related skills are still much in demand around the world, modern technology has added some new opportunities for cruising sailors. The most frequently mentioned overseas short-term jobs seem to be open to those with computer skills, electronic repair skills—both afloat and for shoreside applications—and electronic communication skills. The key to finding work as your cruise is the same as it always has been—be willing to flex a bit and be creative. If you insist on looking for work in exactly the same field as you left, you may have far less luck than you would if you tried something slightly off the normal track.

3

Thirty Feet Is Enough

Now that it is time to buy or build your cruising yacht, have you ever considered why most yacht brokers, builders, and designers will recommend the largest boat you can possibly finance? It is to their advantage to sell or design you a 45-foot yacht instead of one only 30 feet long. Their commission is dependent on a boat's value—the more expensive the boat, the higher the profits.

But yacht brokers, designers, and builders *very* rarely take two or three years off to cruise foreign waters.

Only one group of people can really give you good information on what size boat you will enjoy cruising in: experienced cruising people. We spent three years interviewing these people as we cruised in our own small yacht.

Of the fifty-seven cruisers we interviewed, sixteen had independent incomes or pensions of more than $600 per month. The average length of all included yachts was 37 feet on deck. Those who had been cruising six months or longer averaged 36.6 feet, but subtracting ones with independent incomes, the average dropped to only 32.9 feet. Yachts cruising over one year averaged 31.6 feet. The six vessels we met who had cruised over two years with or without private income had an average length of only 29 feet on deck.

We have since been cruising seven years more and feel that these facts are very positive. If you have an independent income, a yacht of around 37 feet should be the largest you consider. If you have to earn your living as you go, a yacht of about 29 feet is the size you can enjoy and afford.

We are referring to people who plan to live aboard and cruise in foreign waters for extended periods. So, before you dream of all of the comforts of your 40-footer, consider the advantages of the small yacht.

The most obvious advantage of buying or building a 30-foot yacht instead of a 40-footer is the initial cost. No matter how you finance it, if you spend only half of your available funds on the boat, the rest can act as a buffer or insurance plan. Half in the boat, half in liquid assets is a definite contribution to peace of mind as you cruise and explore.

When buying small you can go for quality. Rather than looking for the largest boat for the least money, you can search for the best-built, best-designed, and best-outfitted 30-footer available. Your extra funds can let you outfit the boat to your exact needs before you depart.

Once you sail, money becomes even more important. It's all going out and none coming in. People we interviewed were very aware of their yearly expenses. We found that in boats of about 30 feet, all expenses, including boat maintenance, food, and entertainment, averaged between $200 and $300 a month, depending on where they were cruising. Those in boats 40 feet and over gave averages from $600 to $800 per month. (These figures were for 1975. See the update at the end of this chapter for some recent cruising-cost figures.) Why the huge differences? Boat-maintenance costs rise at close to the cube of the waterline length. Approximately one gallon of bottom paint will suffice for a 30-footer but a 40-footer needs around 3 gallons. Gear replacement on a larger boat is usually more than twice as expensive. A new anchor in the small boat can be less than half the size of that needed for the boat only 10 feet longer, and anchors are sold by the pound.

Another advantage to the smaller yacht is that wherever you travel, shipyard managers, store owners, and fuel docks judge the size of your wallet by the length of your yacht. We have watched the same product or service billed at two different prices for two different-sized boats. As one Latin character said to us, "If they can afford a yacht that large, they must be rich."

One real advantage to *Seraffyn's* small size and limited space may just be personal, but is worth stating. If I had more room, I would buy more things. Souvenirs, toys, clothes. We'd spend much more money on things we have now learned we can do very well without. It's one way of keeping a budget.

Let's forget about money for a moment. Sailing a small boat is much easier. Once you are outfitted with a self-steering vane, your 30-footer can be easily sailed by a couple or single-handedly. You don't need the problems of a crew, and if you are dependent on others for crew, they can be a big problem. A 30-footer is large enough to make having guests a treat, but not a necessity. With a good layout, such as a forward stateroom and quarter berths, you won't be in each other's way.

You may be told, "This 40-footer is designed for two people to retire on and cruise off to a deserted island." But, consider taking in the anchor and chain with a strong onshore breeze blowing. If you are ill, have a sprained wrist, or worse, could your wife manhandle the ground tackle, raise the sails, and get underway? If your engine gave out, could you and your wife short tack up a narrow channel? Could you work into a crowded anchorage under just sail and then lay up to a dock? I've seen the nervous wives 40-footers produce. They're really worrying: what if something gets out of hand; what if I have to sail this boat alone?

I've sailed *Seraffyn* alone. It's fun. I play captain, hoist the mainsail, pull up the anchor, and gain lots of confidence. Should Larry become ill, I know I could sail for assistance. At night during my watches I can reef, tack, or change jibs alone. Larry gets more sleep, and on my off-watches so do I. Remember, there is more to do than just sailing: cooking, navigating, repairing, and sleeping. With only two on board, each person must be able to handle the boat alone.

A few years ago we spent an afternoon on board the 49-foot *Wanderer IV* with Eric and Susan Hiscock in San Diego. They were on their third circumnavigation. The first two had been on board their 30-foot sloop, *Wanderer III*. Susan had several interesting comments to make, woman to woman. "We wanted to have a larger boat mainly to have an after-cabin, but now the cabin rarely gets used, especially not at sea. It's just extra luggage for a boat with two people."

"And it's embarrassing, not being able to sail *Wanderer IV* up to a dock." This summed up her feelings on size.

Remember how much fun it was to take a little boat, load a lunch on board and shove off for an afternoon sail around the bay? A 30-footer makes a fine day sailor. Forty feet is just too much work to get underway. We've challenged friends on other cruising boats to a race to the next bay and a beat back after skindiving; winner has the honor of making cocktails. These races and afternoons are the stuff of memories. They make the sailing part of cruising a real joy.

Maintenance becomes a personal problem as you cruise. No longer can you call your favorite, most trusted shipyard, saying, "My boat needs a coat of paint," and sit back as the work is done. In foreign waters you will have to do the work yourself or put up with endless delays, poor quality, and top prices. It's only one day's work to lay a small yacht up against a seawall, let it dry out with the tide, scrub and paint it, and then float free. Just finding professionals to handle the large job takes more than a day of your time and still the work isn't done.

A well-maintained boat is not only investment protection, and safer, but pays unexpected dividends. People judge you by your boat's appearance. So, if your boat is small enough to make maintenance a pleasurable pastime, you are an all-around winner. I really enjoy varnishing three hatches and the cabin sides. It takes one day in the sun. Give me much more to do and it seems like work.

From the lady's point of view, a small boat means less housework. We go cruising to see how others live. Spending all day taking care of the boat is a drag.

Hal Roth and his wife circumnavigated the Pacific, sailing 25,000 miles in three years. When he was giving a lecture in Vancouver after his return, one of the audience asked, "How come you don't have a boat larger than 35 feet?" Mr. Roth answered, "We cruise to meet people and our boat is almost too large for people to approach. It seems that locals assume that yachtsmen with larger boats aren't going to be as friendly."

We agree with him completely. We sailed into a tiny yacht harbor in the Limfiord, Denmark, on a Saturday afternoon. "Can we tie up next to that blue sloop?" we asked, hoping someone spoke English. "Sure, hand me your line. Can you be our guests at our yacht club dance tonight?"

We accepted with pleasure. Later that evening as I danced with our new friend, I asked, "How come you invited us to this great party before you even tied our dock lines?"

"We knew that anyone sailing in a 24-foot yacht had to be interesting." This has always been our experience. Yet, when we meet people in larger yachts, cruising in the same water, they'll often comment, "The people here sure aren't very friendly."

If after all of the planning and a bit of cruising you find it's not for you, your small yacht has one last advantage. It's easier to sell. Or, if you don't wish to sell it, your investment isn't so large that you'd resent putting the boat on a mooring and getting a home ashore.

Length is not the only factor determining a boat's capacity. Beam increases your space much faster than length does. The 30-foot *Wanderer* had only 8 feet of beam and an overhanging bow. Our 24-foot *Seraffyn* has 9 feet of beam and only 21 inches of overhangs and has almost the same volume as *Wanderer*. Tom Steele's 32-foot yacht with 10-foot of beam is huge inside, as large as a 36-footer with only 9 feet of beam. Since it is your overall length that costs, the beamier boat is a real bargain.

If you are still convinced that you need a 40-foot boat, we suggest that you spend the money to charter a boat similar to what you want. Take a three-week cruise with just the two of you. Go out in some bad weather. Pretend the engine doesn't work, anchor, and then sail off. Let your wife get underway alone while you pretend you have a broken arm. Check with some different yards as to the cost of hauling and painting. Price a new mainsail. The charter costs will be far less than the broker's commission for buying and then selling a 40-footer. Finally, find a friend with a large yacht. Ask him if you can take charge of scrubbing and painting the bottom of his boat. Your friend may think you are crazy, but he will appreciate the help. A few long hours of scrubbing and painting may keep you from suffering from the disease we call "being overboated."

I know that small boats have their disadvantages. You can't carry enough good books. Your guests can't have a private stateroom. You have to sit down to take a shower. It's difficult to carry that motorcycle you'd love to have. But in the final analysis, small boats go and keep and going. Eric and Susan Hiscock cruised fifteen years and 110,00 miles in 30-foot *Wanderer III*. Peer Tangvald sailed his 32-foot engineless *Dorthea* around the world for five years. Tom Steele has spent twenty-four years on board his 32-foot *Adios,* and he and Janet were on their third circumnavigation the last time we saw them. Hal Roth is outfitting his 35-footer and is ready to be off again. None of us is wealthy. We all work along the way, but we all go and have a lot of fun.

Update

After fourteen years on board 29-foot, 6-inch *Taleisin,* we feel even more strongly that 30 feet is enough. This is not to imply that 24-foot *Seraffyn* was too small. For two young people such as we were when we decided to build and get out cruising, she was the logical choice—affordable, big enough to carry the provisions we needed as long as we were modest in our souvenir acquisitions, and definitely easy to handle. We enjoy the luxury of the extra space *Taleisin* offers but have also learned the truth of the maxim—your possessions expand to take up all the space you have. Our costs have risen almost 30% in the boat maintenance and gear category on *Taleisin*.

Are people getting out there in boats under 30 feet in 1997? The answer is a resounding yes. In fact, real bargains in cruising boats can be found, secondhand, in this size range—boats built in the late 1960s and early '70s. It is easier to get marina berths for this size of boat than any other along the California coast and in most other countries.

Costs for those cruising on boats around 30 feet still run much lower than those for larger-boat owners. In a poll taken for the seminar tour we did during early 1997, we spoke with 14 crews who had been out cruising for two years or more. They definitely reflected the numbers mentioned on page 35. Several American sailors cruising on 40-to-45-footers in Europe mentioned budgets of $1,800 per month, with the average probably around $1,200 to $1,600. We met two cruisers on boats under 28 feet, plus a couple on a 35-footer, who were enjoying exploring on budgets of $500 to $700 per month. The couple with the 35-footer were the most cost-conscious we met, doing all their own work, keeping gear exceptionally simple, and hauling out on the tide wherever possible to cut shipyard charges.

4

Yacht Deliveries

Every business deal has two sides and yacht deliveries are no exception. The owner is handing over his yacht, dear to him as his teenage daughter, to a complete stranger who will take it on a journey full of potential dangers. The owner wants his boat to arrive in the same condition in which it left, as soon as possible.

The yacht deliverer, on the other hand, sees a Pandora's Box of a boat full of hidden problems. All he wants is to move it from point A to point B as quickly as possible with no breakdowns or delays so he can collect his fee and get on with his plans.

In few business relations do the employee and employer have less personal contact. That's why special thought should be given to a delivery contract. The owner should know what he is asking for and who he is hiring. The deliverer must consider the responsibility he is assuming.

THE OWNER

Deliveries cost money and there are few bargains. When you hire someone to sail your $80,000 to $400,000 worth of yacht across an ocean, you need a skilled person, one who will maintain your investment all the time it is underway. The man you hire must know not only how to navigate, sail, handle a crew, and operate engines and generators, but also, and more importantly, how to repair almost everything on board with what spares are on the boat. He must know how and where to find supplies in foreign places. And he must know how to maintain, varnish, paint, and keep your interior clean while the boat is underway. This all adds up to a very skilled person. And remember that your delivery captain is involved twenty-four hours a day from the moment he steps aboard, and you'll understand why delivery fees look high at first glance.

At present a contract delivery will cost you about $1.50 to $2 (U.S.) a nautical mile, plus fuel and airfare for the captain and a reasonable number of crew. Or you can hire a delivery captain on a daily basis for about $150 per day plus all expenses, including crew, food, fuel, and airfares. With a good delivery man, the final fee will come out about the same whether you figure it on a contract or a daily basis.

What is the alternative? You can ship your yacht by truck for continental deliveries or by ship. But if the yacht is over 36 feet you'll often pay more. By ship the rate must include unstepping the mast, building the cradle, paying agents, relaunching and restepping the mast, and transporting it from a big ship's harbor to a marina. The actual shipping fee is based on the cubic area that the boat and its mast will take up. Figures vary greatly, but a friend of ours shipped his 45-foot "gold-plater" from Denmark to New York, and it cost a total of $13,000. A sea delivery would have been about $8,000. But the owner saved 6,000 miles of wear and tear on the boat and its gear. His yacht did receive some damage—a scarred toerail and a dented boom—and his wooden topsides became cracked from being exposed to the sun without being washed down with salt water.

Good professional deliverers are expensive; shipping is expensive; but bargain deliveries can cost you even more. Frank couldn't afford a regular delivery team and gladly accepted when a friend of his said, "I've got two months off. I'll take your ketch back to England for you. Just pay me the food and airfare." Frank had cruised locally for a few weeks with this fellow and knew that his friend's longest offshore passage had been 200 miles, but the man loved Frank's boat. Two months later Frank received a message. The boat had been abandoned in a tiny port 200 miles from its starting point. All of its gear had been stripped off by scavengers. The friend had been scared to leave port after a two-day blow outside of Cape Town. His crew had jumped ship. The engine had quit. In the end it cost Frank his boat. He couldn't leave his contract job in England to go out and repair the damages. No delivery team would go for the boat after hearing a report of its condition. So Frank ended up selling his dream ship for the price of its lead ballast.

Delivering a boat is not fun; it is work. Asking amateurs to do it may be asking for trouble. We can cite stories of cut-rate deliveries that took two months to move a boat 800 miles, of boats abandoned during storms, and of boats confiscated when nonprofessionals used them for smuggling drugs. Without a reputation to protect, a nonprofessional deliverer will think first of *himself* and second about your boat.

To protect you and your investment, don't hire anyone to move your yacht unless you can get the names and addresses of at least two people whose boats he has delivered. Call these people. Ask them what condition their boat arrived in. If the owner tells you his boat arrived on time and in good shape, you've found a good deliverer.

If you are arranging a delivery through an agency, insist upon knowing the exact person who will be in charge of your yacht. Call him and get the names of people whose boats he has delivered. If an agency is very busy they might let relatively inexperienced men handle jobs that seem simple. Four years ago we delivered two yachts from Miami to Puerto Rico. The first time we arrived in San Juan, we noticed a 30-footer laid up at the dock, its transom black with soot, its diesel out of commission. Three weeks later we arrived again to see a second boat, identical to the first, its transom also black with soot, its engine out of commission. Both boats were part of a large contract handled by a firm with an excellent reputation. In both cases, the deliveries had been turned over to sailors on their first professional jobs, since the distance involved was only about 700 miles. No matter what reputation the agency has, check the references of the person who will be on your boat and in charge.

Don't be swayed by the sell a sailor walking down the dock gives you. *Call his references.* The owner of a 50-foot South African yacht came by one day to tell us he'd found a very inexpensive delivery captain. He described the crew of a local charter boat, a young bearded sailor who told excellent sea stories. It was only after the boat was at sea that the owner learned that the longest voyage his captain had made was from Barcelona to Palma, Mallorca, a distance of 120 miles. The owner told us he started worrying when he saw the boat owned by the man he had hired. It was in terrible condition and had been left secured to a mooring in an exposed part of the harbor. As the owner said, "If he takes care of his own boat that way, what will mine look like in two months?"

Once you've located the person you wish to hire, tell him all the problems he may encounter with your boat so he can plan accordingly. If it doesn't have an auto pilot, tell him so he can arrange sufficient crew. Let him know the state of the engine, its fuel consumption, and all about your electronics and equipment. Don't be optimistic about the boat's range or fuel capacity. Give the captain a frank idea of what you have on board. The delivery captain may fly to Europe to pick up your boat and find that he didn't bring the right gear and spares along. Then he'll have to spend your money and his time getting ready to set off. The more complete your description, the more prepared he'll be.

An owner got a transatlantic call from his delivery captain: "Sorry, I can't take your ketch across the Atlantic till it has new standing rigging."

The owner replied, "What? That's only six-year-old wire. I crossed the Atlantic two years ago with it."

The delivery captain, a well-respected, very experienced man, then refused the job, and the owner lost the cost of two airline tickets. He called a second deliverer who came and said the same thing. So the rigging was replaced. If you have hired a good person, trust his judgment. He is the one who is risking his life and reputation when he sets off across an ocean.

The delivery captain and crew are going to be living on your boat for several weeks in possibly rough conditions at sea. So if you have any treasures, either take them off the boat or store them carefully away and warn the deliverer. There is bound to be some wear and tear on a yacht during any passage, and you must expect to lose a glass or two or have some chafed lines or even more extreme damages.

In one case, in which we heard both sides of the story, a well-respected captain was asked to deliver a 48-foot racing boat from the U.S. northeast coast to the Southern Ocean Racing Circuit in Florida during late November. Because of the risks of storms, the job was bid to allow all professional crew. Two days out, the delivery ran into a freak cyclonic storm. For three days the team rode hove-to, trailing warps, lying in the trough, doing anything they could to ease the violent motion. On the last day, a sea turned the boat upside down and the mizzenmast carried away. The crew was able to cut the wreckage loose with no further damage. When the weather eased, they stood into Norfolk, Virginia, and called the owner and his insurance company. Instead of being relieved that no one had been lost, the owner raged over the fact that the eighteen Barient winch handles, stored in pockets on deck, had gone over when the boat rolled. Considering that several fishing boats were lost at sea during this storm and that the four men on board had survived three days of winds that were in excess of 100 miles an hour, I think the owner was being unfair about the loss of winch handles.

If this is to be a windward delivery, expect some wear and tear on your engine. Most delivery skippers must meet a schedule, so will motor sail when they can't lay their course. In the case of a racing boat this may actually be cheaper as the savings on sail wear will more than make up for the added engine hours.

Most professional delivery skippers do not want to take owners along on the trip. Owners want to cruise, learn about navigating, and enjoy the trip. Skippers want to move the boat fast and have a crew who will do the menial work. It's difficult to tell an owner to scrub the bilge or clean out the head. It's harder yet to say, "We're setting sail today" if the owner wants one more day in port. Basically taking owners on deliveries is a conflict of interest.

Finally, as in all business deals, get a contract. Make sure it gives an estimate of delivery time. It should also include the deliverer's expected route and the number of crew he plans to take, plus what expenses he will cover, and what you as the owner must pay for.

THE DELIVERER

"Delivery work looks like a great idea. One hundred fifty bucks a day just to enjoy yourself and go sailing."

It's not that easy. Few delivery jobs turn out to be fun. Job equals work. People aren't going to pay you to take a well-outfitted, fine sailing yacht on a downwind, perfect season cruise. Boats are almost always delivered to windward. Old or neglected boats are delivered. Brand-new boats fresh from the factory, full of bugs and untried systems, are delivered. And whatever the condition, the owner usually wants the boat as soon as possible. In most cases, delivery services figure on a time of one day for every 100 miles plus preparation time. That doesn't allow you much cruising. On our last 5,800-mile delivery, we spent ten days preparing the boat and arranging crew, fifty days at sea and eleven days in four ports for a total of seventy-one days. Two days in each port we devoted to renewing stores, going over the engines, and maintaining the sails and varnish. That left us three days for relaxing over two months—or less than a day per port.

Most delivery captains combine delivering with another profession, because unless they are on the top of the list with a busy delivery service, they'll rarely earn enough moving yachts to support a home and family. But for cruising people like ourselves, or for people with loosely planned schedules, delivering is good experience and a fine way to earn a lump sum of money because it's hard to spend much at sea.

Delivering someone else's dream ship is a large responsibility. Instead of taking a month to get to know the boat, you have to step on board, survey and assess it, outfit it, and get underway in a week or less. Once you're on board you have to be a jack-of-all-trades. You must be able to jury rig, haywire, and maintain a boat you are completely unfamiliar with. You'll have to know what spares are vital. The owner is turning the job over to you so he won't want to be bothered. The last thing he wants is to be called from each port with "The Jabsco pump impellor is burned out," or "The generator's not working right." The people who make the best delivery captains are good mechanics and riggers first, and sailors and navigators second.

An owner is influenced by first appearances just as much as is anyone else. If his or her yacht arrives in port with nice-looking varnish, scrubbed decks, and the interior in immaculate condition, he or she will overlook most small mechanical problems. So it really pays to spend your time at sea spiffing up the boat. It also pays to roll up and store away carpets and curtains. In a factory-fresh boat, avoid using any facilities you can so that the owner has the thrill of stepping into a new boat when it arrives. Most owners are willing to add a tip or a fine dinner on the town for the deliverer and crew that bring in a yacht looking better than when it left. And they'll definitely be willing to give you the reference you'll need for the next delivery job.

Whatever you do, write a contract, then get a one-third to one-half deposit before you leave to pick up a yacht. Make sure your contract states how the final payment will be made and in what currency. Include a clause the allows for expenses during breakdowns and states, for example, "The deliverer will allow three days for breakdowns because of faulty or worn equipment during the entire course of the delivery. After three days the owner must pay an additional $70 per day to cover cost of maintaining crew and boat during time taken to repair any breakdowns." Of cource, if the delivery is based on a daily fee, this clause is not necessary.

As for the final payment, it is safest to ask for cash on the barrelhead in the currency of your own country. Don't turn over the boat until you are paid either by the owner or his agent. We have never had any problem with payment but we've heard of several, including one story about a deliverer who had to wait two weeks for the owner to turn South African rands into dollars to pay the fee. The deliverer missed a berth on the Cape Town-Rio race because of the delay.

To protect yourself in foreign countries, have the owner write up a document making you captain of the yacht with full responsibility during a specified time in specified waters. It may come in handy, especially in African countries.

And finally, keep a log for the owner. He'll really appreciate knowing any problems you had, how many hours the engines were run, and what spares you used up.

Yacht deliveries involve a great deal of money. But, like any good business deal, a yacht delivery should come off with both parties satisfied and ready to do business again.

SECTION II

How Can I Handle It?

At the heart of any cruise is that wonderful three-thousand-year-old invention, the sailing vessel. This simple machine can be operated by the least educated of people, it uses no fuel, and it allows modern man to feel a sense of both cerebral and physical triumph over the elements.

Learning the basic skills of maneuvering under sail can be an exciting sport. The rewards of self-confidence, achievement, and low costs more than compensate for the time this practice takes. In the ultimate situation, your sailing and seamanship skills could make the difference between success or failure.

In all of the excitement of dreaming about and preparing for a cruise, don't forget the simplest, most important item. It's so basic it sounds corny, but don't forget to learn how to handle your cruising boat under sail.

5

Under Sail without an Engine

A few years ago I was speaking to a friend who sailed in company with the late Peter Pye, a well-known English sailor. Hale Field told of sailing *Renegade* and *Moonraker* up to the visitors' floating dock at the San Diego Yacht Club in southern California. Peter was planning to stay for three or four days so he was asked to move *Moonraker* from the visitor's dock to another one 300 yards away. Rather than start his engine, Peter and Ann sailed to the new dock. When Hale asked Peter why he hadn't used the more convenient way, his engine, this was Peter's reply: "It's easy to sail on the wide ocean, so I don't mind powering in a calm. But if I don't practice sailing in close quarters I might not be able to when I really have to."

You too can learn to maneuver your yacht without an engine anywhere there is water to float her. But, you must approach the problem with forethought. Sailing without using an auxiliary requires being prepared for all possible snags. Have your anchor ready to drop. Don't rely on your engine to bail you out of a tight situation; it may not start.

Each time you plan to moor under sail in an unfamiliar place you should go through these steps. First, take a dry run. In other words, sail near the unfamiliar dock or mooring. Check the local problems, the location of bollards, pilings, other vessels. If you plan on mooring alongside another vessel, use this chance to ask permission. Then sail back to less restricted waters. Now you know the problems involved. You have seen what lines or ground tackle you need. You are aware of the local wind and current. During your dry run you have seen how your vessel reacts in the restricted area. You've seen her handling limitations.

Secondly, now that you have taken the dry run, you can explain to all of your crew what you plan to do, in detail. You have lots of time as you reach back and forth in the less restricted waters. This is very important and the poor skipper rarely remembers to do this. Instead he blames his hapless uninformed crew when things go wrong. Remember, it is always the skipper's responsibility to make things clear and his fault when the operation fails.

Third, get out necessary gear and delegate individual jobs. In other words, say, "You handle the bow lines. I'll take the stern lines. Charlie, you stand by the jib halyard and be ready to let it go when we come alongside." Then, don't be reluctant to take another trial pass or two to size up the problems involved. Will I be close-hauled? Will I be running downwind into a narrow channel with no way of bailing out by rounding up into the wind? Or is it the simplest approach of all, a beam reach up a wide channel?

Now you know the rules of the game. You can sail up to the dock or mooring, and you know what is involved.

Naturally when sailing in close quarters, knowing how much room you need to tack or gybe and how long your yacht carries when you head into the wind is essential. When you are sailing an unfamiliar or new vessel, it is wise to spend an hour or two practicing with a plastic marker buoy. Sail up to the mark, heading into the wind. Does she carry less or more than you expected? Try approaching the marker as though it was a downwind slip, dropping your sails as you approach and covering the last bit under bare poles. Your objective is to arrive at the marker with very little way. I like to watch the wake made by *Seraffyn.* I have learned to judge the amount she'll carry by the disturbance she makes. The same type of judgment is needed to come alongside a dock or to anchor in tight spots. Until you can judge the carry of your ship, close-quarter sailing should not be attempted. (Remember the condition of your bottom will affect your carry. A foul one will slow you down substantially.)

The condition of your bottom affects your boat's carry.

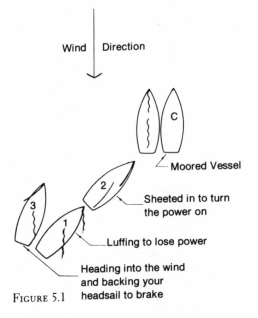

FIGURE 5.1

Wind | Direction

C

Moored Vessel

2

Sheeted in to turn
the power on

3

1

Luffing to lose power

Heading into the wind
and backing your
headsail to brake

When sailing up to a marker buoy you should approach on the leeward or downcurrent side so that when you pick up the mooring line you are swept slowly away from the buoy and not over it. As you practice you will find you can moor your vessel almost as easily and accurately as you can park your car.

Here are some methods we use to speed up or put on the brakes when sailing engineless *Seraffyn*. These tricks can be used when the wind is forward of the beam to save an otherwise perfect approach. In Figure 5.1, yacht number 1, you can ease your sheets and luff. This will slow you down, and by heading closer to the wind you can counteract any leeway. If you lose too much way you can bear off and tighten up the sheets to turn on a bit more wind power (yacht 2). As you come along side yacht C you can either drop all sail or ease sheets until all of your sail is luffing, being careful your sheets or main boom do not hang up on yacht C. Another way of killing your speed if luffing isn't enough is to head closer to the wind and have a crewman back the jib and/or mainsail (yacht 3). On larger vessels with strong winds this usually requires a strong tall crewman. By alternately

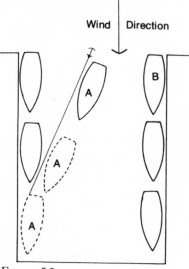

FIGURE 5.2

luffing, filling, or backing your sails you can achieve a surprising amount of control over your speed. But, a crowded anchorage is not the place to practice these skills.

A very efficient braking method used by the Baltic sailors is to have a stern anchor ready before sailing downwind into a narrow channel (Figure 5.2). When A is alongside B, the hook is dropped. In deeper water the hook should be dropped sooner, considering that a scope of at least three to one is minimum for any anchor to be effective. You then take one turn around a cleat or winch with the anchor line, easing or tightening in order to come into the slip under perfect speed and control. The anchor can be left set to haul you out when you are ready to leave. We also use this trick when we want to haul out on a slipway cradle. We tie the anchor rode to a convenient point on shore and haul ourselves off with it when the work is done.

Once you've learned to control your speed, the next step is to bring your yacht alongside another vessel using the experience gained practicing with the marker buoy. If you can, find a small anchored barge or a sympathetic friend with a yacht on a permanent mooring well clear of other vessels or obstructions. With fenders and mooring lines rigged, sail alongside, being careful to head into the wind or current. A few dozen passes and you will probably be able to have a good landing each time. Naturally, the more varied the wind and tide strengths you sail in, the greater your confidence and ability will become.

Now that you can come alongside under sail, you should also be able to sail away. If you can, raise your main and preset your mainsheet to a close reaching position. Have the jib all ready to haul up. Remove the bow line and as the wind carries your bow away from the barge, clear the stern line and give your stern a good shove. Now you are close reaching on the starboard tack. Hoist your jib and you are underway. If your vessel doesn't sail well under main alone, then hoist the main and jib prior to casting off your bow line. As soon as you are clear and the main is full and by, you can sheet in the flapping jib. But, remember, be sure your crew knows what you are going to do and how you are going to do it before casting off your lines.

When you feel you can confidently lay up to and sail away from a moored vessel, you should progress to laying alongside more crowded docks and quays.

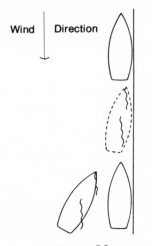

Wind | Direction

FIGURE 5.3

One of the most challenging situations is sailing up to a quay which has only one small space left between two boats (Figure 5.3). Your way must be accurately judged to allow you enough steerage to turn into the dock, clear the downwind yacht, and avoid running into the windward yacht. The most prudent way to do this if conditions are difficult (strong wind or strong tide) is to ask permission and then sail alongside the windward yacht and warp aft to the vacant dock space. With the wind forward this is quite simple, even in large vessels.

Sailing out of this spot would be very much like sailing away from the anchored yacht in rough conditions. Assuming you are tied starboard to as in Figure 5.3, a starboard line is doubled up to the port quarter of the windward yacht. In other words, cleat one end of the line on board, pass it around the port quarter cleat of the vessel to windward and then bring the end back on board. This will allow you to pull your vessel to windward as your bow falls off and your sails fill on the starboard tack. As you gather way you can let go of the end of your line and it will run clear. Then you can coil it back on board at leisure. Don't use a line with an eye-spliced end as it usually won't run free.

Whenever you have to sail out of a tight situation, you should always consider using warps or ground tackle. Especially if you are shorthanded. In the situation shown in Figure 5.4 I would row out

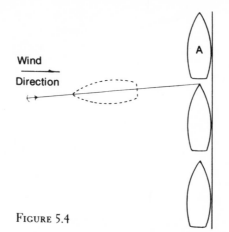

FIGURE 5.4

an anchor and then winch myself out to clear water and sail off the anchor. It's by far the safest way unless you have plenty of strong crew to give you a good shove to windward, clear of vessel A.

Anchoring under sail is very simple when you know how much way is carried by your vessel. You simply select a clear spot with enough swinging room to take care of your scope. Explain to your crew what you are doing. For example: "We'll head into the wind and should fetch up about 100 yards astern of that blue sloop." If you lose way and find you've misjudged, don't be reluctant to bear off and take another pass so you can spot your anchor exactly where you hope to in the first place. You might lose a little face with your crew, but it will be much less painful than having to get up in the middle of the night when the tide swings you onto that blue sloop.

When sailing off the anchor, the trick is to get steerage way as soon as possible. If it is a large deserted anchorage, no problem. But a crowded spot with other yachts close by requires good planning before you sail off. Think your plan through, then tell your crew, "If I back the jib just as the anchor is raised, the bow will swing to

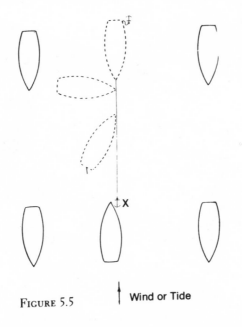

FIGURE 5.5   ↑ Wind or Tide

leeward. That will put you on the port tack, clearing the boat anchored on your port side." In close quarters it is a good idea to have your jib and main hoisted when your hook comes up. This allows you to accelerate and gain way much faster and is therefore safer. Keeping enough way in a crowded anchorage is essential. If you lose steerage and end up in stays, the current or wind can set you down on other vessels.

In order to anchor in a crowded spot, such as in Figure 5.5 with the wind aft, drop your main and sail in under jib alone, in stronger winds under bare poles. On your dry run you have looked over the situation and decided to put your hook down at X. Your ground tackle is all rigged and ready to let go as you approach. One of the crew drops the anchor at X, paying out chain slowly as the anchor starts to bite in. You swing the rudder to turn to starboard if your chain roller is on the starboard side, to port if it is on the port side. This swings the vessel's bow away from the chain so you don't override and mess up your topsides. As you do this the movement of the boat automatically sets your hook, and if other vessels are lying to bow and stern anchors, you can fall aft paying out twice the amount

Figure 5.6

of bow rode you need. Then you drop your stern hook and draw back on the bow rode until you are securely anchored right in the middle of your two anchors. You've done it completely under sail without having to get in the dinghy and row out your tackle. When it's time to leave, you simply reverse the procedure to pick up the stern hook.

I like to stow my anchor as in Figure 5.6, for immediate use and easy restowage. My 100-pound wife can set and restow our anchor in all but extreme conditions. I highly advise some similar easy stowing method if you're going under sail shorthanded.

Handling warps and ground tackle is almost a lost art. Rarely do I see anyone set a beam anchor to hold their yacht off a nasty dock or quay. Warping is hard work unless you have proper ground tackle and warping lines and they are convenient and easy to use.

Three strand lines are almost impossible to use quickly when they kink. Bert Darrell, a well-known practical sailor and owner of a yacht yard in Hamilton, Bermuda, taught me a very useful trick to cure them. His solution: "Starting with one end, coil the line backwards (counterclockwise), letting the kinks fall as they may in an ever-widening coil. When the line has all been coiled, pick up the starting end from the center of the coil and recoil it in the proper clockwise direction. Repeat these steps until all of the kinks disappear." I've tried this and it works very well.

Lines that don't run smoothly or that foul when you need them can be dangerous, especially when you are in close quarters. Another

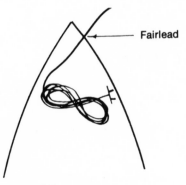

Fairlead

FIGURE 5.7

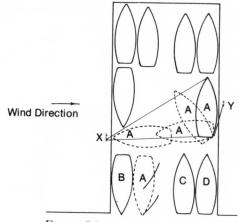

Wind Direction

trick was taught to me by an English sailor as we went through the Panama Canal using four 100-foot lines to position the boat in the center of the locks. He coiled his lines in a figure of eight on deck with the coil at right angles to the fairlead (Figure 5.7). All of the lines ran smoothly without snagging or looping around themselves. Long hawsers can then be conveniently stored by tying marlin with quick-releasing reef knots around the center of the figure of eight and at the top and bottom and then folding them in half. Your hawsers are then quick and easy to use.

These two tricks can help your warping immensely by speeding up your maneuvers and giving you the satisfaction of a job that runs without a hitch.

Warping out of a very crowded anchorage can always be done with safety if you have sufficient lines and fenders. If the wind is fresh in the situation illustrated in Figure 5.8, you could have great difficulties coming out even under power. With only a bit more effort you could warp out in style and complete safety.

Vessel A rows one line from her port bow and one from her port stern to bollard X, leaving one after spring line to hold position. Bow and stern lines are then winched in, pulling the vessel sideways to windward. When you are clear of the dock, winch the bow to windward being careful to fend off vessels C and D. Adjust your bow line so you can step off your transom to retrive your spring line from bollard Y. Now you can use your bow line to warp over to bollard X. Using hand lines and fenders, work alongside vessel B. Coil your warps, have a cup of tea, hoist your sails, and reach off into the blue.

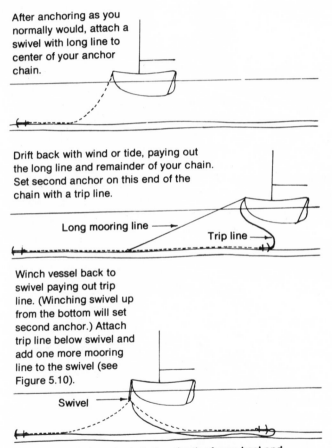

After anchoring as you normally would, attach a swivel with long line to center of your anchor chain.

Drift back with wind or tide, paying out the long line and remainder of your chain. Set second anchor on this end of the chain with a trip line.

Long mooring line →

Trip line →

Winch vessel back to swivel paying out trip line. (Winching swivel up from the bottom will set second anchor.) Attach trip line below swivel and add one more mooring line to the swivel (see Figure 5.10).

Swivel →

Lower swivel into water to below depth of your keel and secure both mooring lines with well-attached chaffing gear.

Figure 5.9*

All this maneuver requires is keeping cool and sorting out what you are going to do beforehand.

When anchoring stern to at a quay or dock, you should drop your anchor dead to windward of the vacant berth, leaving your mainsail set and paying out chain with your winch. As you settle aft toward the berth and the wind or current sets you to one side or the other, you can steer your vessel by pushing your mainboom to windward, either port or starboard. With strong wind or current, set your anchor and row a line into the dock. Then warp in as you pay out your anchor chain. This way you avoid fouling other vessels. If the wind is at right angles to the dock, you can anchor with a minimum scope, then row your long warp ashore and attach it to a bollard. Then ease your bow anchor while winching in your stern. If the wind is not too strong, this can be accomplished with little difficulty.

To set a permanent mooring under sail alone (Figure 5.9), drop your anchor and drift back with the wind or tide, paying out half of the chain you have (in our case half is 150 feet). At the midpoint set a swivel with a long mooring line leading to it. Then drift back again, letting out the rest of your chain. When you reach the bitter end, attach your second large anchor and drop it overboard with a trip

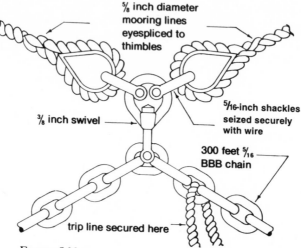

⅝ inch diameter mooring lines eyespliced to thimbles

¾ inch swivel

⁵⁄₁₆-inch shackles seized securely with wire

300 feet ⁵⁄₁₆ BBB chain

trip line secured here

FIGURE 5.10

line attached. Then use the first long line to pull yourself back to the swivel. Attach two large diameter nylon lines to the swivel with properly moused shackles (Figure 5.10). Secure the trip line to the chain near the swivel and lower the swivel until it is below the level of your keel. Secure the two mooring lines with good chafing gear attached.

I can sweep or scull *Seraffyn*, 5 tons gross weight, into or out of many windless tight spots. I use a 14-foot ash sweep. This allows me to scull out of narrow channels or to sweep at about 1¾ knots in calm or tideless waters. Only one oar is necessary in open waters. French sailing yachts under 5 tons are required by law to carry a sculling oar and consequently many Frenchmen sail without power, using their sweep when necessary. See Section 4, Chapter 13 on Oar Power.

Practice under sail alone, and you will have more fun and get into less trouble. In other words, if your engine fails you know how to sail. You are forced to keep all of your sailing gear, ground tackle, and warps in good working order. The more you use them, the more reliable they are. The more you sail, the more skilled you become. But conversely, the more you use an engine, the more it wears and the more likely it is to fail!

6

Be Prepared

Can you handle your boat under sail offshore in all conditions if your engine fails?

Engines should be considered a convenience on an auxiliary sailboat, not a necessity. Sailing vessels have been handled without them for centuries. The British Navy blockaded Napoleon's French coast for twenty years. They never lost a ship except in battle, though they patrolled the English Channel and Bay of Biscay in all weather, winter and summer, working close to shore in extremely clumsy, unweatherly vessels! Surely we can safely sail our outside-ballasted, close-winded yachts at ideal times of the year without depending on an engine to get us out of bad situations.

Time and time again, we've watched people waste cruising time in miserable harbors waiting for parts to arrive for their engine. With confidence in their sailing ability, they could have sailed on to a larger, more pleasant port where parts and service would be available and had fine cruising along the way. The suggestions that follow will help you be prepared to enjoy your cruising whether your engine works or not.

1. Have all of your sailing gear in good order with plenty of spares on board. Have extra food and water in case you are delayed. A simple sailboat should not be hard to keep shipshape. Unlike engines, most potential problems with sails, masts, spreaders, hulls, and rudders can be checked by eye or touch.

2. More important, after you clear port, get a good offing. The greatest danger to a sailboat is the land, not the sea. Very few of the large commercial sailing ships foundered at sea. Most of them were driven ashore due to poor windward ability and an inadequate offing. The distance off that is good enough varies with wind strength, direction, and sea conditions. If you are coasting and the wind is off the land, you can stay quite close to the shore. If the wind increases to a gale, you can go in and anchor. It is better to be anchored in the lee of the land resting, than to heave-to and be blown offshore. (But if you are anchored, be careful that the wind doesn't swing and drive you ashore. When we are in this position with an unsteady barometer, I'd put two reefs in the main, then set the alarm clock for every two hours in case the wind veers or backs. It could be disastrous to be awakened by Force 8 onshore winds and a nasty sea.)

Keep farther offshore if the wind is blowing onto the land, at least two or three miles even in the lightest breezes with a steady glass and good weather report.

If the wind increases to Force 6 or 7, head way offshore, especially if you aren't making port. Twenty-five or 35 miles is a fair margin, but I would keep working offshore because the wind could increase more. The farther off, the safer you are. We have hove-to quite comfortably in Force 10 winds in the North Atlantic for two days. We lost approximately 18 miles to leeward. Our yacht, *Seraffyn,* has a long, moderately deep keel and does not make much leeway. Hove-to with a fin-and-skeg-type boat, with its smaller lateral resistance, you need a sea anchor or extra sea room.*

3. Heaving-to is the classic safety valve of the sailing vessel. If you keep well to windward and become tired, you can stop and rest. You can heave-to and wait for morning or till fog clears to run in on your landfall. During *Seraffyn's* sea trials we left at 1900 one day to sail to Fisherman's Cove, Catalina Island, California. Lin was practicing her navigation, and when we approached the island two hours before dawn, she elected to heave-to and wait because she just didn't like the way things looked in comparison with the chart. It was a good decision, as the bay was blocked with a temporary log boom that was being used in some marine biology experiment; not exactly the thing to run into at night.

4. To sail without relying on your engine you need a boat that will

*See *Storm Tactics Handbook,* by Lin and Larry Pardey

go to windward when necessary, even in gale conditions. You need easy reefing and good strong storm sails, plus real familiarity with your gear *before* the storm conditions are upon you.

5. Keep to windward! What a temptation it is to ease off the wind and roar along on a beam reach, rather than staying close hauled gaining to windward. No matter how tempting, don't start your sheets on a long haul if the wind is forward of the beam. Always keep about 10 degrees or 15 degrees to windward of your rhumb line. If the wind falls aft of the beam you can safely sail your rhumb line course. Many times I have been tempted into easing my sheets and close reaching only to be headed, and then I've had to make several tacks to clear a headland or make port.

6. Sailing without depending on your auxiliary requires thinking ahead. The prudent single-engine pilot is always looking for a patch of decent ground to land on in case his engine fails, especially when he is flying over unknown territory. An alert sailor should do the same, looking at his chart and checking ahead for the depths and bottom conditions near shore in case that nice offshore breeze dies. If you know you can anchor ahead (shoaling water and sand bottom), it is safe to stay near the land. But if the chart shows deep water, steep to the shore, and a rocky coast, keep a good offing. Remember your ace in the hole when sailing with or without an engine is your ground tackle.

I have seen a sailor motoring in a light breeze within 25 yards of a steep-to, rocky headland which was a prevailing lee shore. There was a long, large, onshore swell. He had his sun cover over the boom, mainsail furled and covered, the jib and anchor stowed below. What faith he had in his engine! Just a bit of water or dirt in his fuel and the engine could have died, giving him no time to get sailing or even to anchor.

7. Keep clear of high large points of land because major headlands often have unusual effects. They can create strong currents, sudden downdraughts or a blanketing effect that eliminates your nice breeze. I once got in trouble this way. It was during the first week of our cruise, eight years ago. We sailed into the lee of Isla Guadaloupe less than ¼ mile offshore, all sails set, after two days of reaching along in the lovely 15-knot Pacific northwesterly. The 3,000-foot high cliffs of this narrow island caused a fierce williwaw that laid us cabinsides awash before we could react. Water poured through the open com-

panionway and I prayed as I shoved the helm down. *Seraffyn* rounded surely into the wind and I was able to dowse most of the sails, but not before we had 50 gallons of sea water below. I had learned my lesson.

8. Learn to use tides and currents to your advantage. The merchant sailingmen had to plot their voyages to deliver cargo where it was wanted as quickly as possible and usually weren't able to use the classic round-the-world tradewind route. So they learned to recognise and use every favorable current. They were able to sail in and out of ports and places today's cruising sailors rarely attempt.

For coastal sailing in places with a large rise and fall of tide, you have to schedule your movements with the help of a good tidal almanac. On long passages, the ocean's currents can also be used to great advantage. One passage we made in *Seraffyn* that I am particularly proud of was from the Panama Canal to Kingston, Jamaica, via Cartagena, Colombia. When we were in San Diego, California, on board *Wanderer IV*, I discussed our plans with Eric Hiscock. We planned to cruise to Panama and from there to the East Coast of the United States. Eric's comment was, "I wouldn't try that passage in a straight sailing boat. The wind is against you, the Gulf Stream is against you, and we have spent more time running under bare poles in the Caribbean than anywhere else!" I took this into consideration and sewed a third reef into our mainsail. We left Panama and the usual northeast tradewind was blowing, so we beat along the Panamanian shore using the Caribbean countercurrent (1½ knots average) on our stern all the way to Cartagena, Colombia. We gained much needed easting this way. By studying the pilot charts for each month we learned that the prevailing northeast trades swing more to the east in late spring. We left in May with wind from the east, heading 25 degrees high of our rhumb line to counteract the Gulf Stream. We made our landfall 4 miles to windward of Kingston, five days and five hours later (480 miles). We used the British Admiralty publication *Ocean Passages for the World* and the American pilot charts to turn an extremely difficult beat to windward against the Gulf Stream into one close-reaching tack and averaged 95 miles a day in our 24-foot cutter.

When you are near the coast it is simple to figure out if tide or current is setting you by taking compass bearings astern or on the beam. If you plot them hourly you will know the exact effect for the distance and time run. Offshore, you can use multiple sextant sights to plot the effect of the currents. When we were leaving Cartagena, I took five separate sun sights, a half-hour apart. The first four showed I had not headed high enough. I was being set below my rhumb line. By the time I had taken the fifth sight I had hardened the sheets to steer 25 degrees above my rhumb line to counteract the effects of the Gulf Stream.

9. Don't miss a fair wind. In Gibraltar we watched numerous cruising people who wanted to sail west to the Canaries, staying in port because it was blowing Force 7 easterly with heavy gusts in the harbor. The weather forecasts stated that these gusts were only local. The barometer was steady. But these sailors were timid and waiting for perfect conditions. By the time they left, the easterly winds quit and the prevailing southwesterly Force 4 or 5 set in. So they had to beat against 2 or 3 knots of easterly current or resort to power.

When you are under sail you must be ready to leave the instant the winds are fair, day or night, not always when it's most comfortable.

10. Your boat must be able to move in very light airs. Our log-books show only six-and-one-half days of complete calm during the past eight years. This would probably equal the hours spent just maintaining a diesel engine. But we do have the maximum working rig the designer would recommend for *Seraffyn*, plus a huge spinnaker and nylon drifter. We're glad to have these because we spend about 50 percent of our time cruising in winds of less than 12 knots.

Light air sailing with little or no sea is definitely the most comfortable and enjoyable. You are making 70 or 80 miles a day. The windvane is steering happily. It's warm and dry and the boat is moving like a magic carpet as you lounge back and quietly read a good book. The majority of cruising people miss these idyllic conditions because to them winds of Force 2 or 3 mean "being becalmed." To move well without using your engine in light conditions, you have to sail harder. You must have light air sails and be rigged to control them properly. You must be able to reef quickly and easily when the time comes, i.e., jiffy reefing, jib downhaul, lazyjacks for the mainsail. And you also must keep your bottom clean and reasonably smooth.

If you are going downwind or reaching in very light winds with a lumpy leftover sea, and your mainsail starts to back and slat, you can set a large nylon drifter and drop the main. You'll move just as fast. The drifter will just pant instead of slatting and chafing. When we are reaching without the mainsail, we sheet the drifter normally, but when running we lead the drifter through a block on the end of the main boom and secure the boom forward with the preventer vang. For someone alone on deck this is usually easier to set up than the spinnaker pole. You can also use your spinnaker alone in very light conditions, but I wouldn't recommend carrying it without the mainsail set in anything but the lightest winds as you might have trouble getting it down.

Almost all shorthanded cruising sailors we meet who have boats ranging from 25 feet to 50 feet, with or without engines, say that they average about 100 miles a day on long passages, year in and year out. We find we do the same. I know that when I am sailing larger boats and am alone on watch, I am not so keen to change headsails or reef the main or generally sail the boat near its potential. It's a matter of size and handiness. A genoa on a 40-foot boat is a handful for one man to carry, let alone set, so I suppose the reason boats of 25 feet or 30 feet average about the same as boats 30 feet to 50 feet is that they are easier to sail efficiently. Naturally when a person is sailing without using his engine, he is continually learning to sail better in all conditions and keeping his sailing gear in better order, simplifying sail-handling procedures and smoothing out all the wrinkles to get a better sailing machine. So he too can keep up his 100 mile-a-day average.

If you'd enjoy the idea of sailing without an expensive inboard engine, but your cruising time is limited and you have to be home for work on Monday morning, consider an economical solution: a sculling oar or an outboard motor for your dinghy. Tie your inflatable tender or hard dinghy alongside with good fenders and putt your way through that calm. We've watched sailing boats up to 35 feet long being maneuvered around harbors and at sea this way (see Chapter 12, Section IV—"The Alternatives").

11. You must sail defensively. Only two or three times have I thought I needed an engine and I realize now that these were times when I was not sailing defensively. After we had transited the Kiel Canal by hitching a tow from a fishing boat, we left Cuxhaven with a

strong fair tide flushing us out the river Elbe. The wind was from the northwest so we could just make our course. We had gone 20 miles when the wind lightened and the tide started to turn. We weren't gaining over the ground so decided to work outside the deep channel and anchor in about two fathoms behind the marker buoys until the tide changed. The ships were bumper to bumper. We attempted to squeeze through two or three times, only to tack back into the channel as ships bore down on us. Finally we made our bid. Suddenly we saw the red and green lights of a large coaster's masthead lights in line, and we barely had steerage. As the ship steamed down on us, I was sure we were in for a collision. I flashed our large torch on the mainsail, and Lin ran down and got the freon fog horn and started blasting away. The coaster cleared our stern by 50 feet. We soon safely anchored in 2 fathoms outside the channel. My mistake was in not studying the charts before I left so I could stay out of the big ship channel. There was lots of water and room for yachts outside the buoyed channel. If you study the charts beforehand you can elect to stay well out of traffic separation zones in areas such as Ushant, Finisterre, English Channel approaches, and the Straits of Florida.

12. Don't make more than a daylight passage single-handed, with or without an engine. It is believed that the great single-handed sailor Joshua Slocum, who disappeared at sea, was run down by a ship even though the shipping was much lighter just after the turn of the century. No prudent sailor would sail around today with the massively increased shipping and no watch on deck. Our experience has proven that merchant ships don't necessarily stick to shipping lanes and sea-going tugs rarely do. You must keep a twenty-four-hour watch to be safe.

In Dartmouth, England, we watched an excellent single-handed sailor without an engine wait for three weeks for perfect conditions to make his dash up the channel to The Solent. As he told us and rightly too, he was very concerned about being out in the heavy channel shipping without someone to keep watch all the time. He figured he could make it to The Solent in perfect conditions without having to sleep. But I feel this is a very chancy way to go to sea.

13. Carry a large flashlight (battery operated) and use it to alert ships to your presence and if necessary to flash a D signal on your mainsail (Morse code - - .. meaning "I am maneuvering with diffi-

culty, keep clear"). Also make sure your running lights are easily visible and burning all night.

We have a new freon strobe light which operates on two D cell batteries. It is on its own flagstaff. With this hoisted above the masthead when we have to, ships report they can see us for 3 or 4 miles. The flash is visible up to ¼ mile in extremely thick fog.

Finally, be careful of being towed. If you sail without an engine or your engine breaks down, you might wish to accept a tow someday. But try to avoid this because you will rarely know the ability of the man or vessel offering assistance. Few people in power vessels realize how much way a sailboat carries and the effect of windage on a mast and rigging. If you do need a tow, give the other boat your line and be able to release your end quickly. Also, have your anchor ready. When you accept a tow in close quarters, the motorboat should tie alongside with propeller slightly aft of your rudder for better control.

If you lose your mast or rudder and need a tow, be sure you arrange the price at sea and get it on paper. When we were in Malaga, Spain, we met a sailor with a 30-foot cutter who'd been dismasted off Torremolinos. He was well offshore and in no immediate danger, but his engine would not start so he signalled a fishing boat and asked him for a tow into Malaga. When they arrived in port the fisherman asked for $170 for one hour's towing—not really a lot. The yachtsman didn't have the ready cash so the fisherman was held in port for three full days getting a lien on the boat. The final outcome was that the port authorities awarded the fisherman $1,000 for the tow and the fishing time lost. Whatever the situation, remember you are trusting your vessel to someone else's seamanship the minute you take a tow.

I have delivered a lot of auxiliary yachts and I find myself turning on the motor when the boat's speed drops below 3 knots. I'm lazy and instead of getting out the light weather sails, I take the easy way and mindlessly power along hoping the wind will freshen. When I get into port I don't have the feeling of accomplishment that I do after making a passage on our own engineless *Seraffyn*.

Leave your auxiliary in neutral to charge your batteries and pump bilges, don't turn the prop shaft, and I guarantee your self-esteem and sailing ability will improve immensely as you learn to make ocean passages completely under sail.

Cruising Is a Sharing Proposition

When you look around at the world of longtime cruising people, one thing is immediately apparent. Today the vast majority of cruising boats are owned and sailed by couples or small families. The Hiscocks, the Roths, the Paysons, the Dyers—cruising magazine columns which report the details of cruising boats arriving in foreign ports almost always list ten times as many couples and families as they do single-handers or boats sailed by two or more people of the same sex.

The following chapters discuss some ways to create the type of partnership that will keep ocean voyaging from being a lonely experience. One tells how to meet people when you arrive in some new port.

The last chapter in this section illustrates why I enjoy sailing with Larry. In port or at sea, good weather or bad, it's all better when it's a shared proposition.

7

Free the Galley Slave

There were only two yachts in the tiny fishing port at Carbonara, Sardinia, and it took but a few minutes before the usual questions began.

"Where you coming from?" we asked the two men on the French sloop. Fortunately they spoke English and our conversation quickly advanced till the four of us sat in their cockpit sampling the wine which Joe had made at his own vineyards near Paris.

"Let's make a dinner together tonight," Joe suggested.

"Great idea," I replied. "You can help celebrate our eleventh anniversary."

Joe looked surprised. "You've been cruising eleven years?"

Larry looked even more surprised. "It's our anniversary?" His chagrined look was good for a round of teasing. Then we explained that we'd been cruising eight of the eleven years we'd been together.

"How I envy you two," Joe sighed. "I wanted Jeannie to cruise with me. But she said, 'Go on, find some man to take with you.' I found Mike here, and he's a great guy, but I'd much prefer Jeannie".

Larry and I then left in our dinghy and headed toward a promising reef to skindive for something to cook for our part of the dinner. As Larry rowed he said, "Women want security. That's why so few of them go cruising."

"That's just your opinion," I retorted. "Women don't like cruising because most men are too wrapped up in their dreams to consider a homemaker's needs. They forget to include their wives in the planning of the whole scheme, and they are too impatient to properly introduce their wives to sailing."

As we lazed on a rock after chasing a few fish, Larry and I discussed the whole idea further and came to the conclusion that a woman's first sailing experiences often determine her whole attitude toward cruising. My very first sail was on board the 53-foot ketch Larry maintained and chartered. We had a 30-mile reach along the southern California coast over a smooth sea, sun caressing us as we moved gently along. Then a week later I joined Larry and a keen racing crew on a crack 32-footer, and in lovely 10-knot breezes we won! After that introduction to sailing, anyone would love it. Yet from the stories I hear, many first sails are disastrous. Rough seas, heavy spray, a touch of seasickness. If I'd been introduced to sailing on an average day in the English Channel, complete with fog, Force 6 winds, tidal overfalls, heavy shipping, and cold seas, I think I'd have given up on sailing. If you really want your wife or girlfriend to join you in this wonderful adventure, be cunning. Select your first sailing afternoons with care. The necessary introduction to rougher weather can come later.

"The minute we untied our mooring lines, my husband turned into a Captain Bligh. He started bossing me around—do this, do that—no 'please,' no 'thank you.' " Three women I've met in the last six months have told me this. All of them are anti-cruising. Though I realize that someone on board has to take charge, one of the most important things a couple must learn is that a few minutes of joint planning before you hoist the sails or approach your mooring will eventually eliminate the shouting and foul-ups. Some basic sailing instruction in a dinghy class could give your female mate the knowledge and skill she needs to assist you easily and enjoyably. Many jokes have been told about husbands trying to teach their wives to drive a car. The same jokes apply to sailing. Then add the complexity of a 5- or 10-ton yacht and you will understand why a fifteen- or twenty-hour sailing course may be the best possible introduction to cruising.

Look at your own sailing skills. Unless your mate instinctively trusts your ability, she'll never be able to relax and enjoy cruising. A few hours' special training or a cruise-and-learn charter may prevent you from being a nervous skipper who transmits his fears to his mate.

When we were guests at the Coral Reef Yacht Club in Miami five years ago, the owner of a handsome 28-footer told us his wife loved sailing but didn't like the idea of cruising. In fact, though she would readily go off for an afternoon sail or race, she dreaded weekending. I met her soon after and asked her why.

"It's alright for Sam," she told me. "He just throws some boat gear in the car Friday evening and off we go. But for me, a weekend sail means shopping for special food on Thursday, locating a 50-pound block of ice, and sorting out all the sailing clothes. Friday I pack all the dishes, pots and pans; prepare the food, clothes and wet gear; farm out the parakeet; and make sure I've remembered the toilet paper. Then it's off to the boat, unpack, and cook a three-course dinner. Saturday and Sunday, Sam lounges in the sun as soon as the anchor is down while I still have to cook meals and wash dishes. Then we return home and it's clean the boat, pack the dishes, pots and pans, and take it all to the car. Monday, wash the sailing clothes, unpack the ice chest. Sam has a sailing holiday and I end up with twice the housework."

If Sam considered stocking his weekender with its own set of dishes, pots, and pans, and a store of canned and dry goods; if he pitched in and did half the cooking and dishes; if he poured Sue a cocktail as soon as the anchor grabbed hold—cruising would be a lot more fun for her.

Once your female partner is over the hurdle of learning about sailing and she becomes interested in the idea of shaking off the mooring lines and cruising, you've got to work hard to make sure she stays involved. The couples we see who cruise successfully are true partners. The husband and wife sit down together and plan everything: itinerary, choice of boat, modifications for cruising, work schedules, and finances.

Many women want the security of having money in the bank—a cushion that is there if needed. I know I do. It's easy for Larry to say, "Don't worry; I can always earn more." But I want the security of having enough money to take care of both of us if Larry catches pneumonia, breaks a leg, or worse. I consider the health and feeding of my family first and I want to know where I stand. It doesn't take a lot of money to give your cruising mate the security she wants. The savings in buying a 29-footer instead of a 32-footer could mean money in the bank.

Try to encourage your partner to learn all she can about boat-handling, maintenance, navigation, and the like. Some of the best navigators are women. Mary Blewitt has written one of the definitive books on learning small-boat celestial naviagation. Women make superb sailmakers and good varnishers and some love repairing and maintaining engines and electronic gear. The more involved your wife becomes before you actually select your cruising boat, the better. On a cruising boat there isn't much room for role-playing; the more overlapping skills both of you have, the better.

When I had drinks with Joe on board his French sloop, I could see why Jeannie had opted out. The boat's interior had been built with only Joe in mind. There was a two-way radio, depth-sounder, and wind speed/direction console, but only a one-burner stove. The counter space was an edge of the chart table. There was no dinner table, not one double bunk and the only clothes storage was in open nets. Joe admitted that the few times Jeannie had been on board he expected her to cook and clean because that's what she enjoyed doing at home. He never considered that she foresaw the fact that 365 days a year Joe would demand three good meals. As mate she could look forward to spending three or four hours a day working in a cramped, primitive galley. Yet Joe had used a quarter of the total space in the main cabin for a navigation area which he rarely used more than two hours a day, and then only when at sea. Since few cruisers spend more than 15 percent of their time at sea, simple mathematical logic indicates that the galley would be used eight to ten times more than the navigation area. Joe agreed that if he had thought about it he could have spent a lot more of his time, money, and space on a good galley and interior and less on navigation equipment, and perhaps ended up with Jeannie instead of Mike.

Eight years ago, when we first set off in *Seraffyn*, people were very surprised to see a 24-footer with a separate stateroom forward. Now this arrangement has become standard on small cruising boats, and I think it is a very good one. Not only does it provide a double bunk which lets you enjoy the pleasures of marriage, but it gives both of you a place to sleep that is away from where you sit most of the day.

For most men, this distinction is of small importance. But to a woman who takes charge of the housekeeping, it's the difference between camping out and really living. Being forced to clear the table, lower it, get out the bedding, and make up the bed every night in order to sleep on the convertible dining table is a nuisance.

If you want your wife to enjoy cruising, try looking at every detail in the boat from *her* point of view. Work at making its smallest details a pleasure for her; get her ideas on interior improvements. Arrange a simple but effective solar heated siphon shower. Fix up the galley before you start installing a new radio direction finder. Urge her to make simpler meals underway and save her cordon bleu cookery for days in a calm anchorage. Get her out of the galley with a dinner ashore or by letting her sail while you cook. Let her choose the anchorage or plan a day's sight-seeing. Treat her to a night or two in a good hotel once in a while. These thoughtful gestures give your female mate tangible evidence that you appreciate having her afloat with you.

Otherwise a vicious circle often evolves once you are cruising. You arrive in port. Your wife has to shop for stores, then she returns to cook a meal, then does the dishes. Off to shop for more stores, wash the laundry, cook a meal, do the dishes, and so on till she stops and says, "Why go cruising? All I see is the marketplace, the stove, and the sink. If I'd stayed at home I'd have hot water and a washing machine." There have been times when I've been tempted to throw the laundry bag overboard and quit eating. To make things worse, I'd find myself scrubbing yet another dirty pot while Larry was lounging with a drink in his hand. Finally I blew up. This would rarely happen to a woman in a conventional shoreside situation. She'd watch her husband leave for work at 8 A.M. He'd return nine hours later, tired from the office, and she'd be glad to see him sitting back at ease. But having spent the whole day with Larry, I knew he'd done nothing harder than pull a jib sheet. Once he was aware of this cycle, he worked to help break it by pitching in with the housework. He makes sure we have ice on board so the two of us can do the marketing just once a week. When there is no laundromat nearby, he helps carry water and wrings and hangs the clothes. This way we are free to spend more time together sight-seeing, skindiving, or reading in the cockpit. He also learns more about our boat as he works along with me. My request for a good trash bag arrangement made a lot more sense to him after he had to look for a place to throw the tea leaves.

Cruising has to be a partnership to be fun. Larry and I share the work and the enjoyment of each other's projects. It is important that women have the time to learn to mend sails, work on boat gear, and generally stay involved with the sailing end of things.

Many men embark on a cruise, but the vast majority of long-term cruising boats we've seen are sailed by a couple. That's why I scoffed when Larry said that women like security better than sailing. Many women, just like many men, love excitement, challenge, and change—especially when they are made a true partner in the great adventure.

8

It May Be Worth Your Life to Teach Your Wife

Eric Hiscock wrote, "The only way to get a good crew is to marry one." Being a married crew on board a long-distance ocean cruiser, I can't help but agree with him; but, for every wife who loves sailing and plans for each voyage with as much enthusiasm and excitement as her husband, there are at least ten who go cruising only because they have to. There are another twenty who won't even consider going and probably five times that number who aren't interested in going sailing at all, not even for a balmy afternoon.

Although it would be easy to place all of the blame on the distaff side, I feel that most of this problem is caused by husbands who don't teach their wives to sail.

A husband may protest and say, "My wife is welcome to learn all she wants. I let her take the tiller when I'm pulling up the anchor." But a cruising boat is an impossible place for a beginner to learn sailing. I recently met one couple living on a 35-foot sloop. They had wandered around together for a year and yet Shirley had never hoisted the mainsail by herself. From the first, her job had been to start the engine and then hold the tiller. When I asked Grant why he hadn't taught Shirley more about their boat, he said, "It's easier to do it myself. By the time I show Shirley how to use the halyard winch properly, I can have the sails set and drawing."

Another man said his wife didn't need to learn how to work the anchor winch. "She's got enough to keep her busy in the galley. Why should she learn to set an anchor?"

And the most common complaint I hear from women who don't really know how to sail their cruising home is, "Every time I try to take the helm he nags me: you're pinching, the sail is luffing, you're off course."

Tremendous dividends can be gained by really teaching your wife to sail. If she knows how to short tack up a river, how to adjust and reef the mainsail, and the basics of navigation, sailing is bound to be more interesting for her.

Sailing will also be less frightening when your wife knows what to do in tight situations. I'll never forget how I froze stiff with fear one day when Larry released the staysail sheet in a storm with winds of Force 10. The staysail snapped and flogged, shaking the boat from stem to stern. Larry had it down and bagged only minutes later, with the boat riding easily hove to under a deeply-reefed mainsail. Had I been on deck able to help him and aware of what exactly was happening, I'd have expected the noise and realized it didn't represent danger.

Knowing the more technical aspects of sailing will make your wife aware of the safety built into a proper cruising yacht. She'll be able to look at your cruising home and say, "Yes, this boat is strong and safe." Confidence in your boat will again make sailing more enjoyable for the crew you married.

Once your wife knows how to sail your boat well in most conditions, you will be able to sleep soundly on your off-watches. If you are confident that she will wake you before the boat is overburdened in a squall or before you get too close to a lee shore, you will really be able to enjoy your bunk time. Every time your wife has to wake you to change course or tack or shake out a reef, you lose a half hour's sleep. On a long voyage this can make the difference between a wise decision or a fatigued one when you reach your landfall.

However, the most important reason I'm glad that Larry taught me to sail well is that I really love him. Some day it might be worth his life that I am able to sail *Seraffyn* completely by myself. We were in the outer islands of the Finnish archipelago near Turku when Larry started having severe stomach pains. He is normally healthy as a bull so I was rightly worried. I rowed into a small trading post and called a doctor. From the symptoms I described, she diagnosed possible kidney stones and said to start sailing immediately as the Coast Guard was occupied with a pregnant woman on another island. We had painkillers on board and after Larry had one, I set sail. I ran 30 miles that afternoon and anchored in an open cove for the night rather than try to navigate through the small channels in the dark. The next day I beat into Nagu and the doctor immediately sent Larry off to a hospital. Fortunately Larry had something far less serious than kidney stones, but, had I not known how to sail engineless *Seraffyn*, we would have had to wait for a doctor to be shipped out or a passing coaster to stop.

We met an older couple cruising in the Gulf of California twelve years ago. Six months later we heard that they were headed home, beating northward along the Baja California coast, when the husband went forward to change a sail. He dropped dead of a heart attack. By good fortune his wife knew how to sail well enough to run 150 miles back to Bahia Magdelena where the local fishermen gave her assistance.

Teaching your wife how to handle your boat under power isn't enough. It might work if you are fortunate enough to have your accidents close to civilization, but few boats can be powered 600 or 700 miles on the fuel they carry. It will be important for your wife to be able to sail your boat and save the fuel for maneuvering into harbor when she arrives. I know this all sounds Doomsdayish, but if the same person who spends hundreds on life rafts, safety flares, man-overboard lights, and radar reflectors forgets to teach his crew to sail well, he is neglecting his biggest safety asset.

How do you go about not only teaching your wife to sail, but making it all interesting? The first thing I would suggest is taking a careful look at your own sailing ability. If you have not had lots of experience, your wife will know. She won't be relaxed if it is a case of the blind leading the blind. If you are inexperienced, you are bound to make mistakes such as leaving your genoa up too long and having to fight a wildy flogging mess on a heaving foredeck while yelling at your frightened wife, "Keep her up in the wind, dammit!" It would be far better to invest in a dinghy and spend a season together in your local dinghy sailing club's beginners' course.

If you already know how to sail, I still recommend buying a dinghy for your wife to learn in. Make it one that is cat-rigged and easy for one person to handle. Then your wife can goof off by herself and make mistakes without you rushing to assist. That's how I learned to sail. Larry bought me a 6 foot 8 inch pram that would eventually make a perfect tender to *Seraffyn*, which was under construction. We had a launching party and I proudly set off in newly christened *Rabicon* and knocked myself soundly on the head with her 7 foot long boom. I quickly learned to control my gybes after that. Dinghies react quickly and teach quickly, so after several wonderful evenings with *Rabicon* I was a much more useful hand on board a cruiser. Eventually, when *Seraffyn* was launched, Larry expanded my sailing education from the firm base I'd gained in the dinghy.

Once your wife knows the basics of sailing, start trading positions with her. Don't always take the helm in interesting places; let her do it. You offer to winch in the sheets as she tacks up the river. Let her choose the spot to anchor in and let the ground tackle go. Women make excellent navigators. I learned celestial navigation in a class of forty men and eight women. All eight women got top scores in the final tests. Two years later in Costa Rica I met one of my female classmates on board her cruising home. "I do all of the navigation on board," she told me. "Sure is an interesting change from the galley."

Look around your sailing home and think of the most interesting jobs. Let your wife do them for a change. She'll like you and your boat better if she isn't always assigned to scrubbing the bottom. How about having her whip the lines and do the final varnish coats while you scrub?

Finally, as you teach your wife to sail your boat, look at your gear. Is your sheet winch too small to give your wife the power she needs? Would a simpler reefing system allow her to shorten sail without waking you? Would a jib downhaul help? Simplify your gear to meet your wife's needs and sailing will be more fun for both of you.

To learn to sail well, I had to acquire the skill of telling Larry not

to nag me when I was trying something new. In fact one day I
banished him to the headstay at the end of the bowsprit while I beat
up Newport Bay. I couldn't hear his comments that way and soon set
my own pattern for tacking and getting the jib in quickly. My final
reward came when Larry was gone for a month and I sailed *Seraffyn*
single-handed along with south coast of England, making a passage
of 40 miles from Plymouth to Falmouth. I don't know which of us
was prouder. Larry heard of my little voyage and told a friend, "I
knew Lin could do it, but now I don't have to worry about either of
us because Lin knows she can take care of herself if she needs to."

If I can learn to sail a cruiser, anyone can. I'm 4 feet 10 inches, one
hundred pounds (7 stone) and a mechanical idiot. All your wife
needs is what Larry gave me: patience, encouragement, and a dinghy
of her own.

9

The Mate You Scare Could Be Your Own

Sam rushed on deck to meet us as we rowed across the still starlit patch of water between our two boats. "Hey, good to see you two. When'd you get back? How was your delivery job? Climb on board and meet my wife. She's decided to join me on this cruise."

We secured our dinghy and went into the glowing oil-lit cabin on *Delsamb*. Sam poured us a drink as he introduced his tanned, twinkling-eyed wife. "This is Beatty, hasn't done much cruising yet, but she's giving it a try. I'm breaking her in the easy way. Short day hops till she knows the boat. Now sit down and tell me about your transatlantic sail. Get into any storms?"

"Not till we were only 35 miles from New Orleans," Larry began. "We were powering happily along over a flat sea, getting the boat ready to hand over to its owner, crew cleaning her up. About midnight the wind came up, dead on our nose. By 0200 we were hove-to in 50 knots, temperature dropped from 60 degrees to 18 degrees Fahrenheit. So cold we had to change watch every hour. We were hove-to for two-and-a-half days. Kept the engine running to try to warm up the galley. Second morning Lin got a weather forecast— waterspouts for our area—sure enough, over six of them formed up over the smoking sea. Kept the engine ready to throw in gear so we

could take avoiding action if we had to. Frightening thing; never
been around waterspouts before. Only way we could keep the man
on watch from freezing was to use everyone's warm clothes plus wet
gear and socks on his hands. Only two days before we'd been sunbathing, planning on what we'd do when we got in. Boat rode well
though, hove-to."

I noticed Beatty shaking her head and I thought, "Here we go
again, telling 'sea-fearing' stories. Why is it no one ever tells about
the good times?"

It's hard to remember and describe all of the wonderful days
because they are definitely in the majority. During that same delivery job, we had fine days such as one when a tropical sun warmed us
thoroughly and our American crewman Richard, who'd hitched a
ride back from a walking tour of Europe and the Middle East,
grabbed his huge duffle bag and pulled out a hammock. He strung
the hammock from the forward shrouds and as the *Vagrant Gypsy*
surged over the seas, beam-reaching at close to 7 knots, we took turns
swinging in the sunshine. Our English crewman, Chris, made his first
attempt at making yeast bread after three weeks of watching the
cook. So at tea time we all tasted a very successful loaf, smothered in
butter and jam. Richard strummed his guitar and we discordantly
tried to sing Beatle favorites, "Here comes the sun it feels like years
since it's been here. . . ."

It's not only men who are guilty of telling sea-fearing stories. I hate
heavy weather and love cruising and sailing, yet as soon as the re-
union kissing and hellos were over after a two-year separation from
my parents, I caught myself telling two people who enjoy sailing but
have done no offshore cruising, "We stayed too late in the Baltic.
Everyone warned us, 'Leave by September 15 or take your boat out
of the water.' But we were having too much fun. We waited out a
nine-day gale and all of a sudden it was the middle of October. So as
soon as the one hundred fishing boats clustered in Ronne on Born-
holm Island finally set off to fish we wanted to be underway.
Weather report was fair. Well, to make a long story short, as dark fell
the following wind increased till it was blowing Force 10. Dropped
all sail but had to keep running, couldn't heave-to 'cause all the
fishing boats were trying to work back toward the island, and we had
to have way on to maneuver around them. Could have been run

down otherwise. *Seraffyn* was running beautifully under bare poles when all of a sudden one wave broke right on top of us. Covered the boat completely. Mast must have been at least 30 degrees below the horizon. Companionway was partially open. Every oil lamp lens burst and as soon as we righted I crawled out of my bunk and stepped into water 10 inches deep. Boy did I start pumping! Bent our stanchion 45 degrees. Ripped the dinghy almost completely off its chocks. Washed our binnacle overboard. A 400-ton freighter sank in the same storm and a 200-ton coaster that limped into the same port we did, lost its whole deck cargo and needed assistance to make port."

My mother asked me, "And you enjoy this?" I realized my mistake at once. Why hadn't I told them instead about sailing for three months under the wonderful midnight sun, through the maze of 20,000 Swedish islands and 30,000 Finnish ones, safe anchorages less than 2 miles apart? I should have talked about the time we were whispering along on a following breeze, wearing just shorts, jerseys and bare feet. Tree-covered islands crowded down on the narrow channel. The navigation marks on our excellent charts corresponded perfectly. We glanced behind to see a Finnish Eight-Meter yacht running up the channel, slowly gaining on us. We rushed for our cameras; they ran for theirs. At the narrowest part of the channel they caught us. We joined their laughter and shouted greetings as the skippers on each yacht pulled in their winged-out mainsails so we could sail closer together and miss brushing the trees on either side. For six of eight lovely minutes we traded sailing gossip. I noted the special anchorages they told us about as Larry kept *Seraffyn* gliding along on course, less than 20 feet from the beautifully varnished racing machine. Then they slowly pulled ahead in the 8-knot breeze and we settled back on our sunlit deck, happy to be alive.

Because we've led a cruiser's life for the past eleven years, we're constantly meeting new sailors. Often they are on the verge of making that big decision. They want to set out and go cruising. So they come on board to gather all the information they can, just as we used to when we were building and preparing *Seraffyn*. Soon the conversation turns from iceboxes and water systems to the question of storms. Or, three or four cruising boats arrive in the same port and everyone gets together in the largest cockpit to trade news.

Inevitably one of the couples is new to cruising and the question comes up, "What about the storms?" And so the frightening tales begin. Yet when Larry and I went through our log, we found that in ten-and-a-half years and almost 42,000 miles of cruising on board *Seraffyn*, we've spent less than thirty-one days in winds of Force 8 or above. Most of the time we had wonderful sailing spiced by hard beats and slow drifts. On the six deliveries I've been on, we've covered about 16,000 miles and had only two-and-a-half days of winds over gale force. If you figure that out, it's less than 1 percent of all the sailing we do. We've discussed this with other longterm cruising people and they confirm it. With proper planning, there is little reason to spend much time in storms. Yet let a new sailor come on board and we all drag out the sea stories, rarely considering their effect.

I know happy days don't make nearly as dramatic an impression, but aren't they worth telling about? What of working slowly into a deserted anchorage just at sunset, then rowing ashore to start a small bonfire so you can roast some sausages or a steak? What about the delights of a wall-to-wall suntan carefully cultivated while you watch the porpoises weave their magic around your bow?

And then there's that perfect passage, a beam-reach of 20 or 200 miles when you never have to change sails or steer by hand, when your dinners are a gourmet's delight to an appetite whetted by a 12-knot breeze over a sea specked with smiling whitehorses. Next time you're in a crowd of sailors and would-be voyagers and catch yourself starting to tell a sea-fearing story, look around. Could your story be the one that makes a sailor chary of his dream? Would some sailor's mate, just ready to go along on this great adventure, stop and reconsider after your tale of flying spray and soaked bunks? Instead, how about telling of the wondrous days when the winds blew fair, those days we really go sailing for?

I know it's hard, but I'm trying to do it, even if I'm dying to tell you about the time I was on watch alone, running out of Palma, Mallorca, in 25 knots of wind, when I noticed a ferocious squally cloud racing up behind, rain hissing at its foaming base. . . .

10

The People You Meet

Ten years ago, when we were just getting used to the thrill of cruising, when we were unwinding and learning to live without a clock, our lives directed by the winds and currents, we sailed into La Paz and anchored next to a little American trimaran registered in Las Vegas, Nevada. The couple on the trimaran rowed over and asked us if we'd been in La Paz before. When we said we hadn't, they offered to share their knowledge with us. They'd been in La Paz for two weeks.

We invited them on board and mixed up a rum punch. The four of us spent the rest of the afternoon sheltered from the sun under our awning. As Annabelle and Gordon Yates prepared to go home, we thanked them for their helpful advice and made plans to try a new restaurant with them the next day. While he was climbing into his dinghy, Gordon commented, "Cruising is great, and the bonus of cruising is the people we meet."

At the time, Gordon's comment didn't register with us. We were too busy trying to deplete the Gulf of California's supply of lobster with our trusty trident. We spent two or three weeks at a time hiden in deserted coves, sunbathing, swimming, puttering on the boat and skindiving. Every third week or so, we'd sail back to La Paz for fresh supplies and a dinner out.

Then, after about four months of cruising, his words began to make sense. We started looking around us and noticed people. Not only the other cruising people, but the people of the towns and villages, the fishermen and merchant seamen. We worked at meeting them and found our cruising life growing added dimensions.

By far the easiest people to meet are other cruising people. You all have something in common. The ice can be broken by just calling to another yacht, "How is the holding ground?" before you drop your anchor. Most market towns in popular cruising areas turn into week-long parties when ten or twelve crusing yachts arrive at the same time. One yacht will look rather like a mother duck with five or six dinghies trailing astern.

Cruising friends are a great source of information, and even though you sail on in different directions, you always seem to stay in touch. We've crossed paths with Annabelle and Gordon in three different countries now. The cruising village is rather small in population, and after you've been cruising for two or three years, each new cruising friend seems to know someone you met in the port before last.

In Europe, we've found that most cruising yachts seem to prefer tying to a seawall or quay instead of anchoring. Then the next yacht ties alongside and so on. We've seen boats seven or eight abreast. This is a fine way to meet people, but is really only good if you leave after one or two days. The strain of having no privacy at all and listening to people constantly walk across your decks would be hard on old friends, let alone people you met only that day.

Because other cruising yachtsmen are so easy to meet and generally very interesting, we, like so many other people, have to remind ourselves why we went cruising. If we'd only wanted to meet sailors, we could have done that in our own local cruising area.

Cruising is a way of getting to know how people in other parts of the world live. Your boat is a floating home that puts you in a front row seat. It's your calling card and since you went to the trouble of sailing instead of taking an airplane, local people are going to be a bit more interested in meeting you.

Among the first people we tried approaching were the local fisherman. Armed with my Spanish-American dictionary, a bucket, and a 10-peso note, Larry and I rowed over to a Mexican shrimp trawler that anchored near us in Salina Cruz. The fisherman watched us coming and grabbed our dinghy painter and tied it. They motioned us on board immediately. I tried asking the price of some shrimp in spanish. The captain knew some English and we ended up sharing a beer and being shown around the trawler from engine room to galley. When we asked how all of the complicated-looking trawling gear worked to catch shrimp, the captain tried drawing pictures on his deck with a penknife, then threw his hands up in disgust. "Enough!" he said, "You come fishing with us tonight."

He radioed to a trawler anchored near *Seraffyn* and made arrangements to have the fishermen watch her. Then his crewmen lifted our dinghy onto the trawler's cabin-top, and we were off for a night's trawling. What an education! We returned the next morning laden with a bucket of still bouncing shrimp, another of shiny sea-shells, stomachs full of turtle stew, and heads full of new impressions.

Our experiences everywhere have been the same. Fishermen want to be friendly. Their advice can be invaluable. In fact, I'd trust a fisherman's advice about the sea more than I would a local yachts-man. We often start a conversation just by asking for a weather forecast and end up getting tips on good harbors and local signs of bad weather.

Language can be a difficulty, but even in Finland, where we had absolutely no knowledge of the language, we found the fishermen willing to try sign language to communicate.

Another great source of knowledge and interesting people are merchant ships. Especially in smaller harbors where there are only one or two freighters anchored, merchant seamen are easy to approach. They seem to really enjoy the diversion of unexpected company. We've found that almost all merchant shipping officers speak English.

And how do you approach them? We often get into our little dinghy and row out to where they are moored. We approach their boarding ladder and simply ask the first person we see, "Do you give tours of your ship?" We've never been refused, and going from one end to the other of a 120,000-ton tanker—down five flights of stairs to see the engines, and up another seven to the bridge—can be extremely interesting and informative.

Since we have our home with us, we can easily reciprocate for any hospitality by offering a dinner on board, or an afternoon's sailing. In Mexico we took the chief officer of a Stateline ship skindiving. He

caught a bucket of crabs which he gave to the Chinese ship's cook.
The cook made us a great dinner in exchange.

The hospitality we have been shown by yacht clubs worldwide has
been overwhelming. Members offer us assistance, the use of their
homes, and entertainment. In fact it is only the hospitality of yacht
clubs that induces us to visit some big harbors. The lure of hot
showers and people interested in sailing overcomes our dislike of
crowds and busy cities.

To reciprocate for the friendship yacht club members show us, we
carry a large supply of burgees from our own club in West Vancouver. We present one to the secretary or commodore of the club
we're visiting on the day we leave. It's a small thing, but it always
seems to be right.

Introductions from friends really help in foreign countries. We
keep every address we are offered. Then when we arrive in a port near
an introduction we write a postcard, "We are cruising in a small
yacht from Canada. So-and-so said we would enjoy meeting you.
Please join us for a drink on board *Seraffyn* at cocktail time tomorrow or the next day. Contact us at. . . ."

This way, people are left a choice. If they are too busy, or if our
timing is inconvenient, they aren't obliged to answer. We've met
some great people this way. On the average nine out of ten people
answer our note by appearing almost immediately. And, since these
are the people who are living and working in the country, these are
the people who can really teach us a lot.

We almost always find ourselves being invited out to meals and
given tours, so as a small way of repaying the hospitality, we have
made a habit of collecting small gift items from each place we visit. A
necklace made of passion fruit seeds in Colombia costs us very little,
but makes a lovely house gift for a hostess in Bermuda. We keep a
stock of these items, handcrafted pottery, wooden carvings, whales'
teeth. We're never sorry to have them.

In England last year, we were tied alongside the quay that faces
the main street in Poole. All day long, people strolled by stopping to
stare and dream. Often they would work up the nerve to ask us
questions about our voyage. "Where did you come from? How long
did it take? Where are you going?"

I decided to turn the tables on the next person who asked. After his first question, I countered, "Where are you from?" He looked very surprised and said, "Originally from London, but I live here now." I continued asking him about the area, and a few minutes later, after having a drink on board *Seraffyn*, Larry and I were in Lee's car while he and his wife showed us their favorite spots in Dorset.

Cruising keeps confirming our opinion that people everywhere are the same—great! But sometimes a bit shy. Meeting them makes it all fun. We've tried learning Spanish and even the little we know makes us more friends. But, English and a smile seem to be an international language around people who like yachts.

As a visitor in a small boat, you have a wonderful advantage. You come into a new place looking for adventures. You are interesting because you are foreign. You stay long enough to learn the good things about people and then hoist your sails and leave before you learn their bad habits or they learn yours.

It's a bit like seeing life through rose-colored glasses. But then that's why we all want to cruise. We're dreamers escaping the old and looking for a shiny new world. It exists, and the people we meet make that world even better.

11

On Watch

"The paddock oak came cracking down a few minutes before 5 A.M., the rending, whickering snack of heavy timber rocketing her from sleep. . ."

I glanced over the top of the book at our compass and then around the horizon. Still on course, no ships in sight. I rejoined Henrietta as she heard a knock on the kitchen door. Eight pages later I glanced up again. The mainsail and genoa glowed fuchsia as the sun sank slowly to kiss the horizon. The warm following wind caressed the hairs that had struggled loose from my braids and made them tickle my cheeks the same way the little white horses tried to tickle *Seraffyn's* transom.

Our traffrail log hummed softly just behind me. I glanced to port where 5 miles away the revolution torn hills of Portugal were just starting to release the full moon. Three thousand miles to starboard my family and friends were fighting the fears of inflation, unemployment, and mortgages. Fifteen feet from where I sat my watch Larry lay sleeping, secure in the knowledge that our boat was strong and I was well able to handle most emergencies.

To port the moon showed its pink bald pate, to starboard the sun shot its last rays through the clouds. Ahead lay adventure, behind, our self-steering vane controlled an ever-unraveling, bubbling wake. I returned to Henrietta as the stormy night burst through her kitchen door.

I was glad to come on watch when Larry called. It was warm, I needed only a light sweater and pair of shorts. The velvet black sky twinkled with stars. A light breeze kept us whispering along about 3 knots, close-hauled. Cabo Blanco, 6 miles off and abaft our beam, flashed its light two times every ten seconds. I leaned back against the boom gallows and listened to the sounds Larry made as he climbed into the bunk.

One hour later I heard a new sound. I thought it was a lone porpoise coming to investigate us. Regularly I heard it blow, coming closer and closer from behind.

Suddenly the moonlight glistened off an enormous black whale 20 feet from our quarter. *Seraffyn* is 24 feet long. That whale looked twice our size.

I ran to the companionway. 'Larry, come up quickly," I whispered urgently. He emerged seconds later rubbing his eyes, "My watch already?"

'No, Larry, there's a whale. He's awfully close."

"Why did you wake me for something as silly as .... OH MY GOD!" Larry exclaimed as that giant expanse of black flesh arced slowly, inexorably out of the water 10 feet away from our beam.

"Lin, turn on the radio real loud," Larry suggested, 'Maybe the noise will drive him away." I did.

We stamped on the deck and shouted. We blew the foghorn. But regularly, every two minutes, the whale surfaced beside us saluting us with the over-whelming odor of his rotten breath.

"We'll come about," Larry said as he unclutched the windvane. "Maybe he'll just keep going." We settled *Seraffyn* on the other tack and headed dead off the Costa Rican shore. I steered as Larry watched for our unwelcome companion. The sound of his blowing told us our friend wasn't at all interested in us. He was headed south, no detours intended.

As the sound of his blowing grew fainter, we tacked and Larry set the windvane for our original course. "I'm for a stiff drink. How about you? Then do you mind if I take the rest of my off-watch?"

Larry woke me gently, "Your watch, Lin. We're becalmed again. I got a fix off the lights on Berlenga and Peniche. But it's misted over now."

I climbed reluctantly out of our warm sleeping bag. Larry handed me my shirt and gave me a hug, then disappeared into the forepeak. I pulled on my boots and jacket and set some water to boil, then went on deck.

The huge blue and white drifter hung limply on its whisker pole. The last wind must have been from aft. Two days now we'd had these shifting, sporadic winds. With 15 miles to go we had no wind and little visibility. I went below and poured a cup of tea. Then I opened the almanac to see when the sun would rise. One more hour to wait.

I heard the foghorn of a ship passing nearby. I stood on deck and soon saw its lights as it came into view about a mile away. Visibility wasn't too bad.

I felt a light southerly breeze as I sat sipping my tea in the cockpit. "Should I or shouldn't I," I debated, staring at the 16-foot whisker pole. I waited five minutes more. Then I started. Very quietly I lowered the whisker pole topping lift. I unclipped the pole and slid it carefully along the deck. I dropped the drifter and stored it below. Finally I stored the spinnaker pole on its brackets along the bowsprit.

The sun just began to brighten the sky. *Seraffyn* began to trickle slowly through the water. I caught sight of the lights of Peniche and Berlenga and took bearings. Rushing below I checked our position. We had a good margin of safety now in the 6-mile-wide channel. I went outside to make one last check before waking Larry.

"Your watch, Larry," I said feeling a bit disappointed. "We're becalmed again. I got a fix off Berlenga and Peniche but it's misted over now."

A very light kiss touched my cheek. Larry's smiling face caught my opening eyes. "Hi bug, we're really moving along, beam reach."

As I crawled into my sweater Larry poured himself a glass of rum. "Remember what Pedro said when we left El Capitan? 'Get south of Cabo San Vicente before November and you'll miss winter.' From the look of things he sure seems right."

I pulled on my favorite yellow sea boots, not because it looked wet on deck, but because they kept my feet so cuddly. Larry snuggled into the still warm sleeping bag.

I glanced around deck, no ships in sight, calm sea, sails pulling well. I went below and got the book I'd been reading on my first watch. Before I'd read a chapter, *Seraffyn* heeled sharply to a gust of wind.

I went on deck and another gust heeled us till the scuppers ran with foam. Dropping the mainsail eased our heeling, but I stayed on deck watching the genoa pull us at over 5 knots. I strolled forward just ahead of a burst of spray. For some reason that spray made my decision. I took two gaskets from the deck locker and then dropped the genoa, controlling it with the downhaul Larry had rigged for occasions just like this. Then I eased out on the bowsprit and lashed the sail down.

Resetting the mainsail got us moving, but it wasn't quite enough canvas so I pulled the staysail from its bag and up it went. The sound of the sheet winch must have awakened Larry. "Why aren't you wearing wet weather gear?" he growled at me from his sleeping bag.

I cleated the staysail sheet and growled back at him, "Because there wasn't a drop of water on deck two minutes ago. Go back to sleep."

I went below and dragged out my wet weather pants just in case. As soon as I'd struggled into them I went on deck to see a flash of lightning to windward. 'Damn," I said to myself, "better get that genoa off the bowsprit." I banged my toe on the forehatch, then slid on my rear out the bowsprit, glad of my wet weather pants. I had most of the jib hanks off when I heard Larry's imperious shout, "What the hell are you doing out on the bowsprit at night alone without a safety harness and the boat doing over 5 knots."

Furiously I yelled back to him, "Taking the bloody jib off the headstay," as I slithered on deck with the unruly mass of Dacron.

"You'd better put a reef in the mainsail," Larry snarled as he ducked below just ahead of a good dollop of spray. "And put your wet gear on now! Dammit!"

I bagged the genoa, eased the main halyard, ripping a nail off in the process, and pulled the reefing pennants. Nothing happened. I looked aloft. Nothing fouled up there. Then I went aft to get a flashlight. A fine mist of spray burst over *Seraffyn's* side, effectively wetting me down. I lit the light and found the reefing outhaul line staring happily at me from where it had hooked itself round the cockpit locker latch. I cleared it and pulled the reef into the sail, sheeted in, checked our course, then rushed below for my wet weather jacket.

Back on deck I started tying the reef points into the forward part of the mainsail, clinging to the boom with my chin and getting furious as our motion became worse. I had four reef points to go when I heard the ship's bell ring six times—3 A.M. Larry's turn, thank God!

I called to Larry as I came below, dripping salt water. I began stripping down, reciting the tale of my watch's woes. When I was down to socks and sweater Larry slowly climbed out of the bunk. He smiled at my exasperation and said, "Sail changing sure helps your watch go fast, doesn't it?"

If You Can't Repair It, Maybe It Shouldn't Be on Board

Tom and Janet Steele who cruised on 32-foot *Adios* for almost twenty-two years and two circumnavigations told us, "The farther you sail away from yachting centers, the harder it will be to find paying work on boats around you. The people who cruise to really far-off corners of the globe are the self-sufficient ones. They've got their boat rigged so they can repair everything by themselves." Tom was right. The modern gear that looks like a wonderfully innovative aid to sailing and cruising can be like a lead weight around your neck when it breaks down far from the nearest repair man. Do you send for a new unit? Do you give up two months of cruising or risk a voyage during hurricane season because of delays caused by gear failure?

Most the people in your home port will urge you to buy one more guaranteed-to-be-necessary, got-to-have-it item. The long-term carefree cruising man will say, "If you can't fix it yourself, save the money right now and the aggravation later."

Think simplicity. Maybe our extreme style of simplicity is more than you would enjoy living with. But the following chapters may give you some ideas that start you on the road to technical freedom.

12
The Alternatives

Rebel against the axiom: "The only way to go cruising is with an inboard auxiliary engine." Without an engine you may be able to go one year sooner, have extra money in the bank, and have an odor-free, more easily maintained boat. The inboard engine that is supposed to be a necessity may be a liability to the person who wants to go cruising now aboard a boat 32 feet or under. Rethink the question of auxiliary power and consider two alternatives: an outboard motor or a sculling oar.

The most obvious disadvantage of an inboard is money. Even the simplest 8-horsepower diesel engine costs $4,000 when you include the shaft, tanks, through-hull fittings, and controls. To that you have to add installation costs, which can easily run $3,000. That equals $7,000 for a simple, small-engine installation. We have ten friends who spent less than $7,000 for all living and long-distance voyaging expenses, for a whole year!

Once underway, you continue to spend money on an inboard. Fuel is usually the lowest expense; what costs more is the spare-parts inventory. Then there are repair bills. If money equals cruising time, the costs of a diesel engine could cut months or years off a cruise.

The most tidy engine installation takes up space on a boat—possibly not living space, but on a cruising boat storage space counts. The fuel tank could be used to hold extra water instead. The compartment used for the engine could hold five bags of sails or twelve cases of canned food. In a 32-foot medium-displacement hull, the engine installation, tanks, and spares use approximately one-fifth of the hull volume. This means that an engineless 28-footer would have the same space as a boat 32 feet long with an inboard. The smaller size translates back to cost. A smaller boat to buy or to build means you have cash in the bank to go cruising sooner.

Eleven years ago when we first started cruising, we met a family reaching the ultimate stages of frustration because of their diesel engine. Theirs had broken its crank shaft. They were in a beautiful tiny port called Zihuatanejo, Mexico. The closest mechanic was in Acapulco, 120 miles and a six-hour bus ride away. The mechanic arrived, pulled their engine out, and hoisted it on deck, liberally spilling dirty oil on carpets and teak decks. Then the mechanic left to take the bus to Acapulco for more new parts. Two weeks later, decks stained, tempers and budget strained, the engine was still not repaired and the family was ready to give up cruising.

I thought they were an unusual case until we cruised onward and I found that nine out of every 10 cruisers with inboard engines had tales of frustration. Even if you do all your own repairs, you still have the annoyance of trying to find parts or of waiting for them to arrive by post. Then there is the problem of clearing them through customs, especially if you don't speak the language. Finding a good mechanic is a hassle, and you may have to put up with a fishing boat mechanic who has no regard for the neat, clean work needed to keep a yacht a home.

Friends we met in Malta told how they missed the northeast monsoon season for their passage across the Indian Ocean because of a four-week engine-repair delay. They *had* to wait for the engine to be repaired. Without it they had no lights, no water-pressure system, no refrigeration, and no radio receiver. Instead of sailing the 4,000 miles from the Straits of Malacca to Aden in light reaching breezes, they had to spend fifty days motorsailing to windward in Force 6 and 7 winds when the southwest monsoon filled in.

Few people have a hand-start engine with absolutely no accessories. Most have at least an alternator with batteries for electric starting, electric interior lights, and electronics. Then they have the worry of electrolysis.

The most common alternative to an inboard engine is an outboard motor. A slow-speed, high-torque 7-horsepower long-shaft outboard will push even a 32-foot cruiser along at close to 4 knots. An outboard well in the quarter or stern lockers is an effective way of using an outboard motor and gets the prop down where it belongs. A third way to use an outboard is to secure it on a dinghy, then lash the dinghy alongside with fenders as a yawlboat. In Javea, Spain, we watched the owner of a 32-footer with its damaged prop shaft power to the shipyard with a 3-horsepower engine mounted on his inflatable. He came putting back and said, "They're ready for you right now. I'll power you in." He tied alongside and that tiny engine pushed all 5¼ tons of *Seraffyn* along in spite of the 8-knot headwind.

Of course an outboard means gasoline with its danger of explosion, but this problem can be solved by storing the outboard and its fuel in a well-ventilated deck locker or in the upright dinghy. Better still, have a detachable fuel tank and bleed the outboard when you are finished using it. Store the motor wherever convenient and put the fuel tank on deck in a well-ventilated spot.

The fuel consumption of an outboard can be double that of a diesel, but most people find they use the outboard only to maneuver in harbors or in flat calm when they want to get the anchor down before nightfall. On long offshore passages, the man with the outboard learns patience and how to get the most out of his boat in light winds, so the lack of range seems to matter very little. For local cruising, an outboard with about 1 horsepower per ton of displacement should be enough to get you home in time for work Monday morning if the winds and tides don't cooperate.

You can generate electricity for navigation lights and small accessories such as a stereo system with an outboard, but it is difficult to power a freezer unit or a mechanical bilge pump with one.

Not only is an outboard cheap and easy to install, but it also takes little storage space and, most importantly, it can be removed from the boat and set on the dock when it needs servicing. If an outboard reaches the final state of complete exhaustion, replacement is simple, whereas new diesels never seem to fit the same engine mounts or exhaust connections.

We've sailed with a 14-foot sculling oar as our only auxiliary power for eleven years and 42,000 miles and have rarely been on time anywhere. Come to think of it, we have had some daysails end at midnight. But who cares? One of the special joys of having no motor, no noises, and no dirty fuel oil is the feeling that you have quit the madness of today's world for the slow easy pace of a world controlled by winds and currents.

Being without fueled power on a cruising boat does limit use of electricity to uncomplicated equipment powered by dry-cell batteries or to natural methods of generating electricity, such as wind and water generators or solar panels. But this means fewer gadgets to buy or to break down.

Canals and rivers present a problems to the auxiliary-less cruiser, but for big canal trips, such as the Panama, Suez, or Keil, it is often possible to rent an outboard and to build a temporary bracket or to arrange a tow. It is also possible to scull or row your cruiser up small creeks or through short canals, although you might have to get up before dawn to catch a calm hour.

A boat without a motor must perform well in light breezes and you will have to work harder sailing than the person with power. But this is one of the benefits of depending almost exclusively on sails. You'll have to learn to sail well. You'll also have the joy of working into the same anchorages that Columbus, Drake, Cook, and Nelson entered under sail alone. Then, when your anchor hooks into a firm bottom after a passage filled with varied winds, you will have a feeling of accomplishment untainted by the roar and smell of an engine. Your cruising fund and your health will benefit from a smaller boat with no engine or fuel to buy and no repair bills. A new 14-foot oar costs less than $100. In calm situations, it can move a 5-ton yacht like ours at 1½ knots. And your stomach and leg muscles will be all the stronger for the exercise.

What about safety? "I wouldn't go without a good strong diesel to get me out of trouble!" How often we've heard and seen that statement. Yet we've seen many yachts with engines lost or damaged each year. In almost all these cases people had put their cruisers in compromising situations and then had depended on their engines either to start or to keep running. I watched a 50-foot sloop tear herself to bits on a California breakwater after her owner depended on an engine that got a fuel blockage. With sail covers on and no anchor ready, he had no time to set more sail in the 8-knot breeze before the boat hit the rocks, holed, and sank.

Jane DeRidder wrote an interesting article for *Pacific Yachting* a few years ago about voyaging through the Tuamotos, or dangerous archipelago. One fact caught my eye. Nine yachts left Victoria that season, four with no engines. Four of the nine yachts were wrecked in the Tuamotos. Of the five Canadian yachts that eventually arrived in Papeete, Tahiti, four were engineless.

Sailing without an inboard engine is not necessarily safer. In fact if you could remove Murphy's Law (anything which can go wrong, will go wrong), then an engine would add safety. But engines do fail at unexpected times and we know that people who have no engine are always aware of the danger of getting into compromising situations. The prudence that should be the main part of every sailor's seamanship becomes standard procedure for the motorless sailor. He has an anchor ready to go overboard immediately when he is near shore. He studies his chart and works offshore if the coast ahead is too deep or steep-to for anchoring. He avoids the centers of busy channels and heavy shipping lanes. He chooses his anchorage more carefully. He plans how to get underway easily in case the situation changes.

If money means very little, if you love tinkering with an engine, or if you must have a boat larger than you can handle under sail alone, then a diesel engine is your first choice. On the other hand, if the money you save means a year of your life free to sail where you wish, look into an outboard or, for the smaller cruiser, a sculling oar. You can cruise anywhere in the world without an inboard engine, even in the so-called windless Mediterranean. Hundreds of people do it.

13

Oar Power

How would you like to move your cruising boat completely by yourself when there's no wind? Consider the old standby, an oar. It can work you into a harbor in a calm or from one anchorage area to another, scull you out of a channel that's too narrow for tacking, help you overcome a modest current if you don't quite catch the tide, work you out of the lee of the land into that nearby breeze, or move you clear of a danger that is uncomfortably close.

Your self-made oar can do all of these things without causing noise to disturb your cruising neighbors. It is easy to repair, cheap, and parts are available worldwide. An oar won't drip oil on your teak decks, won't pollute the ocean, requires no fossil fuel, and is as reliable as the wheel. And finally, rowing and sculling provide good body exercise. Sound like an advertisement? Yup, it's for the do-it-yourself movement or move-it-yourself movement. Get an oar and go cruising now with the price of an engine in your pocket.

In calm weather any easily driven sailboat under 30 feet can be sculled or rowed at 1½ to 2 knots by a fourteen-year-old. If you are dragging a three-bladed propeller and large aperture, this speed will be cut considerably. Larger yachts have been rowed and sculled for years. Gary Hoyt rows his engineless *Freedom 40* when he runs out of wind. But I would like to concentrate on yachts under 30 feet as owners of these would most benefit from the extra storage space gained and money saved by eliminating an inboard engine and its

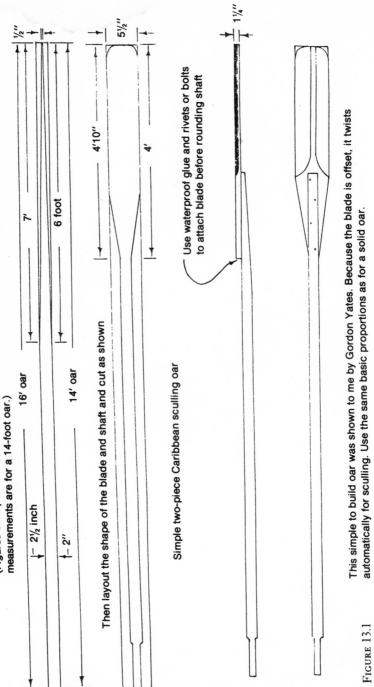

Build your own 14- or 16-foot oar

Use rough sawn ash, spruce, or fir. Mark blade taper as shown then saw this taper out first. (Figures on top of oar show appropriate measurements for a 16-foot oar, on the bottom measurements are for a 14-foot oar.)

16' oar

2½ inch

7'

14' oar

2"

6 foot

Then layout the shape of the blade and shaft and cut as shown

4'10"

4'

Simple two-piece Caribbean sculling oar

Use waterproof glue and rivets or bolts to attach blade before rounding shaft

½"

5½"

1¼"

This simple to build oar was shown to me by Gordon Yates. Because the blade is offset, it twists automatically for sculling. Use the same basic proportions as for a solid oar.

FIGURE 13.1

fuel tanks. This extra space could increase the 30-foot yacht's cruising range by adding space for at least a month's worth of water and food while still leaving extra storage room for a light weather nylon drifter or another case of duty-free rum.

The yachtsperson with a small boat can buy a secondhand lifeboat oar, rig up an oarlock, and find out it's easy to move around in calm weather under oar power. But it's even easier to sail than row. The bonus is: the more you sail and row, the more skillful you become. Each time you use your oars and sails you are visibly aware of their flaws and can take care of the repairs when they are needed. On the other hand, the more you use your motor, the more its unseen parts wear until any one of them could fail at a critical moment.

HOW TO RIG YOUR OWN SCULLING OR ROWING OAR

It is easiest to buy a used lifeboat oar on the waterfront or at a ship breaking yard. If you can't buy one see Figure 13.1 for dimensions to build your own. Try to get the oarlock fittings complete if possible, as it is hard to find large oarlocks in the marine boatique stores. If you can't buy an oarlock have one fabricated from stainless steel or mild steel which you have galvanized, or make a wood pattern (simply a wood oarlock) and have it cast in manganese bronze at the local foundry as I did for *Seraffyn.*

When you select your oar, make sure the shaft is straight when the blade is horizontal. Two or 3 inches of curve or sag is acceptable in the other direction on a 14- to 16-foot oar (see Figure 13.2). This curvature helps twist or feather the oar automatically as you scull back and forth athwartships. In fact Oriental Ullows are built with a definite angle in the shaft. On the other hand, a curve in the incorrect direction will make sculling difficult. Find a way to stow your oar so that it will not sag from its own weight.

The correct oar length for each boat is relative to freeboard. If you have extremely high freeboard aft, you will need a longer oar to reach the water. The oarlock on *Seraffyn* is 3 feet 4 inches from LWL to the center of the oarlock hole, and we use a 13 foot 9 inch oar. Our new 29 foot 6 inch cutter is 4 feet from load waterline to oarlock and the new oar length is 15 feet 9 inches. I think these examples are

The oar shown on this folkboat is too short. The idea is to be able to stand up and still have the oar at approximately 40 degrees to horizontal with three-quarters of the blade below water.

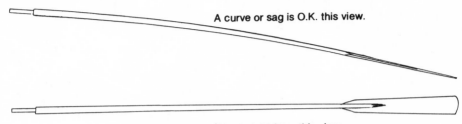

A curve or sag is O.K. this view.

Sculling oar should be straight from this view.

FIGURE 13.2

about right. The idea is to be able to stand up and still have the oar at approximately 40 degrees to horizontal with about three-fourths of the blade below the water.

I secure the leather oar protector on our oar with contact cement and scarf or feather out the joint. I don't like to use nails or tacks because the tack holes weaken the vital stress point of the oar (Figure 13.3). Since twisting the oar is the tiring part of sculling, any way to reduce friction on the oarlock helps. I use grease or cooking oil on my leather and also have a lanyard to position the oar so the oarlock rides on the leather. This way I don't need a shoulder on the protector. Without the traditional leather shoulder, there is less area to rub on the oarlock, therefore, less friction.

Now that you have an oarlock and oar, where do you position it for sculling or rowing? First get a scrap piece of 4 inch by 4 inch fir or

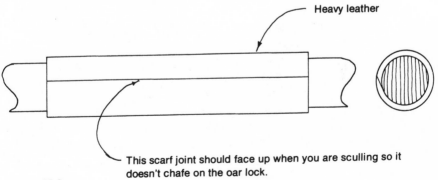

Heavy leather

This scarf joint should face up when you are sculling so it doesn't chafe on the oar lock.

FIGURE 13.3

hardwood and drill a hole in it at about the angle of your transom. If your boat is a double-ender, angle the hole 15 degrees. This hole should easily accommodate the stem of your oarlock. With some G clamps and plywood protectors, clamp or lash the temporary oarlock socket securely onto the taffrail, or the stern pulpit. This gives you an adjustable oarlock socket to experiment with so you can find the best spot to scull standing upright on deck. Where you place the oarlock is not too critical except that you should have the inboard end of the oar chest high while you are standing to one side of it. You also need room to move the inboard end athwartships about 2 feet.

If you have an outboard motor bracket, you might be able to use it as a base for your oarlock. Or simply notch out the vertical wood part that the outboard motor clamps to and lock the oar in this.

Use your temporary oarlock socket for awhile. Change positions until you are positive you have the ideal spot. Then finally fasten down your metal socket. Ideally *Seraffyn's* socket should have been 4 inches to starboard. Oh well, live and learn.

To find your rowing oarlock position, use the same 4 by 4 and experiment so you can row standing up, looking forward with the inboard end of the oar about chest high.

THE SECRET OF SCULLING

When we first took off on *Seraffyn*, we had a second hand 14-foot lifeboat oar with two separate oarlock positions, one on the portside of the cockpit for single oar rowing and one on the port side of the taffrail for sculling. For several years I rowed the boat whenever necessary, only sculling when we were in tight quarters. I row fisherman-style, standing in the cockpit with the tiller between my legs. I can make slight course corrections this way.

When you row with only one oar, you need quite a bit of searoom. As you start to row your boat, it tends to sheer away from the thrust of the oar until you get some speed through the water. Rowing with

This lanyard eliminates the need for a shoulder on the leather oar protector.

Our rowing position, with the tiller between my legs for course corrections.

one oar does give you a bit more torque or power than sculling, but rowing long distances is hard and tiring since you are moving the heavy oar on the powerless back stroke.

Sculling works far better than rowing when you are maneuvering in tight places such as between finger piers or closely moored yachts. You can literally scull in a 360 degree pivot on your boat's axis point. This is handy if you are working into a cul-de-sac dock arrangement. To turn around you simply row or stroke in one direction. Once you are pointed in the right direction, start sculling again. These tight quarter maneuvers are not possible with an oar sticking out 10 feet on one side of your boat.

Two years ago in British Columbia's Gulf Islands we met Ron Wall, who lives and cruises on his engineless 26-foot San Pierre dory. He showed us the secret of the Oriental lanyard system for sculling. Before this, Lin at four feet 10 inches and 100 pounds hadn't had the strength to row or scull *Seraffyn*. When I rigged Ron's lanyard connection, she immediately took over and powered our 5½-ton cutter like a veteran sampan lady.

The Oriental lanyard connection is simply a 3/16-inch low-stretch Dacron line that fits through a 3/16-inch hole in the oar approximately halfway between the oarlock and the handle. This hole is drilled at right angles to the flat of the oar blade. The lower end of the line is attached to a fitting directly below the hole in the oar. For experimental purposes, lash up a temporary connection using an existing cleat or fitting.

Once you learn to keep this line tight at all times, the lanyard will take the upward load or thrust as you scull back and forth with the oar blade at about 35 degrees to the surface (Figure 13.4). The lanyard also helps twist or feather the oar in the correct direction at the end of each stroke to minimize the necessary wrist-twisting effort. You will be able to take a completely novice boatperson, scull with them for a minute, then watch as they carry on alone and move the boat at about 70 percent efficiency. Practice for a bit tied to your mooring or when you are in open water. It is dead simple with the lanyard.

The classic standing position is most comfortable for long-term sculling as it allows you to pendulum your upper body. This body swinging motion is easier and less tiring than using just your arms.

The Oriental lanyard connection.   The classic sculling position.

When you get your sculling oar rigged and use it for a season or two, you will come to appreciate the simplicity and extra manueverability it gives you. Of course for safety you should have an anchor ready, dock lines and fenders readily available, and sails bent on even if you are in a calm anchorage. A sudden gust of wind, one that is stronger than you can row against, might blow in at any time.

Male sailors all over have asked why Lin is so keen on sailing and cruising. I believe that women are smarter, i.e., have move survival instinct. They don't like to place themselves in dangerous situations by going off to war or climbing killer mountains. Their instincts are to take fewer risks so they can live to raise the next generation. This concern continues the human race. Smart women know that their men can get sick or break a leg. Their survival instincts rebel at being on a boat which is too difficult for them to handle—be it sails, ground tackle, or the engine which needs repairing if it breaks down or quits. If they can move the boat with an oar, let go and hoist the anchor,

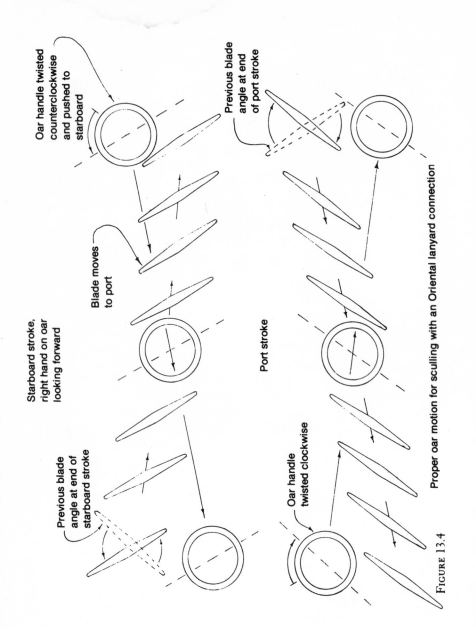

Oar handle twisted counterclockwise and pushed to starboard

Previous blade angle at end of port stroke

Starboard stroke, right hand on oar looking forward

Blade moves to port

Port stroke

Previous blade angle at end of starboard stroke

Oar handle twisted clockwise

FIGURE 13.4   Proper oar motion for sculling with an Oriental lanyard connection

and set and trim the sail, their confidence in these skills will allow them to relax and hang loose. They know they can do something if their mate is out of the picture. I know that since I rigged up our lanyard system, Lin feels more able to take the boat our sailing by herself since she can scull clear of the mooring area.

Even if you have an auxiliary motor, an oar is a good cheap back-up and will always work. It could also serve as a temporary rudder if your main rudder should fail.

But the main reason I use an oar instead of an inboard motor is that it makes sailing and cruising a sport. An engine takes much of the challenge and sense of accomplishment out of cruising. I know that people who have to get back to work on Monday morning realistically require an engine. But I would still have an oar on board in case of engine failure. It could allow you to continue on a two-week cruise instead of sitting in a harbor frustrated and waiting for engine repairs.

For those free souls who can blow away to Mexico for a year or two, time is in abundance, and any money saved on engines or fuel increases the length of their cruise. This is where an oar comes into its own. It can cut down overhead, bolster your feeling of sailing accomplishment, and help you identify with the engineless yachtsman of fifty or sixty years ago. Try it—it still works today.

Update

Sculling a dinghy so you can move easily between moored boats or through tight marinas is essentially the same as sculling your bigger yacht, but far easier. Because the top of your dinghy transom is closer to the water, you can use a short oar. We have sewn a protective leather band 10 inches long on one of our 7-foot, 6-inch dinghy oars, halfway between the rowlock shoulder and the oar blade, to protect the oar shaft. Our dinghy transom has a notch cut in it, about ¾ inch wider than the oar shaft and as deep. The dip serves not only as a sculling lock but as a fairlead for setting out ground tackle. We find we do not need the hold-down lanyard for dinghy sculling since there is far less pressure exerted on the oar.

An afterword on this chapter is that for *Taliesin*, at 29 feet, 6 inches length on deck and a cruising displacement of 17,900 pounds, our 15-foot, 9-inch oar works well. Lin can propel us at approximately 1½ knots in calm conditions.

14

Electricity—There Are Other Ways

What surprises most people who are new to cruising is how unreliable their electrical system becomes after a year of continuous hard use. If they aren't electrical wizards, corrosion, overloaded batteries, generator or alternator failures and lack of skilled repairmen make them slaves to their conveniences.

We once took a survey of yachtsmen cruising outside their own country for a minimum of one year. Among the questions we asked were, "What electrical aids do you have? Which units are working today?" Not one of the fifty-seven sailors surveyed could report all of the electrical aids were working right at that time.

I do not believe you have to give up your conveniences to eliminate the problems of delicate, moisture-sensitive electrical equipment. Not if you choose mechanical, hydraulic and engine-driven accessories plus simple dry-cell electronics instead. Thinking of every way you can to avoid electronics will provide not only more reliable, less interdependent systems, but will also take the load off your batteries so they can be, reserved for real luxuries, like a good stereo, or reading lights over your bunk.

Fortunately, all of the indispensable electrical items required by the self-sufficient voyager can be reliable, self-contained, inexpensive, and portable. This last advantage will come in handy if you occasionally sail on or deliver other people's boats. A portable radio receiver, two quartz watches, a collection of flashlights, two strobe lights, and a cassette stereo powered by a 6-volt dry-cell battery are the only electronics we had on *Seraffyn* for eleven years of voyaging.

On *Taleisin* we find the same electronic simplicity has worked wonderfully.* We started our cruise with a Zenith Transoceanic just as we had on *Seraffyn*. We later switched to the well-recommended Sony 2001D with fine results. The full-band receiver picks up weather reports and gives us the correct time via WWV or BBC anywhere in the world. It is not fitted with RDF, as in our experience the signals picked up on a sailboat's RDF are not reliable.

With the advent of affordable quartz watches, we now carry three, two of which are always kept with the sextant, another of which I usually wear. We keep a regular schedule of battery replacement and check the watches against the time signals twice weekly on passage, so I always have three sources of Greenwich time—radio plus two navigation watches.

In addition to an ever-changing inventory of regular flashlights, we have a 6-volt lantern (EverReady No. 108). This shines a very good beam for about ⅛ mile. In heavy shipping we use it to alert ships to our presence by shining it on our mainsail or flashing the D signal.

Our latest electrical simplification is an emergency masthead strobe light that we can hoist aloft on our spare spinnaker halyard. A pennant staff positions the strobe firmly in place, a foot above the masthead (Figure 14.1). We use the strobe in fog or when we are hove-to near shipping lanes. This dry-cell operated unit is waterproof and so far has been very reliable. Its flash can be seen 5 miles in clear weather and up to ¼ mile in fog. If you can hoist the strobe aloft, you have no wires to install in your mast, no electrical connections to worry about, and, best of all, you can easily haul the strobe down and exchange it if it fails. These neat little Honeywell waterproof strobe units are about $20 each. We usually carry two or three

---

*In 1990 we began making videos. To power the cameras we added a solar panel and a 23-amp gel-cell battery. This led us to try a bevy of small electrical additions—vacuum cleaner, reading lamp, a hook-up to our stereo system. We did keep all essential electrical items isolated and working on their own dry-cell batteries. This soon paid off when a short in the solar panel left us with a flat main battery. After six years with a solar panel we do not feel we would interconnect with any vital items.

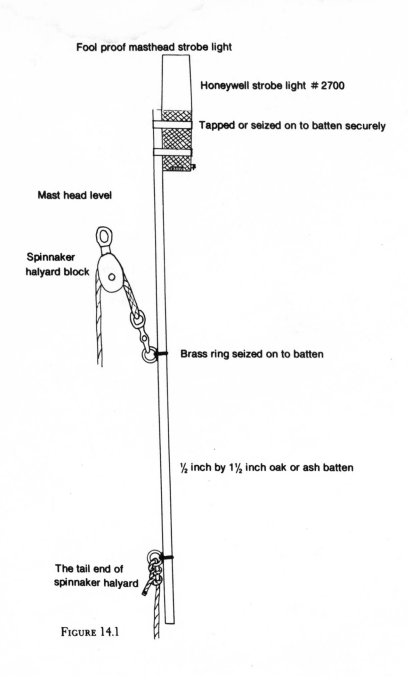

Fool proof masthead strobe light

Honeywell strobe light # 2700

Tapped or seized on to batten securely

Mast head level

Spinnaker
halyard block

Brass ring seized on to batten

½ inch by 1½ inch oak or ash batten

The tail end of
spinnaker halyard

FIGURE 14.1

with one in our jacket pocket or wet weather gear for a personal man-overboard light.

The items just listed are the only absolutely necessary electronics needed for the safe navigation of a simple sailboat. But there are two other self-contained electronic devices that could be considered. If you cruise in a foggy area, a depth sounder would be useful. If it has a 100-fathom range, you can run along the 50 or 75 fathom curve in safety. Depth sounders are the most popular and reliable electronic aid available to yachtsmen today. Brookes and Gatehouse makes one that is dry-cell battery operated, fully waterproof with a retractable transducer that can be cleaned easily from inside your boat. The transducer is set through an all bronze through-hull fitting. The readout unit is hermetically sealed and all electrical connections are gold plated. This makes it the most reliable and probably the most expensive yacht depth sounder on the market today (see page 289 of *Cruising under Sail* by Eric Hiscock). If I owned this unit I'd like to figure out a way to make both the readout unit and transducer totally portable. Then I could take it on deliveries or use it from the dinghy to sound new anchorages or unmarked channels.

Whatever type of unit you choose, try to get one with a transducer that can be mounted without cutting a hole in your hull. This cuts down the chances of leaks, electrolysis, and damage to the transducer.

An EPIRB or Emergency Position Indicating Radio Beacon is dry-cell battery operated, self-contained, waterproof, and it floats. Since it is portable it can be taken with you into your lifeboat or on deliveries. It is supposed to send out a signal that alerts aircraft within a 125-mile radius of your position. Reports are that aircraft have picked up these beacon signals as far as 250 miles away. Ideally this unit will send out signals for up to eight days. It is better than a ham radio for calling emergency help since its beacon can be used by aircraft to actually home in on your position. This is important because if the people in a lifeboat aren't able to give an exact position, search efforts are going to be difficult. This trend towards carrying radios to call for outside help is a recent phenomenon and may be encouraging unprepared neophytes to take a chance and cross oceans. The Hiscocks, the Guzzwells, the Smeetons—most long term, self-reliant voyagers choose to sail with no transmitter at all. But if you choose to have an emergency radio, an EPIRB is probably the most practical and inexpensive ($249 in 1997) way to call for help. One of the most worrisome things about the boats we deliver is that if the engine won't start, everything dependent on the charging system soon quits. Most of these yachts are 40 feet and over with four-cylinder diesels which can't be hand-cranked. But one handsome motor trawler we delivered up the Mexican coast had a hydraulic starting motor instead of the usual electric starter. The main engine was turned over by a vane-driven starter motor activated by hydraulic pressure, stored in an accumulator. The accumulator was pressurized by a pump run off the engine. But most important, the accumulator had a hand-operated pump which could also be used to repressurize the system. This in effect made the four-cylinder, 85-horsepower Caterpillar diesel hand start. I was very impressed, especially when I found the hydro-start turned the engine twice as fast as an electric starter. One charge by the engine would keep the starter turning for thirty seconds. When the accumulator was pumped by hand it would turn the engine for twenty seconds.

These starting systems were developed by General Motors, Caterpillar, and Westerbeke for rugged wet conditions such as water-pump engines, small tug boats, net boats on tuna clippers, and lifeboats where it is impossible to keep the batteries charged up and isolated from salt water. These starter units are completely waterproof. They can be submerged in salt water without suffering any damage. A hydraulic starter theoretically could start your diesel in a completely flooded engine room as long as the diesel engine's air intake was above the water. The accumulator will hold its pressure indefinitely so it will turn your engine over even if you only use your boat once every three months.

Another excellent, non-electrical engine-starting solution is spring or mechanical starters such as made by Startwell in England. This spring-operated starter requires no external energy source. It can be bolted onto the bell housing of the engine as a backup to your electric start, or as a complete replacement. It is required equipment on the British lifeboats as well as being used on larger vessels as an emergency starter.

Hydraulic starter—American Bosch Company, Springfield, MA 01107, USA—ask for information on the Hydrotor Fluid Power cranking system. Mechanical starters—Startwell Ltd., Unit 1A, Peonix Estate, Rosslyn Crescent, Harrow, Middlesex HA1 2SP, England.

The Edson bilge pump. CREDIT EDSON CORP

The most efficient way to handle very heavy ground tackle and chain is with a hydraulic anchor winch. The British Navy used hydraulic winches extensively on their 70-foot MFVs during the Second World War. Commercial boats have been using hydraulic winches for decades, not only for ground tackle, but to lift their seine nets and lobster pots. But for some strange reason, hydraulic anchor winches, though available, have never become popular with yachtsmen. Maybe it's because of the fear of oil leaks on teak decks. Fortunately this problem has been completely solved by the introduction of a flexible air-quip hose.

The beauty of a hydraulic winch is its continuous positive power which it develops directly from your main engine. The Pacific Hydraulic anchor windlass produces 3,000 pounds of line pull *as long as the main engine keeps running.* The same winch with an electric motor is good only as long as your battery charge lasts, and its pulling power diminishes as the battery loses its power. If you've ever been aground in a deserted bay, you'll appreciate the idea of a powerful windlass with a long supply of continuous power which could help you pull your boat with your ground tackle.[*]

One further note of simplicity if you choose hydraulic systems is that the same engine-driven pump that will recharge your start will also power your windlass.

Electric bilge pumps can be eliminated by adding an engine-driven mechanical pump which will work as long as your engine will run. This is far better than choosing an electric installation in which your pump won't work for long if your batteries or wiring become flooded. Simpler yet is the powerful solid bronze hand-operated bilge pump made by Edson, which pumps a gallon a stroke and can be made portable if you wish.

There are two good substitutes for electrically powered compressors to run refrigeration. The first is to trade for a belt-driven compressor run straight off the front of your engine. The second way to have ice cubes and refrigeration on board is with a kerosene refrigeration unit. Eric and Susan Hiscock have used kerosene (paraffin) to run a top-loading chest with great success. Their unit was rather bulky and would probably not fit in a boat under 38 feet. But other people have taken the working parts out of a commercial kerosene refrigerator and adapted them to a custom-built well-insulated chest.

A gravity feed deck tank and a small hand-pressurized shower tank can be installed to simplify your water-pressure system (see Chapter 24, Section VI). The use of electricity to run lights can be cut down tremendously or even eliminated with cabin and navigation oil lamps (see Chapter 22, Section VI). On long passages a windvane can steer your boat without requiring any electricity at all.

If you choose a combination of portable, hydraulic, or mechanical solutions to replace the usual array of electronics offered today, you'll find that cruising will be less of a hassle. Since fewer of your

---

[*] Each of the hydraulic windlasses listed can be converted to hand operation for emergency backup.
Pacific Windlass and Simpson Lawrence Windlasses, Simpson Lawrence USA, 6508 28th St., E. Bradenton, FL 34203; 800-946-3527
Lighthouse 1501, Lighthouse Mfg. Co., 2944 Rubidoux Blvd., Riverside, CA 92509; 909-683-5078
Ideal Windlass Company, P.O. Box 430, East Greenwich, RI 02818; 401-884-2550
Edson Corporation, 146 Duchane Blvd., New Bedford, MA 02745

Two examples of electrolysis. Each piece of wiring you eliminate will cut your chances of electrolysis.

systems are hooked up to your bank of batteries, you'll never have a total power failure if a short drains the batteries or an alternator fails to charge them. With this self-contained equipment, you'll eliminate expensive switch panels, fuse boxes, and the cost and labor of doing a neat, moisture-proof wiring job. Because dampness induced by a salt water atmosphere starts little dribbles of electrolysis, causing current to leak out of various connections throughout your hull, each piece of electrical equipment you eliminate will cut your chances of electrolysis.

Ted Swartz, the general manager of Electro-guard, San Diego, which produces an electrolysis detection unit, said, "No wiring, no wet batteries, no dissimilar metals under water will add up to no electrolysis. But he added, "Most people won't give up their electrical conveniences to eliminate electrolysis."

If you are one of those people willing to eliminate wired systems in favor of self-contained units, you'll not only avoid electrolysis, but you'll be able to scrub out the whole inside of your boat regularly, then hose the whole interior down with fresh water. This removes the salt accumulation that sneaks into every part of the boat no matter how careful you are. Since there was absolutely no wiring or permanently installed electronics in *Seraffyn*, we were able to do this once a year and even our books, stored for up to eleven years on a 24-foot wooden boat, have remained mildew free.

In foreign countries even more than in your home port, good electronics repairmen are hard to find, parts next to impossible. Much of today's solid state and printed circuit stuff can't be repaired without factory replacement parts. These parts usually have to be pulled through the mails, the customs offices, and agents. Believe me, what started out to be a convenience can become a drag. The hydraulic and mechanical equipment I recommend instead are much more durable than electrical units. Because of their workboat origins, it is easier to find repairmen to work on them and parts to repair them. Just sail into a fishing port.

The highly electrified yacht is also anti-social because you have to run your generator or main engine to charge batteries in harbor. My feelings align exactly with Eric Hiscock who writes, "However, unless the engine is used for a considerable time when the yacht is underway, it will have to be run when she is at anchor to keep the batteries charged. The noise may be a source of irritation to the owner and his friends, though they at least will have the benefit of using the current when it has been produced, but it will completely destroy the peace of the anchorage for everyone within earshot, especially on a quiet night. This is a selfish nuisance which no one has the right to inflict on others." (*Cruising under Sail*, page 61.)

Yachtsmen probably end up with all electrical conveniences and aids because electricity is the first solution that comes to mind. Since electricity and electrical motors are dependable and practical in dry shoreside applications, we assume electricity will be as reliable on a boat. But there are three flaws in this assumption. First, household electrical units such as refrigerators are produced by the millions. Research and development teams have had millions of dollars to spend perfecting household refrigerators. Marine systems are usually custom-built and have very little prototyping. Most problems are discovered when boat owners complain. The second large difference is the wet, salty environment found on board boats. It corrodes and shorts out any unsealed connection. And finally, unlike people in a shoreside community, those living on board a cruising boat do not have an unlimited supply of electricity produced by a large company. YOU have to make the current and maintain the generators, batteries, and wiring.

Electrical options are offered to prospective boat buyers instead of mechanical solutions because they can be easily dropped in place and simply plugged into the ship's power supply. Installing things like a mechanical bilge pump will be much more difficult. Yacht sellers will probably have to arrange for special brackets. If the engine installation space is tight this can present technical problems. If the owner is impatient for his boat, the electrical solution will be faster. And finally, I don't think salesmen who handle yachts and their equipment, or designers who suggest this equipment are aware of the mechanical options and their superior reliability. It's the old chicken-and-egg story. No one offers you non-electrical choices because no one asks for them.

Once cruising sailors start minimizing moisture-sensitive electrical equipment and turn instead toward what works and keeps working on fishing boats and other hardworking vessels, I hope this attitude will change.

15

Spars

If you need to build a mast with simple tools and limited budget, wood is the way to go. An extruded alloy spar section will cost at least three times as much as the wood and glue needed to build a handsome, varnished, tapered mast. Price the materials for both before you decide.

If your boat is intended for offshore cruising, a self-built wooden mast has one other great advantage. Once you build a mast yourself, you'll have the confidence and skills to repair or replace it. Materials for your wood spar will be available anywhere in the world. But who can heli-arc weld an alloy spar or secure a pop-riveted fitting in the Azores, Costa Rica, or Malta? Few people, if any.

With modern waterproof glues and reasonable care a wooden spar should last longer than its builder. Its condition can be checked from the outside. On the other hand, since an alloy spar is only anodized on the outside, corrosion can begin from the inside when salt water enters through the joints and pop-rivet holes. This inside corrosion is difficult to inspect without unstepping the mast and removing the heel fitting (see Don Street's *The Ocean Sailing Yacht*, page 107, figure 16).

An alloy spar will *not* act as a radar reflector. You need flat surfaces at right angles to the radar beam to return a signal. If you stack wrinkles of aluminium foil in the hollow sections of your wooden mast it will return a worthwhile signal without the windage, weight, nuisance, and cost of the usual 18-inch reflectors yachtsmen use. The foil-filled hollow mast will in effect be a 40-foot-long, 40-foot-high radar reflector (see Chapter 29, Section VI, "Some Simple Maintenance Tips," for more on radar reflectors).

Fittings can be made at home, inexpensively, for a wooden mast. All the hardware can be easy-to-work bronze, or mild steel that is then galvanized.

It's easy to modify a wooden spar. You can quickly add or reposition a cleat or winch with woodscrews. You only need a hand drill and screwdriver. The old screw holes can be plugged with wood bungs and glue. To do almost anything to an alloy spar you need special tools, special fittings, and special fasteners. The holes left from moving a fitting are difficult to cover up.

This box section mast (Figure 15.1) is a natural choice for the first-time builder or the pro with limited spar facilities. It has ultra simple butt-joints that are easy to fit perfectly. Because it's hollow this section saves on timber and is lighter than the solid mast. It is also stronger because of its extra flexibility, and it won't get the deep longitudinal seasoning checks that are so common on solid spars.

The flat sides of this mast section make a natural base for all of

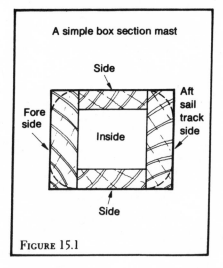

A simple box section mast

Side

Fore side

Aft sail track side

Inside

Side

FIGURE 15.1

your hardware. The hollow interior section is rectangular so it's simple to fit the necessary blocking. Because of this blocking, the job can be done in evenings and weekends, as the gluing up can be done in stages if your time or the number of available clamps is limited.

This mast section can be built without any machine tools. All you need is:

Jack plane
Claw hammer
Ordinary combination ripping and cross-cut saw
1-inch wood chisel
Square
Brace and bits
Pen knife
Plywood straight edge, 36 inches long
¼ inch by 1¼ inch pine batten, 16 to 20 feet long
Old paint brush for glue
Putty knife
Saw horses or temporary supports attached to the side of a building
Clamps—Effective spar clamps can be made of 2 inch by 2 inch scrap wood (Figure 15.2). Use iron carriage bolts or fully threaded rod studding. These clamps are much easier to use if the lower end of the bolt is a tight fit and doesn't turn in the wood because you'll need only one wrench. The inside dimensions of the clamps should accommodate the mast section both sideways and fore and aft so you need a fair amount of thread on your bolts to account for the taper at the head of the mast. Though these clamps are not as quick to use as a G clamp, they will spread the load over a wider surface area and won't crush the soft wood.

A mast can be made of almost any kind of wood. I have seen spars of spruce, Douglas fir, pitchpine, mahogany, hemlock, ash, cedar, even teak. But for this type of section my first choice would be spruce or Douglas fir (Oregon pine). They should be readily available, work easily, and most important, take glue well. Douglas fir is stronger and more rot-resistant than spruce but heavier per cubic foot. If you are weight-conscious and can't get spruce, check with a designer. You

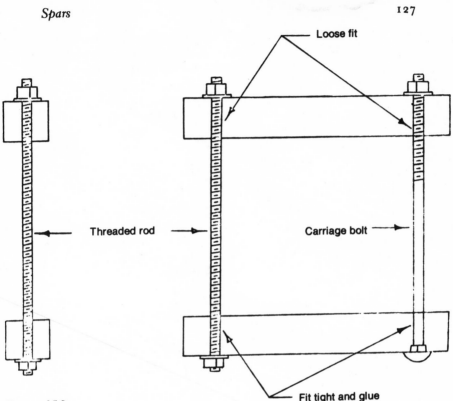

Loose fit

Threaded rod

Carriage bolt

Fit tight and glue

FIGURE 15.2

could probably use a 20 percent thinner mast wall and still end up with a similar weight-to-strength ratio.

If it is possible, order rift- or edge-sawn timber for your box section mast. It's not absolutely necessary, but it will plane easier when you are rounding and finishing your spar. Edge grain also has more resistance to denting and abrasion. It is not necessary to buy airplane grade spruce, the first grade available. Spar grade with its occasional tight knots or blemishes and wider range of annual rings is what you want. Your spar stock should have about 14 percent moisture content before you use it. Your timber merchant can advise you regarding this.

Order enough extra stock to make the scarfs and blocking for all your spars. Instead of ordering mast stock without seeing it, I like to take my mast plans and a scale ruler to the timber yard. There I can look at the lengths and widths in stock and figure out where all my scarfs will be. I choose timber to stagger the scarfs so none are side-by-side on the mast. If you can only get short lengths, this might not be possible, but with today's superior glues you need not worry too much. Have your selected timber machine-planed to an accurate thickness before it is delivered.

Resorcinol glue* is fully waterproof but requires a minimum curing temperature of 70 degrees Fahrenheit for full strength. It's expensive and gives an ugly purple glue line, especially on light-colored woods. If you want to paint your spar, fully waterproof resorcinol is a must. This glue is one part powder and one part liquid.

In England, Aerodux 500 is similar to American resorcinol but is said to cure well in temperatures as low as 60 degrees. This is a two-part liquid glue and the same purple color as American resorcinol. Cascophen compares with Aerodux 500 in being completely waterproof.*

Though not completely water-resistant, a urea glue such as Cascamite or Aerolite 306 (Weldwood in North America) may be fine if your mast is kept well varnished. This type of glue is normally water-resistant, but your joints will delaminate and rot if they stay wet for long periods. Paint is dangerous with a urea-glued spar because you won't be able to inspect the glue joints easily. Urea glue is inexpensive and can be used with temperatures as low as 55 or 60 degrees.

Enough propaganda. On to the actual building.

The thinner-side pieces of this mast are the first to be prepared (Figure 15.5). They must be scarfed and glued together into two pieces the length of the mast. Fair your saw horses or building supports with string. Then lay the timber that will become your side pieces on the supports. If the timber has any defects, mark the poorer side *inside,* the best side *outside.*

A simple scarfing jig will give uniform, tight-fitting, straight joints (Figure 15.3). The identical aligning cleats on the scarfing jig should be accurately positioned and attached to both sides of the plywood straight edge. The jig can used to transfer the exact scarfing angle

*Epoxy would not be a good choice for spars for reasons discussed on page 313.
An update on spar building appears on page 313.

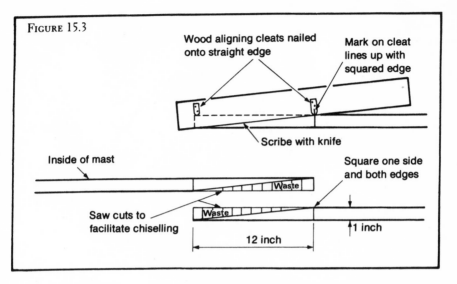

FIGURE 15.3

Wood aligning cleats nailed onto straight edge

Mark on cleat lines up with squared edge

Scribe with knife

Inside of mast

Saw cuts to facilitate chiselling

Waste

Waste

Square one side and both edges

12 inch

1 inch

to all edges of your timber. This jig is figured for a 12-inch-long scarf on 1-inch-thick material. This is the safe minimum scarfing ratio for a spar. If you have extra material you can go as high as twenty to one. Any higher is not necessary and wastes material and labor.

Use the scarfing jig to guide your pen knife. Cut a mark carefully from the squared edge to the end of your timber. Mark each edge of both pieces. This scribe line is your exact jointing line. Now lay the two boards you are scarfing end to end, *inside* up (Figure 15.3) and check that the waste wood is being removed from the correct side of each. Make saw cuts carefully about every inch through the waste materials to within 1/16 inch of your scribed line. Chisel the waste wood off, using the saw cuts as guides, then plane the remaining wood to the scribe lines checking across the scarf with the straight edge on the sole of your plane. Set your plane fairly shallow and work slowly down to your scribe line, keeping the face of the joint fair and true (Figure 15.5).

Now for a dry run. Clamp and check your scarf for fit. One finishing nail from the *inside* will help the alignment and glueing. The feather ends should extend ¼ inch past your squared pen knife mark. The joint should be tight and straight along the scribe line. It if isn't, remove the aligning nail and slightly hollow the scarf across its face

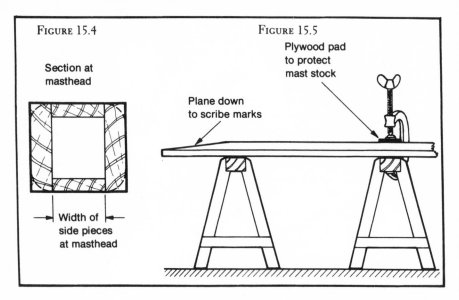

FIGURE 15.4

Section at
masthead

Width of
side pieces
at masthead

FIGURE 15.5

Plywood pad
to protect
mast stock

Plane down
to scribe marks

(about 1/64 inch). Reclamp and check the fit until you are satisfied. For glueing up, replace the aligning nail, brush both surfaces with plenty of glue (wax paper between wood and clamps makes for easy removal with no damage to your wood), clamp the two boards together, and adjust them so they look straight along the edges.

Now scrape off excess glue with a putty knife or you'll waste time later chiselling off globs of glue. When the glue is dry, plane the sides of the scarfs so you end up with two continuous flat mast sides.

A box section mast is normally made with the aft or sail track side straight, forward side tapered. This tapering could cut out some of the defects in your materials so inspect your mast sides and decide which end will be at the top of the mast. Clamp the two full-length sides together, *inside* to *inside* and plane the two sail track edges straight and flush.

This straight after-edge becomes the base line for measuring the gradual taper of your mast. Unclamp the full-length sides and turn them *inside* up. At the top of one side measure from the straight track side, the width of the masthead, minus the thickness of your fore and aft pieces (Figure 15.4). Continue down the mast sides, measuring and marking the width of the mast sides at the appropriate spacing. Now lightly nail your long batten to the markings (the nail holes won't mar your mast as they will be on the *inside*). If the batten bends in a smooth curve, fine and good. If not, adjust the nails till the batten is fair, then pencil in a mark along the batten and saw off the excess wood.

Try to keep your saw as square as possible. If you are a bit wobbly, don't cut exactly to the line. You can true it up later.

Now using the shaped side as a pattern, pencil in your curve and cut out the second full-length side. Clamp the two sides together, *inside* in, and square the fore-and-aft edges of both boards at the same time. Your mast sides should now have a fair curve on the forward edges and a straight square after-edge. Don't be too fussy with this yet as you will probably have to do a little dressing before you glue on the fore-and-aft sides.

All hollow spars should have some solid sections, if only at the butt and masthead. For a more reliable mast, use additional blocking to take the crushing loads of through-bolts and provide extra bearing surface for all fasteners at the shroud attachments.

The internal blocking is the key to glueing up this type of mast easily, in simple stages. This eliminates the panic of glue drying before the whole mast is securely clamped. This is especially important to the home builder who has a shortage of clamps and only two hands.

Your next step is to position the load-spreading internal blocking. As an example of how this is done, I will use a normal masthead sloop with one set of spreaders, stepped on the keel. This type of mast construction works just as well for any Bermudan mast (Figure 15.6).

Start with block A, shape it to fit between the full-length sides, giving the correct dimensions, and taper. The fore-and-aft dimension of block A should be left about 1/16 inch larger than the sides. It will be planed down later (Figure 15.7). Now cut the tapered fingers in the top of block A. These four fingers should be about 18 inches long in an average 40-foot spar to spread the bending load over a large area. With completely solid blocking there is an abrupt change of strength and flexibility at the end of each block which could cause hard spots in your mast and possibly weaken it under strain.

After cutting out the wedges that form the fingers, consider where and how to install your mast wiring and fresh water drain holes. Vertical holes can easily be drilled in the short blocking but the longer butt block might have to be glued together in two pieces with grooves in each to make a drain hole. Now try a dry run by clamping block A between the two mast sides.

Is the mast the correct thickness?

Do you have enough clamps?

Clamp the tapered fingers to the sides using G clamps or slide the cut-out wedges back in place and clamp with your homemade spar clamps. If everything looks fair and square, take it apart and glue up.

Next fit block B and C, one at a time or both together, using the same steps. Check to be sure the mast sides are evenly tapered and straight on the track side before gluing.

With all the blocks glued between the side pieces, you're ready to plane the fore-and-aft edges of the sides and the blocking in between (Figure 15.7). Be very careful of the corners of the side pieces. A dent here will show forever if you plan to varnish your spar.

Now you are over the most difficult part and simply have to fit the bottom and top of the box, the thicker fore-and-aft pieces. These pieces are thicker than the sides, not only to allow for a large good-looking corner radius, but to give extra depth for sail and spinnaker track screws.

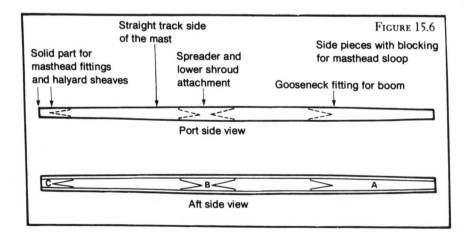

Straight track side
of the mast

FIGURE 15.6

Side pieces with blocking
for masthead sloop

Solid part for
masthead fittings
and halyard sheaves

Spreader and
lower shroud
attachment

Gooseneck fitting for boom

Port side view

Aft side view

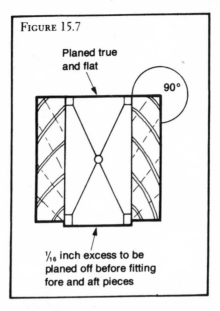

FIGURE 15.7

Planed true
and flat

90°

1/16 inch excess to be
planed off before fitting
fore and aft pieces

Use a straight edge to check your fore-and-aft pieces across the grain for dishing or hollowing. Up to 1/32 inch in 4 inches is acceptable. More than that should be planed out.

Mark the hollow side of the timber *inside*.

Mark all pieces top, bottom, fore, aft, etc.

Then cut the scarf joints.

Clamp the scarfs together dry to check for fit, and adjust if necessary.

Now, measure the previously glued-up side sections between blocks to see if they have collapsed or become hollow-cheeked. If so, make some ¾ inch by ¾ inch spacers and spread the sides to the correct width. A little glue on the ends will permanently locate these intermediate spacers.

Lay on the first plank as in (Figure 15.8, No. 1). Center it using one clamp every 10 or 12 inches. Clamp this in place dry. Check the fit of the jointing surfaces. Be careful to protect the jointing surfaces on the opposite side of your spar and also on the scarf face against dents. Now mark the mast taper on the first plank by running a pencil along the side pieces next to the jointing edge. Unclamp.

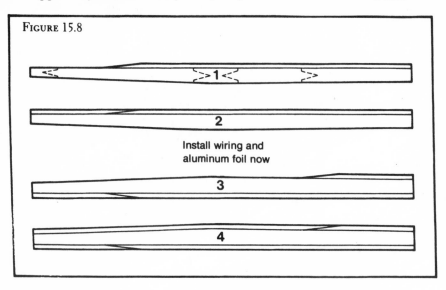

FIGURE 15.8

1

2

Install wiring and
aluminum foil now

3

4

If there is more than a ¼ inch extra width, saw down just to the pencil mark, leaving about 1/16 inch to be planed off when the glue dries.

When everything checks out, brush on glue and clamp up, using a flat block with wax paper to hold the feather edge of the scarf tight. After the glue is set, carefully unclamp and lift the flat block from the feather edge of the scarf. Chisel any glue off the scarfing surface, then clamp the next piece in place, checking the joints, and scarf carefully. Mark, cut to width, and glue it on.

Turn the now three-sided mast over (Figure 15.8, No. 3) but before you button it up, put in your wiring and fasten the wires down so they don't rattle inside the hollow sections.

Don't forget to put in the household variety of aluminium foil for your radar reflector.

Before closing up, check the position of the wiring in relation to the solid sections, then mark the wire positions carefully with a light pencil on the outside of the mast. Otherwise, when you're putting the mast hardware on later, you could pull out a drill covered with bits of copper and insulation. It's a sickening feeling, believe me.

Now the side pieces as shown in 15.8, 3 and 4 can be glued on.

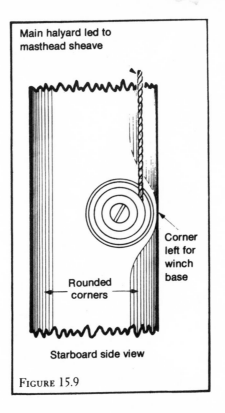

Main halyard led to masthead sheave

Corner left for winch base

Rounded corners

Starboard side view

FIGURE 15.9

Your box section spar will look ready to round off. But don't do it. This radiusing should not be done until the hardware spreaders, fittings, and winches are accumulated and checked for location and fit.

For instance, you probably will want the main halyard winch as far forward on the side of the mast as possible to give the best lead to the halyard sheave (Figure 15.9). If you leave the corners at this spot, you will have a natural winch base. The same applies only in reverse for the jib halyard winch. The mast can also be left rectangular at the mast partners or cut roughly octagonal so you won't have to make concave, convex mast wedges.

Once you have marked where all your hardware goes, you can safely round off the corners and finish up your spar.

16
Build Your
Own Bulwarks

After 25,000 miles of cruising around the Pacific, Hal Roth completely modified *Whisper*, his 35-foot fibre-glass production sloop. One of the many changes he made was to remove the old toerail and fit a bulwark rail. We know why he made this change because we have 8-inch-high bulwarks on *Seraffyn* and they are great. Not only do they give a feeling of strength and security on a small cruising boat, but they have several other advantages.

A high bulwark gives so many things a second life. The winch handle dropped in the scuppers doesn't immediately go over. When you are changing headsails, you and the jib are not so likely to be washed off. A toerail is okay for toes, but an 8-inch-high bulwark really gives a good foothold. Ground tackle, anchors, line, and chain can be left on deck unsecured for a short time without fear of them immediately slipping over. Things, including crew, seem to remain more attached to vessels with nice high bulwarks.

In the tropics it's a real pleasure for the whole crew to sleep on deck. A bulwark lets you select your favorite deck spot and keeps you and your bed on board.

Working vessels usually have a high bulwark that the crew half expects to be damaged when warping alongside quays and docks and when working cargo. It can be repaired relatively easily compared to the hull or deck and covering board. On your yacht this can be a real advantage in case you have a collision or something simply falls down on your boat. The bulwark will absorb some or maybe all of the initial shock and save you expensive repair bills.

Bulwarks with large open scuppers make possible a full-length adjustable lead. This lead can be used for headsails, attaching boom vangs, preventers, and storm or riding sails. To attach a lead to the bulwark rail you use about 4 feet of 1-inch nylon parachute webbing (heavier for boats over 30 feet), lapped 4 inches and sewn strongly into a loop (Figure 16.1). This loop is slipped under the bulwark scuppers and the snap-shackle of a snatch block joins the two ends of the loop above the rail. The block can then be held up snug to your lifelines with shock cord and a quick release snap-shackle. The tension of the shock cord is enough to locate the loops anywhere between bulwark stanchions. To adjust you simply push the block down and slide the loop fore or aft. If a major adjustment is necessary, you have to unsnap the shock cord and remove the loop from the scuppers and move it forward or aft of the next bulwark stanchion. This may not be ideal for racing but is fine on a pure cruising boat.

The scuppers under your bulwark rail should be open 1 inch to allow good quick drainage and ease of adjusting jib leads. On *Serafyn* these scuppers are closed near the transom and bow, but I have seen them open full-length on other good cruising yachts.

In contrast to the traditionalists, I don't think a rail capping is necessary on a bulwark. It only costs more to fit and maintain. Without it the jib leads have nothing to chafe.

I have hawse holes (fairleads) amidships in my bulwark which are very strong and handy, as the spring lines can't jump out. You can also fit large wooden cleats on your bulwark—*cavels* they're called—that are especially nice for making up mooring lines and keeping them up off the deck.

One of the weakest design features in the modern yacht is the way lifeline stanchions are attached to the deck. Many things can overstrain your stanchions, especially people climbing on board and hanging all of their weight on the top of one stanchion, terribly straining the narrow base with its lever of two feet or longer. Once I

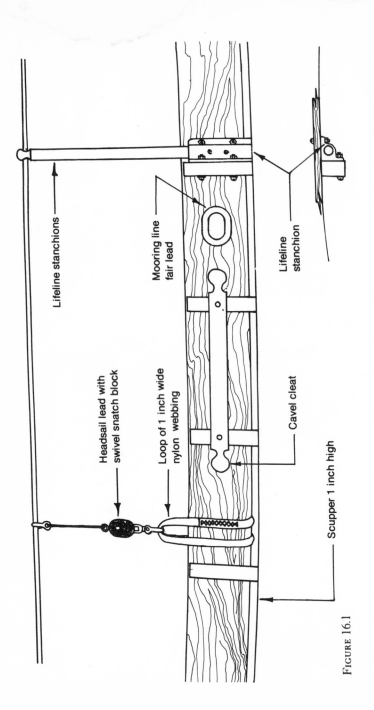

Lifeline stanchions

Mooring line
fair lead

Lifeline
stanchion

Headsail lead with
swivel snatch block

Loop of 1 inch wide
nylon webbing

Cavel cleat

Scupper 1 inch high

FIGURE 16.1

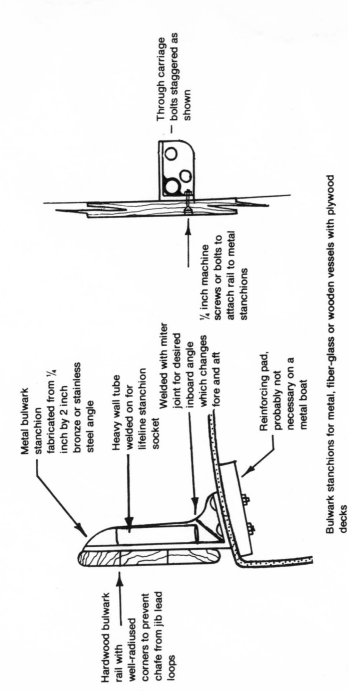

Through carriage bolts staggered as shown

¼ inch machine screws or bolts to attach rail to metal stanchions

Metal bulwark stanchion fabricated from ¼ inch by 2 inch bronze or stainless steel angle

Heavy wall tube welded on for lifeline stanchion socket

Welded with miter joint for desired inboard angle which changes fore and aft

Reinforcing pad, probably not necessary on a metal boat

Hardwood bulwark rail with well-radiused corners to prevent chafe from jib lead loops

Bulwark stanchions for metal, fiber-glass or wooden vessels with plywood decks

FIGURE 16.2

dropped a jib on *Seraffyn's* deck to have the next sea come on board, dragging the sail over the lifelines. The jib filled with green water and bent the lifeline stanchions out board at a 45 degree angle before I had time to haul the sail back on deck. Neither the base of the lifeline stanchion nor the covering board were damaged in any way because the lifeline stanchion was securely through-bolted to the strong bulwark stanchion and to the rail as well. Also, I use heavy wall brass tubing for my stanchions. Under extreme strain they bend instead of buckling as stainless steel will. You can straighten the bent brass stanchion, using a vise with jaws made from hardwood.

A traditional bulwark rail on a wooden yacht is expensive to install and requires a really good shipwright if you want a watertight job. On a fiber-glass or metal (steel, aluminium) yacht, a bulwark can be installed (Figure 16.2) quite cheaply. The savings of not having to purchase genoa track, special lifeline stanchion bases, through-bolts, possible underdeck reinforcing, and fairleads could help pay for your bulwark rail. It would also give you a safer, more secure, and easier-to-sail cruising yacht.

17

Tools and Spares for Offshore Voyagers

A straightforward, simple sailboat can be maintained and repaired with relatively few tools. But as you add machinery and electronics to your boat, the list of necessary spare parts and tools increases. More important, the list of personal skills you need grows proportionately if you wish to maintain your vessel in a self-sufficient manner.

Each of the four lists below are divided into categories that include the minimum tools every sailor should carry, then additional tools for boats with more complications such as inboard engines and electrical equipment. The final part of each list includes the extra tools that will be handy if you want to turn professional to earn a few dollars as you cruise.

Sailmaking tools for the basic sailboat:

Sail needles, assorted, from no. 12 to no. 19
Knife or side cutters
Rope fid
Sailor's palm
Scissors
Awl

Thread

Nylon or tarred marlin for serving

Spare Dacron cloth

Beeswax

$3/8$-inch grommet punch, spare grommets, and dies

Contact cement for emergency repairs

Butane pipe lighter to seal line ends

Additional sailmaking tools needed to earn a living:

Electric portable zig-zag sewing machine with hand-cranking attachment

Dies for brass cringle liners, plus assorted liners and rings

Soft hammer

Seam ripper

Soldering gun with flat tip for hot-knifing Dacron cloth

Rigging vise and fids (priggers)

Nico press tools (talerit)

Various weights of spare cloth and boltrope materials

100-foot measuring tape

Nylon webbing

White electrical tape

Carpentry tools for a basic sailboat:

$1/4$-, $1/2$-, and 1-inch wood chisels

Smoothing plane

Backsaw, hacksaw

Claw hammer

Counterbores for wood screws

Brace and bits $1/4$ inch to 1 inch and expandable bit to $1\frac{1}{2}$ inches

Four or five adjustable clamps

Two-speed hand drill plus twist drills to fit

12-foot tape measure

Paint and varnish brushes

Sharpening stone

Oil can

Putty knife
Wood scraper and fine file
Wood rasp

Additional carpenter's tools for owners of wooden yachts:

Caulking tools including making iron, nib iron, reefing irons
(bent files)
Caulking mallet
Wood plug cutters of ⅜, ½ and ⅝ inches to fit your counter
bores
Screw driver bits for brace
⅜ inch drill motor

This 110-220 step-down, step-up converter (transformer) takes up very little space, costs less than $25 and weighs about 8 pounds. It's a handy unit which allows you to use American-built electrical hand tools everywhere in the world. (In Europe, the Far East, and South America, 220 is the normal voltage available.) I prefer using 110 tools around boats and near the water because it is safer than 220. We know of two cruising sailors who were electrocuted when they were using 220-volt hand tools from the dinghy or off a dock. Be careful when you are using power tools near the water.

Additional tools for professionals:

Assortment of caulking irons
Reefing tools
Caulking gun for paying seams with cartridges
1/4-, 3/8-, 3/4-, 1 1/4- and 1 1/2-inch wood chisels or small slicks
Rabbet plane, jack plane, block plane, bullnose plane
Coping saw, dovetail saw (small back saw)
Long drills 18-inch to 36-inch lengths, 3/16-inch to 1/2-inch diameter
Electric drill motor with 1/2-inch chuck, variable speed for driving screws
3-inch-wide belt sander
8 inch by 12 inch square
Bevel guage, marking guage
50-foot tape measure
Angle grinder for repairs on glass yachts
Wood rasp (fine)
Scribe (compass)
Spoke shave
Various wood scrapers
Step up/step down converter (transformer) for 220 volt to 110 volt so tools can be used in other countries.

Mechanic's tools for the basic sailboat (no engine):

8- and 10-inch crescent wrenches
Assorted screwdrivers
Vise grips
Pliers
Cold chisel
Fine flat file, course half round bastard, various round files
H.S. drill index, 1/16 to 3/8 inches
Hacksaw
Small pipe wrench
Ball peen hammer

Additional tools if you own an outboard motor:

3/8-inch drive socket set
3/8- to 3/4-inch combination wrenches

With an inboard engine, add:

½-inch drive socket set, up to 1¼ inches
Feeler guage
Combination wrenches up to 1 inch
Allen (hex) wrenches
Water pump pliers
Phillips head screwdrivers
Cheap set of taps and dies
Machinist square and straight edge
Inside-outside calipers
Needlenose pliers
8- and 14-inch pipe wrenches
12- and 16-inch crescent wrenches
Small and large assorted metal files and cold chisels
Valve grinding compound
Set of easy outs
Counter sinks
Center punches
Side cutters
Pin punches
Selection of brass rod for soft punches ¼- to ¾-inch × 6 inches
Wire brush
Pry bar
Tin snips

For the professional mechanic, add:

Micrometers
Various gear pullers
Shop manuals for popular marine diesel engines
Torque wrench
Large set of allen wrenches
Quality set of tap and dies

Electrical tools for the basic sailboat (no engine or wet battery):

Small test light and alligator clips to test dry cells
Electrical tape

Add for yacht with wet-cell battery and electronics:

Voltmeter
Soldering gun
Wire stripper
Selection of connectors and wire

For professional electrical repairmen:

Assorted sophisticated and complicated test equipment (a category that becomes so exotic it boggles my mind)

During our eleven years of voyaging on board *Seraffyn* we carried every item on the above lists except for the belt sander, sewing machine, angle grinder, ⅜-inch socket set and items listed under professional mechanic's and professional electrical tools. All of these tools took up about 4 cubic feet of space and weighed approximately 140 pounds.

The Care and Storage of Tools

Iron tools are a hassle on board. WD40 and plastic toolboxes make protecting them much easier. After you are finished with each job, heave all your tools in the toolbox, mist thoroughly with spray WD40 and shut the lid. This mist will oil and protect all the nooks and crannies in your tools, even the grooves in taps, drills, and dies. It will also protect the items you rarely use, the ones that are sitting on the bottom of the box.

For larger tools, such as my handsaw, I have loose plastic sheaths which protect the teeth. I spray the teeth with WD40 and store the saw tooth up so water can't trap in the sheath. All my chisels have their own leather or plastic sheaths which I keep packed with lubriplate grease. When I finish with the chisels, the greased sheath automatically protects the cutting edge.

Electric drills and sanders keep well if they are sprayed with WD40, then wrapped in cotton rags and stored in tightly sealed plastic bags or suitable plastic boxes. Steel hand planes are best protected with a layer of grease on the flat cutting edge of the blade under the chipper, then sprayed with WD40.

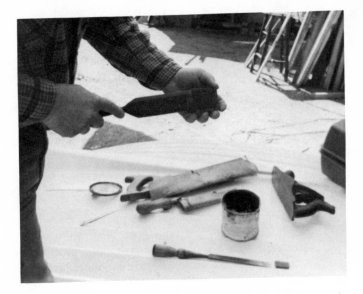

The plastic toolboxes we used on *Seraffyn* for twelve years are made by Adventurer and are about the size of a tackle box. These boxes are available in most marine stores in the United States. They are rainproof, semi-soft plastic which won't dent woodwork, scratch teak decks, or leave rust marks. I plan to use four of these super toolboxes on our new cutter, one for each categry of tools.

Spare Parts

If your boat is built like a fishing boat, with galvanized and steel everything, then you'll need to carry fewer spares. But if she is all bronze or stainless steel fastened, you'll save yourself days of shopping for just the right bolts or metal scrap if you keep a stock on board. Fiberglass cloth, resin, mild steel, wood, and galvanized fastenings are usually available worldwide. It's the more exotic yacht effects like stainless steel or silicon bronze bolts, rod, nuts, and washers that are hard or impossible to find in foreign countries. Stock up on these items plus spare caulking cotton, playing compounds, paints, and varnish. Pieces of metal which match the type used on your boat are handy for fabricating new parts or repairing old ones.

Sailcloth and sail-repair items are only available in the main ports of sophisticate countries such as Japan, Australia, England, and France. So take a good supply with you if you are bound for exotic ports.

Invest in a shop manual for your engine or generator. These manuals contain complete rebuilding and repair information and, most important, usually have a trouble-shooting section. When I deliver yachts I usually buy a shop manual for the owner if there isn't one on board. You should also carry the most concise repair and trouble-shooting literature available for every piece of equipment on board.

Your tools and repair parts become more and more important the farther you sail away from your local chandler and shipyard. With good tools, personal skill, and the correct repair supplies, all things are possible.

Update

If we were working in countries with 220/240-volt electrical power and using 220/240-volt tools, we would also carry a throw-out switch transformer to protect ourselves while working near the water. These transformers, which shut the electricity off immediately if there is an overload or grounding, cost about US$50 for sizes sufficient to handle drills and sanders. They are about the size of a 25-pound package of sugar and probably could have saved the lives of the two sailors we describe in the caption on page 143.

Being Prepared Is the Name of the Game

One of the best things about ocean voyaging and cruising as a sport is its safety record. It's not like skiing, skydiving, gliding motorcycling, or even bicycling, where your safety lies in someone else's hands, be it the pilot who lifts you off, other skiers on the slope, or motorists on the road. Once you sail out the breakwaters, a good watch will eliminate almost all danger of injury or loss due to other people's negligence. Your own preparations, skill, and care will make you safe.

Even better is that this is a sport where age doesn't matter. You're not over the hill at forty-five or fifty-five or sixty-five. Instead if you continue to voyage successfully, the older you get, the more respect you earn. Humphrey Barton at seventy-nine years old was still at it and every time he and Mary reached port, younger sailors were eager to meet "The Bartons."

Physical prowess has little to do with the success of a cruise. So it is a sport for anyone who is willing to accept its most basic premise. The success of a cruise is in direct proportion to the amount of preparation. That preparation can't stop when you've outfitted the boat and bought all of your charts. It has to include careful consideration and reconsideration of situations which still lie in the future.

These chapters deal with three basic areas where preparation now should help you avoid problems later.

18

Make Your Cruising Drag Free

If you trust your ground tackle, cruising can be heaven. You'll be able to lay at anchor and get a good night's sleep. Because you know your boat is safe, you won't think twice before going ashore for dinner or a day of sight-seeing. There is nothing that can ruin your cruising as much as the fear of dragging. Unfortunately the art of drag-proof anchoring is usually learned the hard way, by dragging across a bay at 0200 on a stormy night, or by being hit when some other hapless sailor drags into you. But a careful look at anchoring techniques, a defensive attitude toward your choice of anchorage, and a look at all of the equipment needed for handling ground tackle in changing conditions, can make these lessons less frequent.

In Puerto Andraitx, Mallorca, we watched a high bowed 45-foot ketch drag in a 25-knot wind. The owner tried to reset his anchor at least six or seven times. Finally he gave up and tied alongside a fishing boat at the quay. We'd been in Andraitx for four months and we had to break out our anchor with our winch each time we wanted to go sailing so we knew the holding was fine. The man on the ketch was using good ground tackle, heavy chain, and a large CQR anchor. He later told me, "My echo sounder showed 15 feet of water, so I put out 45 feet of chain. Should have been enough. Must be poor holding ground."

I had sounded that area with a leadline and knew there was 18 feet of water and only 12 inches of tidal rise and fall. So his transducer was probably 3 feet below his waterline and hadn't been calibrated to allow for the difference. Secondly, he was obviously not including the 5 feet from the water to his bow roller in his calculations. This additional 8 feet added to his 15-foot sounder reading gives a total of 23 feet from bow roller to bottom. The absolute minimum scope for anchoring with chain is three-to-one which means he needed 69 feet to be safe. (My preference is five-to-one scope or a minimum of 90 feet in shallow anchorages, no matter what the depth. Chain doesn't do you any good in the locker.)

For proper scope, especially in shallow anchorages you must figure your bow roller heights and measure water depths accurately, then add an allowance for any possible rise in the tide. A leadline is more accurate, cheaper, and more reliable than an echo sounder for this use. If the lead is charged with tallow, soft beeswax, or even peanut butter, it can bring up a sample of the bottom and help you decide which anchor to use to avoid dragging. (Most leadlines have a hole in their lower ends for this purpose. If yours doesn't, drill one at least ¾ inch deep and ¾ inch wide).

Check the depth contours on your chart carefully before you anchor. At Isla Cabrera near Mallorca, Spain, the military commander told us about ten yachts that had anchored in the only possible place, a shallow narrow shelf near his headquarters. A Force 10 squall blew through the anchorage. Six of the ten yachts dragged just a short distance and their anchors dragged over the edge of the five-fathom shelf into 20 fathoms where they hung straight down. All six ended up on the rocky lee side of the bay. If they had been anchored on a gently sloping bottom, the crews could have had time to let out extra scope or set out a second anchor as the boat dragged. If your chart shows little dragging room in the anchorage, put down extra scope or set two anchors when you first hook up.

Anchoring defensively is an art. Hedging your bets by being out of harm's way will save you the work of repairing banged-up topsides and mending frayed tempers. Choose the dead center of the anchorage if you can. This gives you maximum room to swing on your scope, the most time to react if you do drag, and the easiest spot to sail out of when you weigh anchor. Before you let go of your anchor, consider who you want as neighbors. Let's say you have two spots where you can anchor. One is to leeward of a husky ketch with an all-chain rode. This boat is riding stoically to the gusts that periodically rake the harbor. Your other choice is to leeward of a lightweight racing sloop, one that is sailing back and forth across its nylon rode, coming up short at the end of each lunge. If you have to anchor to leeward of one of these, it's almost always safest to choose the one riding to all chain. The yacht with the nylon rode could foul something such as an old hunk of metal that is rotting on the bottom, chafe through its rode, and come crashing down on you. If the wind is strong, the weight and windage of this extra boat could start your anchor dragging too. This scenario happens all too often, especially in ancient harbors with decades of rusty metal waiting on the bottom to chafe through an anchor line.

If you anchor with all chain, you will have to give yachts with nylon rode a wide berth. In a harbor with changeable winds and tides, your chain will lie on the bottom and your boat will move only if there is a fairly good wind or the tide is quite strong. Then your boat will move slowly with the chain dragging over the bottom, but vessels with nylon rodes will quickly swing the length of their scope and bash into you before your chain has reacted and moved 10 feet.

In the Mediterranean, anchoring stern to the quay or docks is space-efficient in the small stone harbors. But if your anchor moves or drags 6 to 10 feet, your rudder, transom, or windvane is bashing against the dock. Choosing to anchor stern to is therefore a risk proportionate to the amount of fetch in the harbor. In places like Rhodes Harbor in Greece, the yacht basin is fully enclosed and only about 500 feet across. So no anchor-dislodging sea can build up. But in Palma, Mallorca, the town quay is open to the south for about 1 mile. A nasty short sea can build up quickly in a southerly blow. It will leave your stern pumping up and down dangerously close to the quay. In this situation if you do choose to anchor stern to, you must anchor defensively. Use twice the scope you normally would so you can pull yourself 50 feet away from the quay in a moderate blow. When you decide to leave, this extra scope will make it easier to winch yourself out to your anchor and give you more maneuvering room as you sail out.

Leaving your boat unattended while it is moored Mediterranean-style is asking for trouble, or at least minor damage. Twenty-nine of the forty-five yachts tied to the harbor wall were sunk in Palma harbor when a strong southerly blew in. This 1977 summer squall did all of its damage in less than an hour.

When you are tied stern to, pay attention when other yachtsmen near you are picking up their anchors to leave. Quite often anchors and chains get criss-crossed. When your neighbor lifts his anchor, he can pull yours up accidentally. A great tangle usually ensues, tempers are frayed, and quite often the anchor of any untended yacht is simply dropped right back in the bay with no attempt made to reset it properly. The man who was not on board when his anchor was disturbed could come home to see his stern bashing the dock.

I think it bears repeating. Always keep someone on board when you are anchored Mediterranean-style. When any boat near you leaves, check your anchor by winching your chain up tight to confirm it is still well set. Whenever possible, we prefer anchoring off and using our dinghy to get ashore. It's usually safer, more private, cleaner, and easier in the long run.

Unfortunately in some Mediterranean ports this just isn't possible because of space limitations. Our choice then is to lie bow to with a stern anchor set. This way, our infinitely less vulnerable bobstay and bronze-strapped stem will be the part of the boat that touches first, if all our anchoring precautions fail. This method has one other advantage. It keeps people from staring down the companionway, so we have more privacy.

Lay your ground tackle carefully to prevent dragging. If you dump your chain on top of your anchor, chances are the whole mess will foul and drag. You must spot your anchor where you want it, then slowly play out scope without pulling on the anchor at all as you drift or motor astern. Only secure the bower when you have payed out full scope. Then set the anchor.

A trip line is a very handy recovery gadget, especially in old harbors with centuries of junk on the bottom, but it too must be carefully set. In northern Spain I managed to get my trip line half-hitched around my own anchor chain and it towed my anchor backwards. I have since been careful to throw the trip line and buoy well away before letting the anchor go.

During a delivery trip we were anchoring in Funchal, Madeira, at night. It was a fairly deep, rocky anchorage, famous for fouled anchors. So we attached a trip line to the smallest fender we could find on board, one that was 20 inches in diameter. Then we tried to set the anchor. It didn't hold. The buoy didn't submerge, but after two tries we realized the trip line was too short and the buoy was holding the 75-pound Herreshoff anchor just off the bottom. We lengthened the trip line and the anchor bit in.

Eleven years ago in Mexico a fierce rain squall came through our anchorage and cut visibility to almost nothing. That's when I learned how to tell if I was dragging when I couldn't see the shore to take bearings. Almost immediately after the first blast of wind, the boat began laying beam to and I wasted valuable time taking the jib off the bowsprit, hoping the reduced windage would allow the boat to head into the wind. Then it dawned on me that the boat was laying beam to the wind because we were dragging. I immediately dropped 150 feet of chain and the boat headed into the wind. When daylight came we were only yards away from the rocks. So we learned a cheap lesson. If you are laying beam to the wind and there is no tidal current, your anchor is dragging.

In less dramatic situations, a few moments spent looking at your chain while it is under tension can tell you if you are dragging. If the chain lifts slowly in the gusts, then lowers itself slowly as the tension eases, you are holding. But if the chain is bobbling in a jerky fashion when it takes the strain, this is a transmission of the anchor bumping and slipping along the bottom.

There have been hundreds of thousands of words written about which anchor is best for this or that type of holding ground. Advertisers have stressed stowability, low cost, or light weight as selling points for their product. But the self-sufficient offshore voyager should look at the facts for himself and carry a variety of the *heaviest* anchors he and his crew can handle. When the chips are down, anchors and the gear to handle them are your only insurance. I plan to buy three types of anchors for my new 8-ton, 30-footer: a 35-pound CQR as a working anchor, a 65-pound folding fisherman (preferably the one designed by Nat Herreshoff) for storm use, and a 20-pound high-tensile Danforth for a stern hook.

In his book, *The Commonsense of Yacht Design*, L. Francis Herreshoff says of his grandfather's original design, "Here is a perfectly proportioned instrument, and if the shotgun and the violin can be said to have reached their final state of perfection, here we see the final perfect state of the anchor." But your rode can wrap around the fluke of your Herreshoff and drag the anchor backwards (Figure 18.1). The fisherman holds well in most bottoms and it's the best anchor for rock or weed. But if there is a chance of swinging, you need to set two anchors to prevent fouling.

On a straight pull in sand or firm mud, the lightweight stockless anchors of the Danforth type hold better than the fisherman. But in soft mud I have felt the lightweight flat palmed anchor floating along the bottom instead of digging in. If the lightweight anchor is dug into firm mud and has to reset itself due to a 180-degree wind shift, a lump of mud can jam between flukes and shank so the flukes don't hinge over and reset into new ground (Figure 18.2). I once brought my Danforth anchor up backwards with the chain wrapped around the rectangular hinge plate after three days in La Paz with a daily 8-foot tidal range. With a Danforth you should use two anchors if there is a chance of changing winds or strong tides. Also choose one

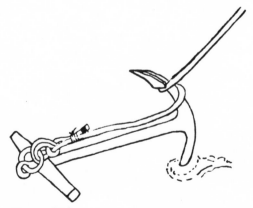

FIGURE 18.1

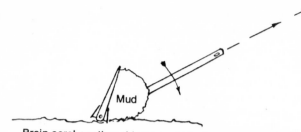

Brain coral or other objects could foul a stockless anchor
in the same manner
FIGURE 18.2

that is at least 50 percent heavier than suggested by the manufacturer. All of the lightweight anchors sold today are welded together
(and in some cases only spot welded). We've seen literally hundreds
of lightweight and stockless-type anchors being straightened and
rewelded in shipyards and machine shops around the world. The
lightweight anchor's straight-pull holding power, with its large fluke
area, is just too great for its construction. The Danforth company
acknowledged this by producing a standard 22-pound anchor in mild
steel and then a more expensive 20-pound model built of high ten-
sile steel. In my mind this is equal to having two models of the Boe-
ing 747, one with wings strong enough for carrying the full potential load of passengers, and another for those days when the plane is
flying only half full.

The genuine drop-forged CQR is the favorite of most cruising
men when it comes to a working anchor. With a CQR you can swing
on tide or wind with only one anchor set with confidence, because
first, it has no protuberances to grab chain as it rumbles past, and
second, the hinged shank swings across to follow the line of strain
and the flukes remain embedded in the bottom. As strains increase
the fluke rotates to align with the shank. It has three catches that I
know of. Though it holds well in sand, shell, or gravel and is excellent in mud, it is not as good as the fisherman for penetrating weed
to get down to a firm bottom. Secondly, the CQR has a bad habit of
jamming under large boulders. So it is wise to carry a fisherman
anchor to use as a backup. Third, the CQR must be used with plenty of adequate-sized chain to hold the stock down and allow the
anchor to dig into hard-sand bottoms.

˙See update at the end of this chapter.

Whatever your position on line versus chain for anchoring, it is interesting to note that insurance companies won't allow anything but chain rodes on commercial ships. The weight of chain acts as a shock absorber so no upward force is exerted on the shank of your anchor until all of the chain is lifted. Because of its weight, chain lies on the bottom and is less likely to loop and foul your anchor. And, if chain rubs against something sharp, it won't chafe through and let you go for an unscheduled moonlight sail. Chain definitely has its drawbacks: it is heavy, expensive, and you need an anchor winch to handle it. It's sometimes dirty, and it must be stowed carefully each time you use it so it doesn't jam in the chain locker when you next try to anchor. But none of these drawbacks affect the holding power of your ground tackle.

Nylon rope definitely has its uses. My second anchor bower on *Seraffyn* is 300 feet of nylon with 30 feet of 5/16-inch BBB chain.*

If I need a second anchor set, this is much easier to row out with a dinghy. It rarely picks up mud. Nylon is extremely strong because of its elasticity and in a ground swell will not jerk the anchor out of the bottom or make crashing noises in its chock. With nylon you can use a sheet winch for an anchor winch. So lightweight stockless anchors and nylon bowers are definitely cheaper than chain and forged anchors. That's why many designers and boat builders recommend them. In fact, this type of gear has become standard on racing boats which rarely lay at anchor. But for extended cruising you spend most of your time at anchor, so the weight and cost of chain becomes secondary to complete dependability.

Nylon line has a special use even if you have an all-chain rode. For safety, 50 feet of heavy nylon should be shackled to the inboard end of your chain to act as a shock absorber in case of swell build-up in an ultimate storm. The end of the nylon should be tied around something very strong, such as a sampsom post with a round turn and two half-hitches. This knot will allow you to untie the bitter end of your rode if you have to slip the cable and get out of the anchorage in a hurry. Simply tie the nylon end to a spare fender so you can pick up your gear later. (Don't use a bowline which cannot be untied under

---

*BBB chain is short link, fully tested American chain. English chain of equivalent strength is short link Lloyds tested. It is unwise to use proof coil or long link chain. Proof coil is cheaper but only every twentieth link is tested.

In a hurricane situation like this, chain makes you feel you've got a little extra in hand.

strain.) Another advantage to the nylon snubber on the inboard end of your chain is that it works as an emergency shock absorber in case the clutch of your winch fails and the chain starts to roar out. Three hundred feet of chain can build up an incredible speed and in some cases it will even start to smoke due to the friction on your cat head. A 50-foot motor yacht in the Caribbean had this happen. The end of their chain was shackled to one of the through-bolts holding their stem together. When the chain came up short, it imploded the stem and left a 2-foot-by-2-foot hole just below their waterline. The boat sank. The stretch in the 50-foot nylon snubber would have minimized this terrific jerk and saved the boat.

Getting an anchor out quickly can save your ship if you go aground, especially if the tide is falling or a swell and wind are pushing her onshore. TIME IS VITAL. Only a hard rowing dinghy will be quick to launch and easy to use. You must get her off fast.

But this fairlead has all the faults—nothing to keep the line from jumping out, sharp edges, weak construction.

You won't have time to dig out the inflatable, pump it up, put on the outboard, and hope it starts. Before you go off cruising, it pays to practice getting an anchor into the dinghy and kedged out just like it pays to have man-overboard drills. Unship the dinghy. Put the anchor in first. Then flake the anchor rode in carefully so it will run easily as you row. Have a fairlead in the dinghy that is protected with brass half round. (A dip in the transom just like a sculling lock works perfectly.) Nylon line with a short length of chain is the easiest to handle in this situation. That is why we have a second bower (bow anchor rode) readily available to load in the dinghy.

In a situation where there is lots of time, I will use my 25-pound CQR and its 5/16-inch chain to kedge away from a dock or to set as a beam anchor when I want to lay away from a dock. To keep the chain from running out of the dinghy too quickly, I put my shoe on it and press against the notch in the dinghy transom. This works as a pressure clutch; ease the pressure, and the chain runs more quickly.

I have learned that a stem dinghy is a must for rowing anchors out in winds over Force 6 with choppy seas. The fine bow cuts through the chop and also carries better with each oar stroke than a pram does. An inflatable is even worse than a pram in these conditions.

When we were sailing down the Red Sea we hooked up behind a reef to wait out a gale. The next morning the wind increased, and I tried to row out my second anchor in our 6-foot, 8-inch fiberglass pram. I just couldn't make headway against the 3-foot chop that built up in the ¼ mile between us and the reef.

I wanted that anchor out so we could get a good night's sleep. There were unlit coral reefs to leeward of us. I tied a fender to my 12-pound lightweight anchor on 200 feet of ⅜-inch nylon. Then I put on my fins and mask and swam to windward with the floating anchor while Lin payed out the cable. It was remarkably easy to swim against the seas. I untied the fender and lowered the anchor to the bottom when I was about 200 feet to windward and well to port of my main anchor. Then I returned to the boat by sliding along the ⅜-inch line. I did the same trick with my 35-pound fisherman attached to three fenders. But this time I pulled myself and the large anchor out hand-over-hand along the small nylon anchor line, and as I approached the small anchor I was careful not to get above it. I let the second larger anchor free from the three fenders, and Lin winched it in tight. I then pulled myself over to the 12-pounder, fenders tied to my waist. I broke the small anchor loose, and Lin reeled me in while I hung onto the anchor. I'd never once been detached from *Seraffyn*. We slept well that night, and since then mask, snorkel, and fins have been added to our list of necessary anchoring equipment.

An anchor winch is at the top of this list. Even Joshua Slocum had one on his low-budget *Spray*. I wouldn't consider cruising without one. Lin can handle our anchors because of our winch. She can easily let the clutch go, and our CQR, which lives hooked onto our bobstay, falls to the bottom (see photo, page 56). Lin can also crank in the chain and rehook the anchor by herself with no fear of a strained back. I think this is one of the main limiting factors on the size of boat two people can enjoy owning: what size of storm anchor can the weakest regular crew member carry and handle with confidence? The proper anchor winch will increase this size.

On boats smaller than 35 feet a good hand-operated anchor windlass made of bronze or galvanized malleable iron is the key to ground tackle handling. I have seen many serious problems with aluminum cast winches. Bronze, iron, and aluminum winches will all seize up if they are not greased periodically. This will not cause any serious problems on bronze or iron winches. You'll have to take them apart, loosen up the seized parts, grease, and reassemble them. But with an aluminum winch the white oxide caused by salt water expands in all the bolt and shaft holes and makes disassembly extremely difficult. Cap screws break off, and the corrosion expansion is often so extreme the castings will crack next to a shaft or bolt. I have seen this happen

This is a well-designed, strongly built fairlead.

on some of the best winches built of so-called marine alloys. Give aluminum anchor winches a miss and get yourself a good strong reliable bronze or iron one with separate gypsies, one for rope and one for chain. Make sure they can be used independently so you can set a second anchor while the first one is locked in place on its own gypsy. Our winch is a Plath 7B, with a separately locking chain gypsy.

If you order an anchor winch from outside the United States, be sure to send the manufacturer 12 inches of the exact anchor chain you plan to use. Chain link sizes vary between U.S., English, and metric sizes. The manufacturers usually have various chain gypsies and can only guarantee to send you the correct one if you supply a chain sample.

Things can sure go wrong if your chain fairlead bends, breaks, or allows the chain to jump out in a swell. The chain can literally saw right through your deck in a very short time. Chain is a real danger to bare hands if it ever gets loose. Your fairleads should be strong enough so that the outboard lip can't bend when the chain exerts a side load. This can be achieved by strengthening the lip or with a bolt through the lip into the inboard plate of the fairlead just forward of the roller. This will also keep the chain from jumping out.

If you mount your fairleads on your bowsprit, they should be banded right around the spar. If your anchor or chain hooks under a large boulder while you are winching it up, the next swell could lift your 10 tons of yacht and yank the fairlead down, then split your bowsprit right at the through-bolts. If you have a swell running into the harbor, it pays to leave your anchor winch clutch slightly loose and the ratchet pawl off so the anchor chain can slip a little if your boat jerks upward against the chain and anchor. This will help protect your fairleads and your nerves.

Make sure your fairleads are well flared, especially on the side lips, so that line rodes will not be chafed. The width of the bow roller should be three or four times the diameter of your anchor line so you have room for chafing gear.

Drag-proof anchoring is a combination of proper gear and defensive anchoring techniques. It should be every sailor's primary insurance plan. When all else fails, your anchor, ready to use, is your ace in the hole. It can save your boat, and, most important, it could save the lives of your crew. When you are exploring foreign waters, you'll find marinas are few and far between, expensive, and crowded. Most of your time will be spent at anchor. Reliable, nondragging anchoring methods and gear are a must for safe, enjoyable, worry-free cruising.

Update

We have no personal experience with anchors such as the Bruce, Delta, or others not mentioned in this chapter. Comments from cruisers we have met who have used both the Bruce and the CQR seem to run against the Bruce as a main anchor.

When we outfitted *Taleisin,* we wanted the strength of ³/₈-inch BBB chain but found its weight (over 700 pounds) hard to handle. We then did research into higher grades of chain and decided on system 4 (hi-test) chain. This let us use ⁵/₁₆-inch chain with slightly higher strength than ³/₈-inch BBB with only a bit more expense but far less weight (320 pounds). A complete discussion of chain appears in *The Capable Cruiser.*

The bronze anchor windlass we used on *Seraffyn* was made by R.C. Plath, 5300 S.E. Johnson Creek Blvd., Portland, OR 97222; tel. 503-777-2441, fax 503-777-2450. Other hand-operated anchor windlasses we have seen come from ABI, 1160A Industrial Ave., Petaluma, CA 94952; tel. 707-765-6200; Marinox Inc., 403 N.E. 8th St., Ft, Lauderdale, FL 33304; tel. 954-760-4702; Lofrans and Muir Windlasses, 30 Barnet Blvd., New Bedford, MA 02745; 508-995-7000; Traditional Marine, 58 Fore St., Portland, ME 04101; 207-773-7745; Vetus Den Ouden Inc., P.O. Box 8712, Baltimore, MD 21240-1712; 410-712-0985.

19

The Self-sufficient Sailor's Emergency Abandon Ship Kit

Years ago someone asked Jean Gau, "What about a lifeboat?" Gau, who had crossed the Atlantic eleven times and circumnavigated twice on his ketch *Atom*, is known for his self-reliant attitude. He simply answered, "*Atom* is my lifeboat."

We agreed completely, especially when we considered that at 24 feet on deck, *Seraffyn* is about the same size as most ship's lifeboats. So we worked at every method we knew of to make sure she stayed afloat.

After one eye-opening encounter with a large ship late at night when we were hundreds of miles from the nearest shipping lane, we decided to stand watches at all times except in very heavy fog. Then we'd have to depend on the 30-foot long radar reflector inside our hollow wooden spar. We've kept extra close watches when we've been near migrating whale paths. Each year both of us have inspected *Seraffyn* inside and out just as if we were surveyors so there would be little chance of hull or mast failure.

Then when we arrived in Gibraltar we met three young English sailors who'd been hit amidships by a Portuguese fishing boat late at night 40 miles out at sea. *Piratical Pippet*, their well-found wooden Folkboat, was badly sprung in the collision. Barry, Will, and Gordon could not have kept her afloat long enough to reach port. But Barry, who is a judo expert, leaped onto the deck of the fishing boat during the confusion in the aftermath of the collision. He threatened bodily harm to the Portuguese captain unless he towed *Piratical Pippet* into port.

Just a year earlier we'd read how Peer Tangvald had been sailing 50 miles off the mouth of the Orinoco River in his 32-foot *Dorthea* and collided with a submerged log. *Dorthea* was holed and in spite of his attempts to patch her, Peer had to abandon ship and seek safety in his 8-foot sailing dinghy. He sailed 125 miles in his tiny lifeboat and reached one of the Caribbean islands.

These two incidents, plus a rash of stories about collisions with whales which sank boats such as the Robertson's *Luccette* and Maralyn Bailey's 31-foot plywood sloop, combined to make us consider that for all of our care there could be a time when we'd have to abandon *Seraffyn* and take to our sailing dinghy.

We'd already been convinced that rubber liferafts were not the answer. The Baileys drifted for 117 days in a liferaft and had no way of propelling themselves into shipping lanes which lay less than 100 miles away. A French couple drifted in their liferaft for twelve days within sight of the island of Mallorca and couldn't reach it for lack of propulsion. So we did a refit of our 7-foot fiberglass dinghy, installed sealed bouyancy tanks, and fitted it so that if we had to abandon ship we could cut one line, then the dinghy, oars, sail, rudder, and daggerboard would float free together. If there was absolutely no doubt *Seraffyn* was sinking and we had four minutes to abandon ship, we could grab the dinghy mast and boom which are held to the upper shroud in a simple holder made of a leather boot at the base and a piece of 2-inch plastic hose aloft. We could unlash the one tie that secures a 5-gallon jug of water that is always ready inside the bulwarks, lash that to the dinghy, and set the whole affair in the cockpit right-side-up, ready and waiting for us while we tried to keep *Seraffyn* afloat. We would never leave the mother ship (*Seraffyn*, or the yacht we might happen to be delivering), until she actually sank under us. There have been too many cases of yachts being abandoned then found drifting later while the crew and lifeboat where never recovered.

If time was shorter than five or ten minutes, we could just let the dinghy and its equipment float free, then right it once *Seraffyn* sank. We'd have both sail and oar power so we could work at rescuing ourselves instead of sitting and hoping a passing ship would see us. We'd also be more visible than a liferaft with *Rinky Dink's* 14-foot-high striped sail. With this plan arranged and a bit of practice carried out, we forgot all about abandoning-ship plans other than preparing the dinghy when we stored it on the cabin top chocks for any voyage of over 30 miles.

Then during the winter of 1976–77, we made the final decision to leave Malta and head east through the Red Sea, across the Indian Ocean, and eventually the North Pacific. This was the first time our cruising plans included more than a single long-distance voyage in one year. An old friend who was also wintering in Malta sold his cruising boat, then insisted, "You take my Emergency Position Indicating Radio Beacon. I'll worry a bit less about you when you are in the middle of the Indian Ocean." His concern and careful analysis of the lack of shipping lanes over the routes we planned to travel finally led us to consider making up some kind of emergency pack that would be ready inside the dinghy if we did have to abandon ship. We looked at a few commercial packs, ones that were used in life-rafts for racing boats. They were far too expensive and also planned for seamen who would sit and wait for rescue. The commercial kits in no way met our requirements. So we gathered up the stores and equipment that would help us independently work at survival in a small dinghy while we tried sailing to either a busy shipping lane or toward land. The kit we finally packed weighs about 30 pounds and fits inside a 10 inch by 25 inch round canvas bag. It is packed so salt water and exposure will do no damage.

Contents

Loose in bag:
    4 handheld red flares in waterproof pouches
    1 orange smoke flare

1 collapsible 10-inch radar reflector
1 watermaker (Air Force surplus, makes 16 ounces of water per day if there is sun)
1 Dacron cover for forward third of dinghy (protection from sun and spray)
2 1-gallon foldable water bags (from wine in a box container)
1 hand-bearing compass

In a tightly sealed and taped 2-gallon plastic container such as paint is sold in:

10 cans fruit nectar
10 cans meat pate
1 pound glucose candies

In a sealed 2-gallon rugged plastic container which is rigged to be used as a sea anchor:

1 pencil
Pad of paper
Passports or photostat of passports

The complete contents of our abandon ship kit. On the left are parts for a radar reflector. On the right is a solar watermaker.

Fifty dollars
Small container of two-part underwater putty
Water resistant 1½-inch wide tape (duct tape)
40 multi-vitamin pills
2 rolls surgical gauze
Hand care cream (medicated)
Extra strong sun block cream
3 sizes Dacron sail thread, 200 feet each
Sharpening stone
Fishing trident (three-prong spear with barbs)
100 feet of ⅛-inch line
Knife
Miniature can opener
3 fishing lures
12 assorted fish hooks (½ inch to 1 inch, single and three prong)
20 feet leader line
10 feet ¹⁄₁₆-inch stainless steel seizing wire
2 white towels
1 signal mirror

Now that we are in an area where health food stores exist, I might substitute high-calorie health bars of some sort for the canned meat pate. Their more concentrated caloric content would be better for providing the energy required to think and work toward rescue.

Our kit was planned to assure survival for four or five days while we learned to live in the environment we found around us. Then we hoped it would provide the tools for self-sufficiency while we worked actively toward our own rescue.

The radar reflector mounted at the top of our 14-foot dinghy mast should send off a better return than a liferaft which would intermittently be hidden by any swell. We decided against including medicines other than the simplest first aid supplies, not only because of space limitations but because we've found communicable diseases are so rare away from crowds and land. Both of us are intimately involved in the navigation on board *Seraffyn*, so we decided against trying to include charts of any sort in our kit. We both confer daily on our position. We are both aware of the course we intend to sail toward land. Larry marks the positions on our chart as he does his sun or star sights. I record it in the log, then give a daily estimate of our distance to land. Twice a week we consult our ocean passages charts which show both low-powered shipping lanes and high-powered commercial routes so we can plan extra careful watches when we cross these points. If we should have to abandon ship, we'd have a pretty good idea of which way to sail or row to find an area where traffic would make rescue more possible. If time allowed, we'd grab a sextant and a small scale passage chart while we abandoned ship.

There is a tag on the outside of our emergency kit which states when it was last inspected. Once a year we disassemble and reconsider each item in it. Then we redate the tag and store the bag under the cockpit, right next to the companionway where it is easy to reach when we set off on any new voyage. During the first morning at sea we follow a reassuringly familiar program. First Larry stores all of the dinghy sailing equipment inside *Rinky Dink*. He gets the emergency kit and lashes it in place under the dinghy's forward thwart. He puts a quick release tie on one of the spare 5-gallon water jugs. This done he seals the chain locker hawse pipes, sets up shoulder high lifelines from the top of the boom gallows frame to the upper shrouds, and then he reminds me or I remind him, "Don't fall overboard. If you do, you are dead." Then we forget about "what if's" and work at sailing *Seraffyn* well, keeping a good watch and navigating carefully.

We did carry that Emergency Position Indicating Radio Beacon (EPIRB) with us for six months. But after careful consideration we decided to send it back to its owner before we sailed up the China Sea and across the North Pacific. First we noticed corrosion on many of its connections, even though it had been stored in a dry place inside *Seraffyn*. With our skeptical attitude toward electronic equipment, we figured it would be inoperable just when we did want to use it. We also felt that if we had the idea we could call for help, we might not prepare to take care of *Seraffyn* or ourselves as carefully.

In Sri Lanka, the owner of a 50-foot sloop knew one of his spreaders had some dry rot in its end and his garboards (the area where the keel meets the planking) were leaking. "Don't worry," he told us, "There's never any rough weather between here and Singapore this time of year. Besides, I'm in contact with people twice a day on my ham radio so I can always get help if I need it." The

Canadian yacht *Crusader* was lost in an unseasonable typhoon ten days later with six hands on board. *Crusader*'s ham-radio calls set off a massive search in which aircraft, ships, and airliners assisted. The U.S. Air Force flew over two days on a search pattern that covered 100,000 square miles of ocean and cost the Canadian, American, and Malaysian governments thousands of dollars. These same ham reports worried our friends and family tremendously because we had left the same port bound for Malaysia at the same time. Other than worrying a lot of people and causing a massive search, the radio did no good. But some work on *Crusader*'s keel or spreaders might have.

We feel that yachtsmen have a deep moral responsibility to take care of themselves if they sail outside the harbor entrance. There is no real reason for us to be at sea other than for pleasure or adventure. Unlike fishermen or merchant seamen, we are not providing food or supplies for other people. We are not earning our living from the sea. *So we have no right to put our faith in radios which call and ask commercial ships and aircraft to divert and search for us.* We are asking them to risk their lives and waste their money so we can feel safer about pursuing our own pleasures.

We decided a long time ago that cruising is a sport and that the object of the sport is self-sufficiency. Sailing in all of its forms is one of the safest sports there is. For miles traveled, it's far safer than driving your car to do the grocery shopping. Even more than while driving a car on streets used by millions of other people, your safety on a sailboat depends on you alone, using your skills and your training.

We assembled an emergency abandon-ship kit for the same reason we carry a spare for every mechanical part of the boat that ensures safe sailing. If you have a spare on board, you probably won't need it. If I felt sailing across oceans was so unsafe that our need for abandon-ship equipment was more than a one-in-ten-thousand chance, I wouldn't go to sea.

See the update to this chapter on page 313.

20

Staying on Board

In the beginning there was the spare jib sheet or a halyard tail. When a worried professional sailor had to go out on the bowsprit and tame a sail in rough weather he grabbed the handiest line, secured it around his waist, and went to work. Then amateur sailors started making long offshore voyages for pleasure. They built themselves rough-weather harnesses for those times when they were worried about going forward without an extra bit of security. In the 1960s single-handed voyaging developed into an ever-growing fad. Lone sailors realized no one was going to switch off their windvane and turn their boat around if they slipped overboard. So they started looking toward their rough weather harness as a wear-it-all-the-time solution to the basically unseamanlike, unsafe sport of singlehanding (see Chapter 6, Section II).

From there it was a simple step to the high pressure offshore racing scene. Racing rules were breeding boats which stole some of the most important basic safety design features from the foredeck crew. The urge to win at any cost meant club racers had to discover some way of freeing their hands to change sails on lightweight boats with wicked, skittery motions, no bulwarks, and insufficient handholds. So sail-makers and equipment companies started designing and marketing harnesses.

Unfortunately, the stories and advertisements these companies promoted started to push heavy-weather harnesses out of the category of equipment that was to be used for emergency situations. Somehow sailors were convinced that these were now safety harnesses to keep them from falling overboard no matter what and save them even if they did. So people began substituting this inexpensive, easy-to-buy piece of equipment for the knowledge and preparation that really keep you safe on an offshore boat.

A boat that is properly designed is the first step toward staying on board even in the roughest weather. The first and foremost thing to look for on a good boat is a seakindly motion. A boat's motion is affected not only by its size and displacement but by its underbody design and weight distribution. A 35-foot fin keel boat with 45 percent ballast ratio and high topsides will have a quicker, snappier motion in a seaway than an old fashioned, long-keeled, low freeboard boat with 35 percent ballast. That's the main problem with choosing an ex-IOR racing boat for offshore voyaging. The racing boat may be faster in some conditions but its motion could increase the danger of falling overboard.

High deck structures and doghouses are features which provide below decks comfort but destroy on-deck-at-sea safety by adding to a boat's motion. We had this demonstrated vividly when we delivered a 54-foot ketch across the Atlantic. Her heavy high deck house and solid plywood sun cover plus high topsides created such a wicked roll that we couldn't run dead downwind in safety. So we added 480 miles to our 2,800 mile voyage by tacking downwind. Even then her motion was far worse than on board 24-foot *Seraffyn* in the same winds and sea.

High deck structures, especially on boats where the mast goes through the cabin top, are unsafe. You have to climb up on the cabin top to hoist, lower, and reef your sails. The higher you climb, the farther you are from the boat's axis and the worse the motion gets. For safe offshore sailing our first choice is always a boat with a one-level deck and working area. This means no climbing to reach the mast and no jumping off the cabin after you've lowered the sails.

Wide clear side decks are another design feature that will keep you safe at sea. Eighteen inches used to be considered the safe minimum. This let sailors move fore and aft confidently while they dragged a bagged sail behind them. Twenty-four inches was even nicer. That gave you plenty of room for those worrisome times when you felt crawling forward was the more prudent way to go. Unfortunately, many designers have sought ever more interior space by widening cabins until some side decks on so-called cruising boats are only 8 inches wide. This interior spaciousness does help sell boats, especially to novices who aren't aware of on-deck safety at sea.

Cruising sailors have also violated this very important safety feature by using the clear side deck area for extra stowage. Fuel tanks, motorcycles, portable generators—this is just the beginning of the list of gear we've seen cluttering this vital seagoing safety corridor.

Bulwarks or 6-inch-high toerails are high on my list of seagoing keep-me-from-going-overboard design features. When a boat is heeled and water is washing along the side deck, anything lower just won't give you a foothold. Without these high rails, gear will slide off the boat if it is left free for even a moment. So instead of concentrating on moving carefully around the boat, you'll be lurching after the wayward winch handle.

Not all so-called non-skid decks are really non-skid and this may be why so many newer sailors are leery of moving around even in calm weather without a rough weather harness. There is a simple test you can try to check your deck's gripping ability. Pour some diesel or kerosene on the deck, let it drain away so the deck is still damp looking, then pour salt water on, and test the grip both barefoot and in boat shoes. Bare teak, Treadmark, bare cedar, and painted sanded decks will pass this test. Many fiber-glass patterned non-skid decks will turn into ice-skating surfaces. This may seem a strange test, but an overflow when you are filling your tanks, blow-by from your diesel vents, spilled kerosene, bits of greasy food, or even oil slicks at sea can cause the same situation. If your footing is slippery, you'll always be a candidate for an unexpected, possibly lethal trip overboard.

A final but very important general design feature for at-sea safety is handholds. These include lifelines at least 24 to 30 inches high with stanchions that can stand the strain of a 200-pound man hitting them with a force that could equal 1,500 pounds. To withstand this, the stanchion bases must be bolted through the deck to some solid member of the deck framing. Screwed-down bases will rip loose. A bulwark with its wooden or metal stanchions will create the best possible base structure for good lifelines.

Cabin top handholds come next. These must be kept clear at sea.

I've seen lovely handholds made useless by mops and boat hooks stored right where you wanted to grab.

If you store your dinghy upside-down on the cabin, it should have handrails on its bottom. It pays to load your boat as if it's ready for sea, then practice going forward and aft on each tack in a rough sea. Make sure there are convenient, easy-to-grab handholds on each side of you and plan ways to keep them clear.

This quest for handholds, plus the need for good foot resting places on each tack make us uncomfortable on board a flush decked yacht. A low cabin with its coachroof decorated with handholds gives you not only a place to cling to, but in rough seas the weather side of the cabin presents a place to brace your knees or back while you work storing sails and gear.

Once you've chosen a good, safe, seakindly boat, the sailing equipment you choose can keep you out of situations where falling overboard is a possibility. A jib downhaul will pull the flogging sail down while you stand next to the mast (see Chapter 32, Section VI). Good jiffy reefing gear with all of the control lines grouped near the mast will keep you from having to move around a canted, plunging deck (Chapter 25, Section VI). High cut jibs with clew rings sewn into the sail and bowlines instead of shackles for the sheets will make dodging lethal flying D rings a thing of the past. Gaskets (sail ties or stops) stored in several handy, easily accessible places on the foredeck, amidships, and near the cockpit will cut down hunting trips when each unnecessary step could be dangerous.

Boom gallows aren't designed just to look salty. Nor are they just a convenient place to store the boom while you are in port. They are an important addition to the inventory of sailing equipment designed to keep you on board in rough weather. A properly set up boom gallows will give you a strong body support when you have to work at the stern of your boat. Even more important, the outboard upper corner of the gallows will make a firm support for sea-going, chest-high lifelines. Larry first used these on the 85-foot schooner *Double Eagle* during a round-trip voyage between Honolulu and Newport Beach. Bob Sloan, an experienced delivery skipper, rigged chest-high lines between the gallows frame and each set of shrouds so the crew had bulwarks, normal lifelines, plus the chest line to grab on the way fore and aft. Larry adapted this extra lifeline on *Seraffyn* so going forward even in rough weather feels and is easier.

Easy-to-release and easy-to-retrieve ground tackle may seem unrelated to staying on board at sea. But if you must enter a small port during heavy weather it is imperative that your ground tackle be ready to let go. If this means climbing around the foredeck handling heavy anchors, searching for shackles and rode ends, you'll be out where the motion is difficult and the danger of slipping imminent. This is why we choose to carry our main anchor made up at all times and ready to release. One of us goes forward for moments only to make sure the anchor is clear and the winch handle ready for use. The less time you spend on the foredeck in a seaway, the less chance you have to slip overboard.

Some of the most frightening stories we've heard have concerned close calls when cruising sailors or delivery teams almost fell overboard because of gear failures in rough weather, and the main cause of these failures were roller furling jibs. These jibs work wonderfully under normal sailing conditions. But the four times we encountered heavy weather when we were delivering boats with roller furling jibs, problems developed. In each case the gear had failed in one respect or another. A 300,000-mile delivery sailor told of a furling gear that became so completely jammed in a half-furled position that for the safety of boat and crew he had to climb aloft during a full gale and cut the fouled sail away. Hanked-on jib systems aren't initially as easy to use, but hanked-on sails always go up and always come down. During a storm no one should ever have to go out on the foredeck or aloft fighting jammed or broken gear.

Proper sailing techniques keep you on board where you belong. The most important of these is, don't be over-canvassed. Shorten down when you first think of it, not when all hell breaks loose. It's better to be under-canvassed for a while than risk sending crew onto the foredeck when the squall is already on top of you. With or without a bowsprit, it pays not only to take sail down before the stronger wind hits but to remove that extra sail from the bow and store it completely away. We once lashed our small genoa down on the bowsprit to ride hove to during what looked like a quick, soon-to-pass squall in the North Pacific 800 miles west of Vancouver.

Three hours later the squall proved to be the forerunner of a two-day, 55-knot storm. So instead of removing that jib when the seas were relatively calm, Larry had to put on his rough weather harness and go out on the plunging bowsprit in 20-foot seas. The normal five minute job became a twenty minute struggle.

Learning to move around on deck properly will save you from many potential dangers. Bob Duke, a husky, 6-foot-plus marine surveyor told me about the teasing he gets from potential buyers when he moves around slowly and surely on each boat he visits. He always has his hand on a secure hold and in his own words, "I probably look like an old lady." He has never slipped or fallen, though he's been on hundreds of different boats. But several of Bob's clients have cooled their own enthusiasm when they rushed along a side deck and tripped overboard. There is nothing sissy about crawling along the side deck in rough weather. You should never go forward without a handhold every step even in moderate weather. Practice moving around on board blindfolded in harbor and you'll find out where the danger spots are on your boat.

After all of these safety items are worked out and practiced, a rough weather harness built for you alone should be added to your equipment list. A two-and-a-half- to three-inch-wide belt designed so that when it is not taking any strain it rests well below your chest will be more comfortable to wear than many commercial harnesses. When normal working strains come on the safety line, the wide belt should spread the load across the middle of your back and in extreme situations the belt should slide up under your armpits where it belongs. A working line that is only 2½ feet long means you can't move too far from convenient handholds nor move too quickly from one place to another. So you are forced to remember the basic at-sea safety procedure of planning each step before you make it. The only improvement we might make to the harnesses we have used for twelve years would be to add a second 2½-foot long working line which we could attach to a second point before we released the first hook.

But no matter how carefully designed any rough weather harness is, it is not an item to be used at all times. It is not a panacea to replace proper equipment and proper training. Nor is it a piece of gear you should come to depend on. There are several reasons we and most other long-term, offshore sailors feel rough weather harnesses should be relegated to their proper place, i.e. something to be used when you consciously think, "This is a situation that demands one more bit of precaution." First, in reality almost no one wears a harness at all times. This would mean wearing it while you slept, while you sunbathed, and while you sat in the cockpit steering on a warm sunny day and always having its clip secured to some strong point. This may actually happen on racing boats where the one long · voyage of the year can be expected to last eighteen or twenty days. But on long cruising passages, which last sometimes thirty-five or forty days, this is an uncomfortable nuisance, so what usually happens is that crew charge out of the companionway to see what is causing all the racket and rush forward to help muzzle a wayward jib or release the offending halyard and don't stop to think about whether or not they are wearing a harness. If the now harnessless person has not learned *proper hanging-on habits* he/she will be prime material for an unwelcome trip overboard. Because these same people have always depended on their harness to act as a third hand, they will not have learned to work with one hand for the ship, the other for themselves.

If you say, "Okay, I'll use the harness everytime I go out of the cockpit in winds over 20 knots," the harness probably won't be there for you to grab when a sudden squall hits. So again, only your carefully learned, limpetlike habits will help you stay on the foredeck.

Safety harnesses hinder your movement around the boat and are liable to break under sudden shock loads. This was proven in the sadly disasterous Fastnet Race. Out of 235 crew who said they used their harnesses during this race, 26 reported the harnesses failed. Either buckles came undone or hooks straightened out, attachment points broke, or safety lines chafed through on the wire lifelines. Six lives were lost directly as a result of these failures. Furthermore, 10 men reported the harness wrapped around some obstruction when they fell overboard. This kept them from climbing back on board unassisted.*

Peggy Slater, a well-known and successful West Coast racing skipper, emphasized this problem of getting back on board if you do fall

* From 1979 Fastnet Race inquiry by Council of the RYA and RORC.

over. She had a frightful experience during a solo passage to Honolulu. When she was washed overboard during a jib change her harness line did keep her attached to the boat, but she found there was no way to get back on board, especially since her windvane kept the boat racing downwind at close to 7 knots and the dragging headsail kept her pinned against the side of the boat while seas washed over her head. In spite of a broken hand, she was able to climb back on board almost eight hours later, saved by her extraordinary strength, determination, and some fortunate circumstances including a surge by the rushing boat that washed her high enough to grab a hold on deck. But after several years of contemplation she concluded, "I've come to feel that if you fall overboard while you are single-handing, even if you are attached by a harness, you might as well be dead. Provisions to make climbing back on board such as steps on the transom, a windvane release line which will cause the boat to head up into the wind, or handrails along the outside of the boat might help. But no sane person wants to unhook his lifeline snap and let go of a sure thing to chance reaching the stern of the boat when he is wearing all sorts of soaked heavy clothes and is already suffering from the shock of falling overboard."

This theme—if you fall overboard, you're dead—seems to run through my personal sailing life. I first heard it when we'd finally figured out our self-steering gear and sat back in wonder as that magical vane kept *Seraffyn* right on course. Larry reminded me that the windvane would not hear my cries if I fell off the boat at night while he slept, nor in all probability would he. The captain of a Costa Rican shrimp trawler warned me again when I was working as his cook. "Men go out at night to use the stern rail. They are sleepy and make a mistake and slip overboard. The helmsman doesn't hear their cries, not with the engine chugging and the bowwake churning."*

Many new cruising people wonder about the problem of keeping their young children safely on board. Some modern cruising boats

* The Costa Rican government found a solution to this problem of losing crew overboard. They made a new law placing the responsibility where it traditionally belongs. Any trawler captain who returned with one of his crew missing went to jail immediately for six months. Captains took steps to teach each man the dangers, and the problem disappeared.

look like netted playpens containing chained youngsters. I've spoken to the parents of children who grew up on ocean-going yachts before harnesses were billed as the be-all and end-all solution. The Stanilands told how they took three-month-old Ian across the Atlantic, then started teaching him to swim at the age of four months. As soon as he could swim he was given free run of the deck of *Carina* with its 6-inch bulwarks. He fell overboard once while his mother stood by and watched. She let him flounder around for a few moments before rescuing him. He never fell overboard again. "That's the way babies learn not to touch hot stoves," Ian's mother told me as she proudly watched 26-year-old Ian sail out of Marsessmett Harbor on Malta, bound on yet another charter. "There are far more dangers in a house on shore—electric cords for young mouths to teeth on, concrete steps to fall down, heavy doors to close on little fingers, trucks and cars passing 50 feet away from the door. Just teaching a child not to fall overboard is easy."

More recently an article in *Cruising World* magazine told of one mother who said, "I decided to tell each child, 'When you can swim completely around the boat, you can sail without a harness except when your father and I use one.' This challenge proved exciting to each of her four children who came to look on the constant bondage of harness and hook as a sign of babyhood. Each child earned his/her badge of honor before the age of three."

Harnesses should be considered in their proper place, as a piece of gear to be used in heavy weather situations. Just like sail ties and reefing gear, they should be kept handy for the times when they are needed. And as with all gear on board, you should consider what can be substituted if the rough weather harness is not at hand when you need it. A jib sheet will attach you to the boat when a squall builds sudden ferocious seas against a strong tide. A halyard end will provide extra security when you rush from below and have to get that jib down now or loose it. But most important of all, please consider the following.

No amount of skill, no equipment, and no boat will keep you immune if you don't develop the most important seagoing skill of all, a complete fear of falling overboard. It is amazing to watch people drive cars cavalierly through crowded cities and along high-speed, heavily traveled highways. They're not the least afraid of driving, but every one of them is terrified of falling asleep at the wheel. They know this could mean instant death. People can learn not to doze at the wheel of a moving car and they can learn not to step off the curb in front of a Kenworth truck. They can also learn not to fall off a boat with or without a rough weather harness.

21

Priorities for Safe Offshore Voyaging

We feel the goal of most cruising sailors is the excitement of compe-
tent passage-making free from accidents and gear failures. These
accidents may make exciting sea stories but in truth mar the joy of
voyaging. The following checklist is in the order that we believe will
eventually lead to this goal. It is based on the premise that self-sufficiency is the law of the sea. Rescue from willing, skilled agencies such
as the U.S. Coast Guard or Royal Life Boat Society is not available
when you are outside American or English waters. In places like the
North Pacific or Indian Ocean, it could take up to five days for a
vessel to reach you and offer assistance even if your calls are heard.
That is why we start this list with learning the basics of good sailing.
We feel that only after you have considered each of the first five
categories carefully, should you think about the items in the final
category, items which are only for use in the rare, extreme emergency.

I. Learn the basic sailing and boat handling skills. This category is
the one most frequently overlooked by prospective cruising sailors.
In the excitement of planning and rearranging their lives so they can
take off for six months a year or more, people seem to look at the
time and expense involved in really learning to sail as an inconven-

ience. They are anxious to make their dream become a reality. Stories of people who learned to sail after they set off cruising are full of mistakes, accidents, and even tragedies. The least advertised tragedy is the fear or dislike of sailing that can be instilled in your prospective sailing partners when your lack of skill leads to a few incidents that could have been avoided if you'd spent a little more time practicing sailing skills. We recommend learning in dinghies or small boats because the quick response of simple boats like these will help you learn the basics of sail trim, balance, and maneuvering. Even if you plan to have a very reliable engine on your eventual perfect cruising boat, there will be times when it fails. Once you've learned the following skills, you can relegate that auxilary engine to its proper place. You can look on it as a convenience, not a necessity for safe voyaging.

a. Learn to sail a dinghy or engineless boat under 20 feet in length confidently before you buy a larger boat.

b. Learn to hang on and move around the boat without a harness.

c. Practice setting anchors and sailing away from a dragging anchor.

d. Learn to reef and change sails in all conditions.

e. Go out sailing in squally, stormy weather.

f. Sail on as many boats as you can so you choose your own boat with opinions based on experience.

II. Choose a boat designed for safe voyaging. Although every manufacturer who sells boats over 20 feet long will tell you his cruising boat is great for crossing oceans, only your previous sailing experience will help you choose a proper offshore boat. Appearance, interior accommodations, price, and ease of financing should not sway you. If you can't arrange for extensive sea trials before you buy, spend the money to charter a boat like the one you are considering buying. After ten or twelve days of sailing you should be able to judge the most important sailing safety features for yourself.

a. Size is the number one safety feature. Be sure any one member of your crew can handle your boat single-handed at sea or in harbor if necessary. Remember the storm anchor necessary for a 40-foot boat weighs close to 100 pounds.

b. Comfortable motion in a seaway.

c. Wide, clear side decks.

d. Good non-skid on decks and working areas.

e. Easy-to-work, one-level deck area.

f. Clear foredeck for working gear and sails.

g. No extreme combings to climb over.

h. Bulwarks or 6-inch high toerails.

III. Learn cruising skills. This category and the first one require time and patience. Peter Pye said it: "To learn to sail you've got to go to sea." He served his apprenticeship exploring the rivers and estuaries of southern England for three years before he set off across the Atlantic. Although there is a tremendous amount to be learned from books, only hands-on experience will give you and your crew confidence in your cruising skills.

a. Learn navigation. Even if you can afford sophisticated electronic gear, for safety's sake learn piloting and celestial navigation using only a compass, sextant, and radio receiver.

b. Become aware of what is absolutely vital and realize that everything else is only a convenience or comfort, i.e., you can exist on beans and rice and water, you can sail with only a main and jib, you can sail without an engine, but you cannot sail without a mast.

c. Learn to inspect all of your own rigging and vital equipment.

d. Learn to maintain and repair every vital item on board.

e. Learn to maneuver in close quarters without your engine. Practice using warps, anchors, and on small cruisers, a sculling oar.

f. Take basic first aid courses and have a second person on board who is aware of the medical supplies and skills needed in an emergency. We are signing up for a paramedic course offered by a local university. (You might consider having your appendix removed before making any long passages.)

g. Attempt to instruct your crew in the basics of sailing, simple navigation, and safety procedures so they can take over if you are disabled.

h. Plan stowage so there are no heavy objects over any bunks, floor boards are secured, and lockers won't open accidently. No fuel tanks or drums on deck. Think of what might get loose or cause bodily damage in a knock-down situation.

i. Show everyone on board the danger of falling overboard and proper hanging-on techniques.

IV. Select equipment for safe voyaging.

a. Jib downhaul lead well aft to muzzle a flogging sail so you can safely go out on the foredeck.

b. No low-clewed deck-sweeping jibs that could block your vision when you are heeled in a seaway. Low cut sails, dodgers, lifeline spray cloths, and doghouses with misty windows can keep you from seeing a ship on a collision course.

c. Easy-to-use, permanently installed reefing (jiffy, slab, or pennant).

d. Lifelines which can stand the strains of a 200-pounder hitting them at high speed.

e. Chest high, at-sea lifelines.

f. Reversible or spare halyards.

g. Sufficient handholds and rails.

h. Boom vang that's easy to set and not only prevents accidental gybes but makes it easy to control planned gybes.

i. Climb-on-board steps so swimmers or someone who falls overboard can get out of the water easily.

j. Sea anchor.

k. Proper bosun's chair with safety line attached for going aloft.

l. Selection of extra heavy ground tackle.

m. Hand-operated, powerful anchor winch to save your back from damage and make warping easier.

V. Carry proper do-it-yourself safety equipment.

a. Strobe lights.

b. Signal torch.

c. Radar reflectors.

d. Freon horn and refills.

e. Backup oil lamps so you can always show running lights.

f. Medical kit.

g. Repair materials and spares for vital equipment, i.e., for sails, rigging, and rudder.

h. Jury-rig plan.

i. Efficient bilgepump, not only one run off your engine, but a powerful hand-operated pump for times when the battery may be down or the engine may not start.

j. Emergency hull-repairing plan and materials.

k. At least 1,000 feet of warping and mooring lines.

l. Spare anchors.

m. Fire extinguishers.

n. Emergency reverse-osmosis manual watermaker.

o. Man-overboard pole and ring.

p. Rough-weather harness.

VI. Optional emergency equipment. We've had the opportunity to spend time with some of today's best-known offshore cruising sailors—the Smeetons, the Guzzwells, the Hiscocks, and Peer (Peter) Tangvald. All of them seem to agree: The sport of cruising is being self-sufficient. We go to sea for pleasure, not for commerce. Therefore if we must call for outside help, we've in some small way lost the game. If you adapt this attitude before you set off cruising and if you can honestly say to yourself that you have considered and acted on each of the previously listed items, it is *highly unlikely* that you will ever need the last five items below.

a. EPIRB

b. Separate CO_2-activated life raft

c. VHF or single-sideband radio transmitter

d. Handheld VHF

e. Boat-saving CO_2 inflatable-bag system. (This is discussed in detail in *The Capable Cruiser*.)

All of the equipment in categories IV and V fit in two lockers on board *Seraffyn*. We did not carry any of the items listed in the last category during her eleven years of voyaging.

On *Taleisin* we carry all of the same equipment and have added only a flotation collar to make our hard tender into a better sailing lifeboat,[*] plus an EPIRB as discussed in the update at the back of the book.

---

[*] For more information on converting a hard tender into a sailing lifeboat, see the video "Voyaging, Upgrading Your Cruising Boat," available from Paradise Cay Publications, tel. 800-736-4509.

Details That Can Make Your Yacht More Efficient, Simpler, and Easier to Maintain

We once had a boisterous discussion with a seasoned boat builder and a young designer. The subject of the debate was the set of plans for a 30-foot cruising cutter which were spread across the floor. While the boat builder talked of appearance, ease of construction, and types of wood, the designer talked of balance and performance in a running sea. What caused the discussion to get heated was Larry's inquiry into fairlead placement, rudder shaft accessibility, working room near the mast, and butane storage. Finally the designer turned to us and said, "Larry, the overall concept is what matters. The details aren't so important."

To this day we both disagree with him. Details are what make any acceptable sailboat into a cruising yacht. Join a gathering of offshore voyagers and the conversation will consist of tidbits about details, from how someone's new galley pump works to a show-and-tell of a keen new type of shackle.

From stem to stern a cruising yacht is a mass of details. The more attention you pay to simplifying each one, the better your cruising will be.

22

Oil Lamps at Sea

Oil lamps work. Engine failure, generator breakdown, or power shortage won't stop them. Lin and I have used kerosene lamps on our 5-ton cutter and home, *Seraffyn*, for eleven years. We've never spent a night at sea without our full regulation navigation lights visible and bright from sunset to sunrise.

The greatest joy of oil lamps is the elimination of one of the petty irritations of life on a small boat at sea or at anchor: "Damn it, turn that light off. You're running the batteries down!" With oil lamps, no one is concerned if you leave all the lights on.

We usually leave our anchor light burning when we go ashore, even if we are in a designated anchorage or on a permanent mooring where lights are not required. Then if we return late, the distinct golden light on *Seraffyn* beckons us homeward. The anchor light will burn for 30 hours on one-quarter pint of fuel without refilling—that's efficiency! Compare that to the diesel fuel and noise required to generate enough electricity to run an anchor light for the same period.

Several visitors on board *Seraffyn* have asked, "How about reading with oil lamps?" We find they are fine. In fact, the accompanying drawings were done using their pleasant glow. Trimming the wick properly so it follows the contour of the center guard and has no stray hairs or bulges, turning it up properly and using a mirror or reflector behind the chimney will make the light bright and clear. But if this is not sufficient, the Tilly pressurized lamp from England and the

Aladdin nonpressurized mantel lamp made in the United States both give off bright white light. Sooting and smoking with any type of oil lamp is usually the result of poor wick trimming or sudden drafts of air.

Oil lamps below decks are very safe if they are gimballed and fastened with a locking set screw. If you do happen to hit one or break the lens accidentally, the flame will simply blow out. But after one miserable experience we learned to turn interior lamps down when we leave the boat in the evening. That way we return to a cheerfully lit but soot-free boat.

Smoke bells are necessary to stop the heat produced by the lamps from scorching the overhead unless there is 2 or 3 feet of clear space above each lamp. The small amount of heat produced by oil cabin lights is nice in a cold climate and with proper ventilation can be unnoticed in warm weather.

In 1972 we met Bert Darrel, an all-round shipwright, rigger, and

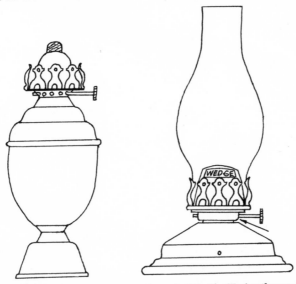

The drawing above shows a properly trimmed wick. It will give the most possible light and will smoke far less than a wick that is trimmed flat. The lamp used for the illustration is a Perko-type cabin lamp. The drawing on the right shows a running lamp modified to have an internal chimney. It uses the same fringe as the cabin lamp. I bought spare cabin burners, sawed off the fringe, and soldered them to the navigation lamp burners.

practical seaman who lives in Bermuda. When the subject of seasick navigation lights came up he gave me this tip: "When you are carrying oil lamps high in the rigging, what generally causes them to go out is the oil swishing in the base. So if you three-quarter-fill the base with caulking cotton, you make the whole container into a wick without greatly decreasing the oil capacity. Then the amount of fuel on the wick is not affected by motion."

He was right. For two nights we hove to in winds of Force 9 and 10 between the Azores and England with the anchor light high in the rigging. It burned perfectly, no sooting, no blowing out.

Our oil lamps are standard Perko fittings which I have modified to have an internal chimney which stops excessive drafts. We've done the same with an English-built Seahorse brand lamp. We've also increased the efficiency of our port and starboard lamps by using reflectors behind the burners. The shiny side of aluminum foil works great for this. We find it is easier to replace the foil every few months than to polish or rechrome a reflector.

Underway I carry my 360-degree anchor light about 6 feet above deck on the backstay. Hung like this (just as Joshua Slocum did on *Spray*), the light shed is enough to allow comfortable working all the way up to the foredeck. Since the light is above eye level it doesn't spoil night vision.

Electric lights are initially more convenient to use, but if failure does occur, it is rarely possible to find a short circuit or corroded connection or to replace a masthead light bulb at sea, especially with a strong wind blowing. These are only a few of the simplest problems that can keep you from showing running lights with an electrical system. If your alternator, regulator, starting motor, or main engine fails, you've got no electricity. Solar panels should be a viable backup for engine-supplied electricity. But there is still the problem of salt water deterioration that is ever present with wired systems.

Oil lamps on the other hand are simplicity itself and can always be returned to service by trimming the wick, replacing the burner, or draining the oil and refilling the reservoir if condensation deposits water in the fuel (sputtering is usually a sign of this). Since all of the servicing on oil lamps can be done right on deck or below in the galley, it's far more likely that you will return your running lights to full service even in rough weather.

To make oil lamps convenient, a gravity fill tank is imperative.

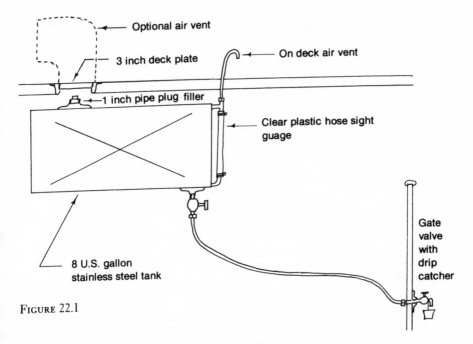

Optional air vent

3 inch deck plate

On deck air vent

1 inch pipe plug filler

Clear plastic hose sight guage

Gate valve with drip catcher

8 U.S. gallon stainless steel tank

FIGURE 22.1

Chasing a funnel and 1-gallon can around the cabin sole will frazzle even the toughest sailor. Fit copper tubing from the tank to a tap mounted in a convenient spot in the cabin. Then you can fill lamps with ease and no spillage, especially if you remember to do it before dark (Figure 22.1). We have found that this instant tap of kerosene has many uses: cleaning grease off our teak or topsides, cleaning brushes, thinning paint and varnish. Using a butane pipe-lighter for lamps makes light-up time easier than with matches and is less messy.

Fuel for oil lamps is available and cheap almost everywhere. The best we ever had came from Colombia, South America, England, and Malta, places where most of the population use kerosene for cooking or heating. Number one jet fuel works but it will make your eyes smart and it leaves a brown film on chimneys. I don't recommend using it. In the United States wick test kerosene is what you want. In England look for Esso blue. In less sophisticated countries, the kerosene sold for home use is usually excellent. But it pays to buy a small sample and try it out before you fill your main tank. If the fuel burns for two nights without leaving a deposit on your wick or chimneys, it's good oil. We find we use about 1 gallon of kerosene a month for all of our lighting. Our gravity tank holds 8 gallons of fuel so including paint clean-up at haul-out time, our tank holds a six-month supply.

It pays to carry six or eight spare cabin lamp chimneys at all times. These are the same as the internal chimneys for the navigation lamps. The chimneys store easily, wrapped in newspaper and arranged among our least-used linens. Four spare burners with wicks for both the cabin lamps and navigation lights complete our spare parts inventory. We've had difficulties getting these parts in some foreign countries, but usually we've been able to turn up reasonable substitutes for wicks or chimneys.

When you are buying burners for your lamps, take a magnet along. Some burners have iron parts that will rust and eventually jam your wick.

Maintenance of an oil system is simple. If you drain the fuel before each passage, scrub the lamps and lenses well, and trim the wicks, that should be it for at least a month. If the lenses do get sooted because of faulty adjustment, clean them with dish soap and a plastic scouring pad. After that it's simply a matter of refueling the lamps when they need it.

All the components of an oil lamp system will approximate the costs of the components in a comparable electrical system, excluding installation labor costs. Both systems require running lights, anchor light, cabin lamps. The oil system requires a gravity feed storage tank, smoke bells, bulkhead mounts, and spares. In place of these the electrical system needs its storage batteries, generator or alternator, wiring, and fuses, plus spare bulbs, fuses, regulator, and spare generator or alternator. Labor costs would probably be less on the oil system, depending on how the gravity tank is installed.

Since they have only one moving part, nonpressurized oil lamps are very durable and unaffected by moisture or salt water. I have seen proper brass or copper ones on fifty-year-old yachts and the lamps are still in perfect working order. Electrical systems with their dozens of moving parts and wiring connections do not like salt water and therefore are not as long-lived.

The oil lamps we used on *Seraffyn* were manufactured in the

United States by Perko. They are small and rather handsome. The cabin lights come in various sizes ranging from 9¼ inches high including chimney, to much larger sizes. The navigation lights are 10½ inches high with a 5¼-inch base and are also available in larger sizes. The only modification we made was the addition of internal chimneys as described in the beginning of this article.

Daveys Company of England makes an excellent set of lamps with internal chimneys as do some of the Dutch and German manufacturers. This type of oil lamp is used by the Dutch salvage tugs for their dead tows and for barges which do not have electrical systems. Most maritime countries insist that commercial ships carry oil navigation lights in case of electrical failure. I believe that all yachts with electric lights should have at least backup oil lamps for their navigation and anchor lights.

There are some small problems with an all-kerosene system. It's difficult to find a good binnacle with an oil lamp. When we first set off we had an oil light lifeboat binnacle that worked very well. But when we lost it, we found we really didn't need a binnacle light since our windvane held our course and occasional checks with a flashlight kept us on course. We do carry a good supply of flashlights and lots of batteries, plus a masthead battery-operated strobe light for when we have to lay hove to in a storm. This system of oil lamps plus strobe is what we plan to use on our new 30-footer.

Electric lights are convenient for the weekend sailor, but oil lamps are the epitome of reliability and simplicity for the long-distance cruiser. I've never been able to run all of the proper navigation lights on any of the boats we've delivered unless I was under power. If we were sailing all night we ended up with a flat battery in the morning. So we usually ran with only a masthead light, a good watch, and instructions to the crew to turn on the running lights if another vessel was in sight. This is not a good practice, but electric light systems forced us to do it.

On the other hand, my oil lamps have never let me down this way. And furthermore, the soft golden glow of an oil lamp gleaming off a glass of Barbados rum while we lie in a snug anchorage reminds us of years gone by. Oil lamps definitely contribute to the esthetic pleasures of modern cruising.

* Oil lamps can be purchased from suppliers listed on page 317.

23

Rudders for Cruising

Yacht designers and builders quite often forget how important "unrepairability" is when they design and build rudders. Sure the rudder will steer the boat when you put the helm up or down, but what about the nuts and bolts of maintaining and repairing the rudder, the stern bearing, the shaft, or propeller? The location and construction details of a rudder can make various interrelated repair and maintenance jobs either simple or a hassle.

A friend of mine bought a yacht in southern Spain. It had a loose stern bearing. We planned to haul the boat, paint the bottom, replace the rubber stern bearing and be off in three or four days to cruise in company. But the rudder location beat us. The shaft and stern tube had to be replaced due to excessive wear. The rudder's skeg was located aft of and in line with the propeller shaft. So it was impossible to pull the shaft aft (see Photo 23.4). We had to completely unbolt the engine and pull it forward into the main saloon in order to take the shaft and tube out. We spent three extra days of labor, slip charges, and frustration doing what should have been a two-hour job. We lost three irreplaceable days of cruising in the Balearic Islands for the lack of built-in repairability.

Here is a photo discussion of various rudders. The photos were taken in the Malta Yacht Yard where over three hundred cruising yachts were dry stored for the winter. Compare these photos to the rudder on your dream cruiser for simple repairability.

The large hole in the rudder (Photo 23.1) is for easy propeller shaft removal. (Note small holes in the trailing edge of the rudder for emergency steering lines.)

A similar arrangement in (23.2) allows the propeller shaft to be removed without the hassle of unbolting and moving the engine forward. But in spite of the hole through the skeg, the rudder must still be removed to get the shaft out.

Photo (23.3) is a study of built-in maintenance problems. Unlike the arrangements in numbers (23.1) and (23.2), it is necessary to remove the rudder before removing the propeller, or shaft, or before servicing the stern bearing because the rudder shaft is too close to the end of the propeller shaft. This rudder installation was on an amateur-built boat.

Photo (23.4) shows a modern fin-and-skeg yacht. There is enough room between the shaft and skeg to remove the propeller and service the stern bearing. But if the shaft has to come out, the only way is to remove the engine forward. A hole such as in (23.2) would allow the shaft to be pulled aft once the rudder was removed, but the hole could weaken the skeg.

Photo (23.5) shows a practical outboard rudder that can be lifted off its pintles in minutes. The shaft, stern bearing, and propeller can be pulled aft without removing the rudder because of the cut-out in the leading edge of the rudder. Having the propeller in an aperture makes fouling lines less likely.

Photo (23.6) is its own story. Try this on a concrete shipway! A travel lift will facilitate this painful extraction, but few primitive shipyards in far-off cruising areas have such sophisticated, costly equipment.

The older yacht in (23.7) has a wooden rudder shaft and if this were my boat I would be keen to inspect the shaft alley and rudder stock regularly for worms. But I would guess it is rarely removed for inspection as the rudder needs about 4 feet of clearance under the keel before it will drop out. If you are considering buying a boat like this, make sure the surveyor removes the rudder to inspect the shaft alley and rudder stock. (A copper or plastic tube in the shaft alley and copper sheet, tacked behind the creosote-painted stern post, will eliminate worm worry.)

With the steel yacht in (23.8) we have the reverse logistical prob-

Photo 23.1

Photo 23.2

Photo 23.3

Photo 23.4

Photo 23.5

Photo 23.6

Photo 23.7

Photo 23.8

Photo 23.9

Photo 23.10

Photo 23.11

Photo 23.12

Photo 23.13

Photo 23.14

Photo 23.15

lem. The propeller and shaft have to be removed first to allow the rudder to be dropped out of the hull. The rudder is also at the same level as the after part of the keel. A grounding on a hard bottom could damage the rudder shaft and cause it to bind. For safety, all rudders should be at least 3 inches higher than the bottom of the keel.

Photo (23.9) shows an inboard rudder on a motor sailer that can be removed without digging a hole. The four bolts at the rudder-to-shaft coupling can be unbolted. The shaft is then eased up into the hull enough for the rudder to lift out of the heel fitting, or as in (23.10) the heel fitting is unbolted from the aft part of the keel.

The rudder on the steel yacht in (23.11) has a good grounding clearance. This with the removal coupling on the rudder shaft makes a very practical inboard installation. Also of interest is the fact that this rudder is hollow and filled with used engine oil to reduce internal corrosion and provide some buoyancy for easier turning.

In (23.12) we see an easy-to-remove-and-service outboard rudder. But the wooden stern post on this boat is too close to the propeller shaft. To remove the stern bearing or propeller, the owner will have to shift the engine forward.

This rudder (23.13) has a small heel fitting added later to discourage fouling warps, lobster pot lines, and anchor chains. Without this fitting you could end up anchored by your rudder. Note too the water path for the rudder prop shaft bearing.

This boat (23.14), like most shoal draught vessels, has a problem getting the rudders deep enough for rudder control. Small skegs on the hulls, built lower than the rudders, would stop damage when taking the ground. It would also help prevent fouling lines.

With an outboard rudder such as this (23.15), simple, cheap owner-built self-steering gear can be fitted.* This rudder also has prestretched Dacron (Terylene) line stops. If you lash the tiller with stretchy nylon line when you are hove to in heavy seas, the rudder is controlled by the combined efforts of the tiller lashing and Dacron stops and kept from being jammed hard over. Otherwise it is possible you could shear the pintles from the stern post. External rudder

* (See John Letcher's very informative book, *Self Steering for Sailing Craft*, page 120, diagrams 5-41a and 5-41b. Published by International Marine Pub. Co., 21 Elm Street, Camden, Maine 04843.)

stops are rarely rigged on inboard rudders because of the extra drag they create.

I would not consider anything but an outboard rudder on my own cruising sailboat, not only for ease of removal, inspection, and repair, but also for the final bonus of being able to have the simplest-to-install type of effective self-steering gear.

I hope this photo discussion will give you some ideas for modifying your existing rudder. Or if you are planning a new yacht, maybe it will help you design a rudder with built in "repairability."

24

Plumbing Ideas

This chapter is not a complete compendium of ways to plumb a proper yacht. It is just a collection of thoughts and ideas that come to mind when we consider the problems of keeping a cruising boat comfortable and properly maintained. Each of the ideas will be listed in my order of preference starting with the simplest way to plumb up to the more complicated.

Anyone who has cruised for a long time is aware of the almost fanatical search for the mythical hot shower. Yachtsmen go to great lengths to get what they take for granted in a shoreside home. If you can have your own bathing facilities on board, you'll be free to choose whether or not you want to stay in a marina or at a yacht club. If you can devise a simple, neat way to have a hot bath without using a ton of fresh water, your floating home will be more comfortable and more self-contained.

In warm climates a deck shower can be easily rigged. On *Seraffyn* we used a 5-gallon black plastic jerry jug. If this jug was left out in the sun for a few hours, it provided a warm or even hot shower. We would take our showers just before sunset and if the water in the jug wasn't warm enough, a transfusion from the kettle would sort it out. We lifted the jug onto our spinnaker pole fitting, then used a siphon hose with a simple swing valve to start and stop the water flow. Five gallons of warm water would give us both a luxurious hair shampoo and shower. If the anchorage was crowded we would wear bathing suits and scrub ourselves under the suits. If water was limited, both of us could shower and shampoo using 3 gallons. If we were really watching our fresh-water supplies, we could both wash first in salt water then rinse with 2 quarts of fresh water. This is the simplest possible shower system and will work on any size boat if the weather is warm. If the weather is cool and your boat is too small for a built-in shower, inside baths must be done the hard way—with a basin and wash cloths. This is not our first choice, but it does work. A 5-gallon bucket set on the floor between the settees worked as a shampoo basin during our 49-day, 45-degree North Pacific crossing.

On a large boat, say about 30 feet, a sit-down tub with a hand-pressurized shower tank would be my first choice. On colder days, water could be heated on the stove and added to the pressure tank to achieve a comfortable temperature. This system is almost foolproof. You have no pipes or hoses to clutter the bilges or leak. The water is heated simply and cheaply. The separate pressure tank automatically meters the water each person uses.[*] This pressure tank could also be used in a standard toilet and shower arrangement, but I prefer the sit-down shower tub because it contains the spray so you don't have to wipe down the whole head after each shower when you feel clean and are looking forward to going out for dinner. More important, sitting in a tub is less dangerous in a sea way than standing in a shower.

Hot water for a shower can also be produced with coils running through a diesel or solid fuel stove, or by circulating your engine's cooling water through a hot-water heater. This system works quite well but is space-consuming and means pipes in the bilges. This system can also be quite expensive and, worst of all, means you have to run the engine in harbor just to have a hot shower.

There are also "demand" propane water heaters which work well. ("Demand" means that it activates when the hot-water tap is opened.) They must be vented well and have a pilot light which flares when the water is turned on. But these devices worry me. I would rather heat the kettle on the stove than be concerned about explosions or carbon monoxide/dioxide poisoning.

---

[*]A portable pressure system can be made by adding a handheld shower head and hose to a plastic 3-gallon insecticide sprayer. (See *The Care and Feeding of Sailing Crew*, 2nd edition, for more on bathing afloat.)

The most complicated way to produce a hot shower is electrically, with an auxiliary 220-volt generator producing current to operate a household-type electric water heater. This system is common on large motor sailers or motorboats with sophisticated engine rooms. Once again, the noise caused by running the generator could irritate your neighbors, the pipes and wires will clutter your bilge, and water consumption will be hard to meter.

Water transfer from your tanks to your drinking glass can be achieved in various ways. The simplest is the system we saw on a tiny globe-girdling trimaran, *No Name*. Her crew carried twenty, 1-gallon jugs of water and took out one jug a day, set it on the counter, and poured when necessary. Only slightly more complicated but hundreds of times more convenient is the gravity tank system. This is a small version of most cities' water systems which usually have a reservoir or large tank above the town. The tank drains down to various facilities. On a yacht this tank can be small (8 or 10 gallons). It can be installed on deck in an unused corner, inside the corner of the deck house or even in the flattish triangular space above the chain locker. This tank can go anywhere as long as it is above the valves in your system. It is backed up by other tanks under bunks or in the bilge which are used as spare water storage. This may sound inconvenient since it means transferring water by hand from storage tanks to gravity tank. But it is only during long passages that you have to transfer water and then this system forces you to be aware of how much water you are consuming. In harbor or when you are coasting, your day tank can be topped up directly from shoreside facilities.

The next choice and the one most common among cruising sailors are foot- or hand-operated pumps. These are easier to install than gravity feed systems, but the pumps used on live-aboard yachts wear out surprisingly fast and require a supply of spare parts plus regular rebuilding.

The electrical demand pressure systems are my least favorite choice. They are reliant on battery power. If anything in the electrical power chain fails, you can't get water unless you have a hand pump backup. Electrical systems are usually bilge cluttering and a source of breakdowns. These systems have been known to develop leaks and pump all of the precious water supply into the bilge, and finally, few things are more irritating than sitting below and hearing the noise of the pressure pump frittering away your diminishing water supply while some guest or crewman takes a leisurely shower or lets the water run while he brushes his teeth. On the more positive side, an electrical pressure system is convenient to use and has pressure similiar to that found in a shoreside home. If water and electricity are available in unlimited supply, this system works fine. But for some reason, no matter how careful the crew, water seems to evaporate on boats with a demand pressure system. So if you have one, isolate one tank for emergency water supplies.

If you are regularly tied alongside a dock with fresh water supplies nearby, there is one more way to achieve pressure water. Simply plumb the shoreside water hose into your system. This can be done by using a pressure-restricting valve so you don't over-pressurize and blow up your water system. A gravity water system can also be pressurized for those times you spend alongside the dock by isolating the day tank and only pressurizing the pipes. If you use a dockside hose to pressurize your system, remember to turn off the hose whenever you leave the boat. A leak in the system could sink your floating home.

Conserve fresh water with a salt water tap in the galley. The easiest way to do this is with a garden variety tap plumbed as directly as possible to a through-hull that is as far away as possible from your sink and head discharges. Attach this tap to a bulkhead below the waterline close to the sink. When you can use salt water for such tasks as boiling eggs or washing dishes just put a pot under the tap and turn it on. This below-the-waterline tap has another bonus use. You can wash out your bilge with it. Attach a garden hose to the threaded tap and you have salt water pressurized up to the level of your waterline. A final rinse with fresh water can be done using a hose from your gravity feed tank.

Our second choice for a salt water tap would be a foot- or hand-operated pump in the galley. The salt water pump is used much less than the fresh water ones so it is not likely to wear out as fast. We prefer foot-operated galley pumps, as this way you have both hands free to work or hang on.

Another plumbing option for the galley is hot salt water pumped directly into the sink or even bathtub. This is achieved whenever the engine is running. Hot water from the heat exchanger or exhaust manifold is routed overboard via the sink. If you have to run your engine to cool your iceboxes or charge batteries, this engine time can serve double by producing plenty of hot salt water to make scrubbing that pile of dirty dishes easier. It will also conserve fresh water.

The simplest type of sink you can have on a boat is a plastic or stainless steel bowl that you empty directly overboard. (Remember to check for silverware.) But most cruising boats, even the tiniest ones, now have self-draining, fixed sinks. Our choice for a 30-foot cruising boat would be two deep sinks as close as possible to the centerline of the boat. This way the sinks would drain well on either tack. If your sink backs up when you are heeled, it is best to have a swing-type shut-off valve right under the sink. This is more convenient to use than the through-hull fitting in the bilge. A clear plastic hose for the sink drain is handy when you have to clear the stoppages that are inevitable in a galley sink drain.

Some yachts have drains which let the shower and icebox water go directly into the bilge. This is a smelly practice and should never be allowed in a wooden boat as the fresh dirty water in the bilge could encourage bacteria and eventually cause rot. The installation of a sump tank can be simplified if you use your bilge pump to clear this tank also. Just install a two-way valve near the pump. This valve switches the suction line on your pump from the bilge to the shower or icebox sump.

All of the hoses you use on board should be clamped to the through-hull fittings with stainless steel clamps. Check this with a magnet even if the clamps you buy come off a shelf labeled "stainless steel." Often the bands are stainless but the screws are iron. A magnet will not be attracted strongly by proper hose clamps. If any hose could possibly be kicked or hit by items stored near it, double up the hose clamps and, if necessary, use steam hose for extra strength. Inspect the fittings the hose slips onto. Make sure it has a proper boss or raised section so the hose can't slide off by itself. Proper swing-type seacocks have this boss plus a flat flange which can be bolted through the hull and backed up with a wood pad. This pad strengthens and stiffens the hull around the through-hull hole. Remember, seacocks and hoses below or near the waterline should be as reliable as the hull itself. Carefully, research each fitting's quality, strength, and method of installation. Almost all floodings and sinkings in harbor are due to poor hoses, poor clamps, or cheap through-hull fittings (often only gate valves). Please don't try to save money here. Use only the finest quality.

Bilge pumps are supposed to pump the water out. But one night we came home to *Seraffyn* to find the floorboards floating. The bilge pump overboard hose was looped above the waterline and exited underwater at a through-hull. Somehow it had started to siphon water back through the pump into the boat. Maybe a passing fishing boat's wake had given it the needed push; we'll never know. If we hadn't lived on board, *Seraffyn* could have sunk right at her mooring. I had installed a marine check valve at the top of the loop on the overboard hose. But this had frozen shut because we used our bilge pump so rarely. The check valve is vital in any bilge pump or toilet overboard hose. The check valve lets air into the hose above the waterline and stops water from siphoning back into the boat. When you pump the bilge or head, you should be able to hear this valve sucking air on the back stroke. This means it is working properly. We now listen for this sound each time we use the bilge pump, and we close the seacock when we leave the boat, just to be sure.

Effective, carefully installed plumbing alternatives can save you time, money, and aggravation. They'll also eliminate most of the piping in your bilge. An empty bilge is easier to clean. But more important, an uncluttered bilge is a space ideally suited for your shipboard wine cellar.

Update

The sit-down, tub-type shower described here has worked wonderfully on *Taleisin*. Ours is under the companionway where an engine might be on other boats. The pump-up sprayer (a plastic 3-gallon insecticide sprayer with a demand-type shower head in place of the spray head) is right next to the tub, concealed in a locker. During fourteen years of voyaging on *Taleisin,* we haven't felt like looking for showers on shore. It has always been easier to shower on board.

25

Reef, Don't Buy

Sails for a pure cruising boat should be purchased with the following thoughts in mind: they must be strong; they should be reliable and hold their shape; they should be simple to reef, and easy to maintain. Above all, they must be as inexpensive as possible. Yet many designers of cruising boats show sail plans with six headsails, storm trysails, drifters, spinnakers, possibly twin running sails, and the sailmakers and fitting manufacturers chuckle all the way to the bank. So, if you are planning your sail wardrobe for a cruise or if the forepeak of your small live-aboard cruiser is jammed full of seven or eight expensive, wet sail bags, and you would like to use that space for something else such as a private stateroom with a double bunk, here are some simple, well-proven ways you can save space, make sail changes easier, and save money to go cruising.

When it was time to replace the lapper on *Seraffyn*, we built one with a 5-foot-deep set of reef points. When it's reefed it is our working jib. For the price of a set of reef points (about $50), we gained another sail. We've used this sail for over six years and found it ideal. We also put a reef in the working staysail which gives us a storm staysail. On certain yachts with cutaway underbodies, this will also work well as a backstaysail for heaving to. Our mainsail with three sets of reef points works well as a storm sail.

Seraffyn is cutter rigged, and designed with a large working sail plan so these three sails give us almost all the balanced combinations we need for winds over Force 2.

FIGURE 25.1, nos. 1–9

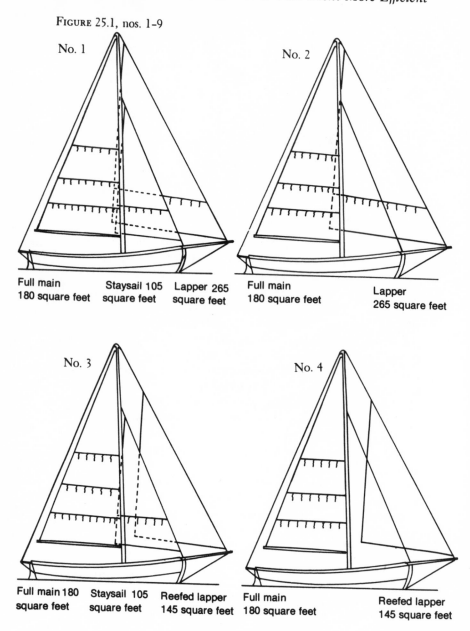

No. 1

No. 2

| Full main | Staysail 105 | Lapper 265 | Full main | Lapper |
| 180 square feet | square feet | square feet | 180 square feet | 265 square feet |

No. 3

No. 4

| Full main 180 | Staysail 105 | Reefed lapper | Full main | Reefed lapper |
| square feet | square feet | 145 square feet | 180 square feet | 145 square feet |

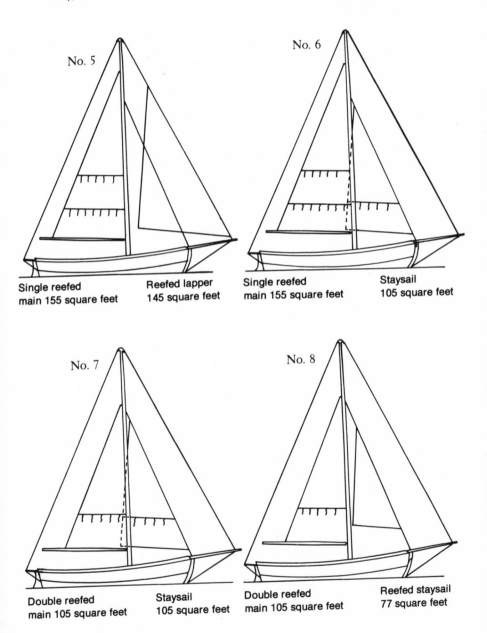

No. 5

Single reefed
main 155 square feet

Reefed lapper
145 square feet

No. 6

Single reefed
main 155 square feet

Staysail
105 square feet

No. 7

Double reefed
main 105 square feet

Staysail
105 square feet

No. 8

Double reefed
main 105 square feet

Reefed staysail
77 square feet

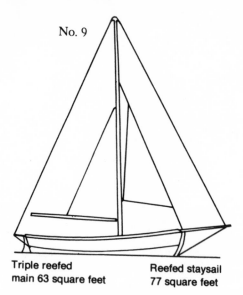

No. 9

Triple reefed
main 63 square feet

Reefed staysail
77 square feet

		SQUARE FEET
No. 1	Lapper, staysail, and main (all plain sail)	550
No. 2	Lapper and main	450
No. 3	Reefed lapper, staysail, and main	430
No. 4	Reefed lapper and main	325
No. 5	Reefed lapper and one reef in main	300
No. 6	Staysail and main with one reef	260
No. 7	Staysail with double-reefed main	210
No. 8	Reefed staysail and double-reefed main	182
No. 9	Reefed staysail and triple-reefed main	140

Reefing a headsail is much easier than:

1. Hauling down the jib
2. Taking the jib off the headstay
3. Bagging the jib
4. Bringing the new jib on deck
5. Unbagging it

6. Changing the sheets
7. Hanking on the new sail
8. Hauling up the new sail

With a reefing headsail you:

1. Haul the jib down on deck
2. Tie the jibsheets into the reefing clew
3. Fasten the tack down
4. Furl and tie the reef points
5. Haul the jib up reefed and ready to go

Reefing a main is even faster and easier, for you have no sheets to retie. You simply haul down the reefing clew, secure the reefing tack, then haul the sail up loose-footed. Your reefing pennants should be permanently rove and led to cleats near the main halyard winch. Tie your reef points in when you get around to it.

Another plus with reef points is that if any of your working sails are badly damaged in the foot area, you can immediately tie in a reef and carry on. Since most sailboats rely on their mainsail to beat off a lee shore, it is wise to have reef points in addition to your other reefing gear in case the foot of the sail rips or the furling gear itself breaks down.

We have never found we needed a storm trysail. During the past seven years and 20,000 miles, we have only used the triple-reefed main three times, going to windward in winds of over 50 knots. I think this works well on *Seraffyn* because her stoutly built main is much smaller and farther aft than a sloop rig of similar size. For heaving-to in extreme conditions, it would be worth trying a reefing staysail/backstaysail (Figure 25.2).

When we were in Poole, England, I worked with a sailmaker for two winters to learn about sailmaking and to earn a new main and lapper for *Seraffyn*. I spoke to the owner of the sail loft about making a roller-reefing 10-ounce jib. He didn't like my idea and suggested the simpler route, a set of reef points. The reasons he gave were: A reefed jib has no expensive furling gear to break down and will set just as well reefed as unreefed. A furling sail won't do this because the draft of the sail accumulates aft as the sail is rolled. You end up with a baggy, inefficiently-shaped intermediate jib. A jib rolled on

Figure 25.2

Reefed staysail
on back stay 77 square feet

the headstay creates considerable windage forward when you are trying to heave to, making it harder to keep your bow close to the wind. And finally, you can't hank a different light-weather jib on the headstay easily because your furling jib is in the way.

Repairing piles of damaged sails at the loft, I saw various methods of sail construction that work on cruising yachts and others that don't. For offshore long-distance cruising, I want all my working sails triple-stitched. This holds the shape of the sails longer by strengthening their weakest point, the seams. And three rows of stitching are more resistant to chafe.

I like bolt ropes on all the luffs of my working sails, either hand-sewn or with a rope inside a strong luff tape. This allows draft control, reefed or unreefed, that you can't get with a wire-luffed sail. If you are using a jib downhaul, the rope-luffed sail will come down the headstay without twisting the hanks and jamming because it isn't stiff like wire. Your sails will be easier to bag and take less space to stow without wire luffs.

I prefer handsewn rings with the ring sewn into a wide area of cloth spreading the load. A stainless-steel clew ring flogging around in the air might knock you out if it hits you just right when you are working the foredeck (Figure 25.3).

Patches at the reefing tacks and clews of your cruising sails should be almost as large and strong as those for an unreefed sail. The forces on the corner patches are about the same, reefed or not.

I like heavy taped leeches on my working sails. This takes the strain off the panel stitching and makes it almost impossible to split a seam horizontally from the leech forward.

All cruising headsails should have a hollow leech and foot to prevent flutter and flogging. Your main can also have a hollow leech, like a genoa, without battens or headboard. Torn or chafed batten pockets, incidentally, are the commonest repairs in a sail loft. Having a battenless mainsail allows small boats to raise and lower their mainsails on any point without fouling the shrouds (see next chapter).

Nothing is more impractical on a cruising boat than a maximum luff, deck-sweeping, large overlapping genoa. It chafes against the pulpit, lifelines, blocks, and spreaders. A large portion of your field of vision is blocked. It's difficult to tack with because of its long foot. With high-cut, small-overlap jibs you have less chafe and you can see steamer lights. If your running lights are on the shrouds or cabin sides they will not be obscured by the foot of the sail. The foot of the jib won't scoop up water when you're going to windward. Only racing men put up with all unseamanlike disadvantages of the deck sweeper. I know, I've done it racing but it isn't comforting to me to be on watch alone and not have 360-degree visibility.

Space inside 24-foot *Seraffyn* is at a premium and anything we don't have to store below gives us more living or storage space. So first we eliminated a working jib, storm trysail and storm main by adding reef points. We also furl and cover our main on the boom. The staysail is bagged on its stay. We don't use a staysail on a boom as the boom clutters up the foredeck too much and makes it harder to handle the anchor gear; the sail rarely sets perfectly on a self-tending boom, and the boom and its gear all cost extra money. Our lapper is removed from the bowsprit and stored in a bag on deck. That way our three working sails are kept out of our living space and are right at hand in case we want to go for a short daysail, or we have to move to a new anchorage quickly.

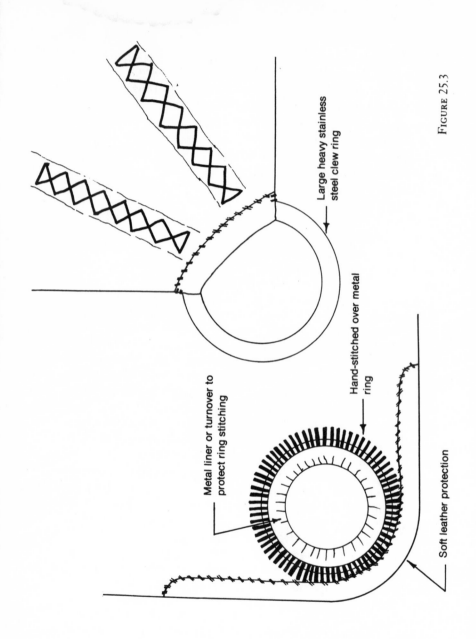

Metal liner or turnover to protect ring stitching

Hand-stitched over metal ring

Soft leather protection

Large heavy stainless steel clew ring

FIGURE 25.3

All bags and the sail covers are waterproof PVC-covered Dacron fabric which keeps the water and, most important, the sun, off our sails. My first mainsail was 3½ years old and looked as though it was in perfect condition, but you could poke your finger through the two lower panels. We had been furling the sail on the boom without a cover, and the foot had been exposed to the constant tropical sun. The ultraviolet rays had done their dirty work. Now we take the two or three minute's extra to put on a cover or bag our headsails every time we take them down. We use these three working sails 80 to 90 percent of the time. It's only in winds of Force 3 or less that we have to go below for our light sails.

We sail *Seraffyn* with no engine and only three working sails, a light-weather genoa, drifter, and spinnaker—six sails in all. These are more than adequate for simple cruising. And we don't seem to have any serious gaps when we are invited for the occasional informal cruiser race. A small part of the money we saved by having only six sails instead of nine or ten was spent on having those sails made to extra strong, longer-lasting ocean-cruising specifications.

The next time you see an old photo of a commercial schooner or skipjack from around the turn of the century, notice the area in the large working sailplan. Note the multiple reefs in the nonoverlapping headsails, reefs in the foresails, and multiple reefs in the mainsail. The old timers didn't waste their time sewing together three jibs when one with two sets of reef points, strongly made, would do the job. Try it. It's simple, well proven, and in these inflationary times, wondrously cheap.

26

The Cruising Man's Mainsail

When you decide to be purely a cruising sailor, you should analyze each piece of gear on board, including your mainsail. Is the mainsail easy to reef, furl and set? Is it efficient to windward? Will it be easy to repair and maintain in primitive countries? Is it, above all, strongly constructed?

I used a standard mainsail with headboard, roach, and battens for four years on *Seraffyn* and got tired of replacing battens, stitching, and repairing batten pockets. I also hated having to disturb Lin at night to set or reef the mainsail. If I could eliminate the battens and headboard, no matter what our course, the windvane could be left in charge while one person reefed or unreefed the mainsail on any course. With no battens or headboard to foul the shrouds, it wouldn't be necessary to head into the wind to raise or lower the sail.

I discussed my mainsail problems with Paul Lees of Crusader Sails in Poole, England. Battens, large roach, and headboard were developed to give a boat the maximum amount of sail area under any particular racing rule, and since until recently purely cruising boats were not too common, a cruiser got a racing mainsail whether he intended to race or not. Paul said he could cut our new mainsail like a genoa, without battens or roach. He went on to say that a leech line would be necessary, as even careful cutting and stable cloth could not prevent curling and fluttering as the fabric aged.

I also spoke to *Seraffyn*'s designer, Lyle Hess. Lyle felt that the roach area would not be missed going to windward and would only slightly affect *Seraffyn* on a reach or downwind. I took all of this information into account and chose the simplified mainsail since it wouldn't affect our ability to beat off a lee shore.

Battens are generally a nuisance on a cruising boat. Their pockets chafe badly on the inboard ends, splitting the pocket stitching and tearing the sail if they happen to break at night. Sailing in light winds with a leftover choppy sea, a mainsail can make the most agonizing slatting and banging noises, even though it is prevented and vanged well. By eliminating the weight of battens on the leech of the sail, the strain and wear of slatting can be greatly reduced. About half of your mainsail repairs will be eliminated when you get rid of battens; ask any sailmaker.

The twist of the headboard can cause your halyard to chafe on the sheave box and possibly derail and jam when running downwind. By eliminating the headboard you eliminate this problem and have the bonus of one less thing to foul the shrouds. A headboard mainsail is simply built like a genoa or boom staysail (Figures 26.1 and 26.2).

Now someone will say that removing the roach area will give the vessel lee helm. If any helm does develop, it can be relieved by raking

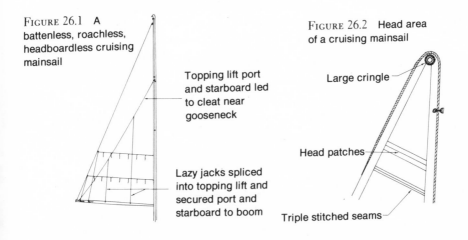

FIGURE 26.1 A battenless, roachless, headboardless cruising mainsail

Topping lift port and starboard led to cleat near gooseneck

Lazy jacks spliced into topping lift and secured port and starboard to boom

FIGURE 26.2   Head area of a cruising mainsail

Large cringle

Head patches

Triple stitched seams

the mast slightly aft to balance up. Most of the newer boats I have sailed on suffer from weather helm, so possibly a roachless main can be an improvement.

If you want a new mainsail, speak nicely to your local sailmaker about eliminating roach, battens, batten pockets, and headboard. They represent considerable labor and extra material. He could probably use this saving to triple-stitch each seam for no extra cost. Most sailors agree that panel stitching failure due to chafe is an extremely common sail problem. Using three rows of stitching will give you 50 percent more resistance to chafe and more threads to rub through (Figure 26.3).

While on the subject of chafe, a problem that besets most mainsails, may I mention that I have found ways of eliminating it. Clear plastic tubing, fitting over all shrouds which the mainsail touches, gives a nonchafing smooth surface. Then, when running or broad reaching, I use a preventer vang tackle with nylon line to secure the

FIGURE 26.3   Triple stitched seams

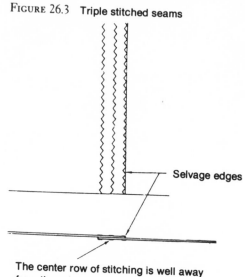

Selvage edges

The center row of stitching is well away from the selvage edges therefore has full holding power on both layers of cloth. This prevents any distortion such as may happen near the cloth edge.

boom firmly. This stops the mainsail and boom from pumping up and down against the shrouds; hence, no chafe.

My downwind rig is main and headsail wing and wing, with wind-vane steering. I attended to these antichafe details and my mainsail lasted four years and 14,000 miles. No extra gear such as twin stay-sails have been necessary just for dead downwind sailing. Back on the subject of triple-stitching. Dacron or Terylene sailcloth is very stable; therefore, most loss of sail shape is due to relatively weak panel stitching. Triple-stitching will stabilize your sail panels and your sail will hold its shape much longer (Figure 26.3).

While on the subject of cruising mainsails, one cannot ignore reef points and pennants (slab reefing) with lazy jacks for the following reasons:

1. No expensive or complicated geared mechanism is necessary.
2. If the tack and clew patches for each set of reef points are strongly sewn in, you can reef without immediately tying in the reef ties. In squally weather this is very convenient. As soon as the squall is passed, you can quickly rehoist the sail by just releasing the pennants and winching up the halyard. If lazy jacks (Figure 26.1) are used, they will contain the foot of the reefed sail, and when or if the reef points are to be tied, will contain the loose area at the foot of the sail, making the knots easier to tie.
3. If your sail is badly damaged along the foot or lower panels, the upper portion is still useable with a reef tied in.
4. With pennant reefing, you can tie in the necessary reef, then hoist the reefed sail and get underway smartly; but with roller reefing you have to hoist the whole sail and then proceed to roll it as the sail slats and bangs around.
5. When using a reef, one can control sail shape by loosening or tightening reef ties or clew and tack pennants.
6. A vang or preventer can be secured under the bolt rope without use of a roller claw.
7. When roller reefed, the leech and luff of the sail take most of the sailing strain, causing premature stretching and leech flutter.

8. Cutting back the tack of a sail for roller reefing gear is definitely a compromise. As the sail is rolled, the bolt rope tries to climb the reefing gear, causing vertical wrinkles, chafe, and general nasties.

9. The extra cost of having reef points sewn into your new mainsail will, in a new boat, be offset by not having to purchase furling gear, which can be quite expensive.

A person committed to roller reefing can still have battens and roach removed from his mainsail, allowing him to roll the sail completely without concern. For safety I would have reef points even if I had roller reefing.

If at all possible for cruising, one should have handsewn rings everywhere, though this does increase the cost of the sail. These handsewn cringles are more secure and spread their load over a wider area of the sail. On sails with punched spur tooth grommets, I have taken the time to sew each luff and foot grommet as shown (Figure 26.4). Large handsewn rings accept jury-rig-type repairs much easier than do the hydraulically pressed rings used on many racing sails.

I'm sure my triple-stitched, battenless, roachless, and headboardless mainsail will be stronger and last longer, and will definitely be easier to use than a misplaced racing main.

FIGURE 26.4   Sewing in a spur tooth grommet

Spur tooth grommet

Seizing

Hand stitching should be done with slide or hank in place. This allows the slide or hank seizing to bear on the metal grommet and prevents chafe. This stitching spreads the load over a wider area of cloth.

Slide

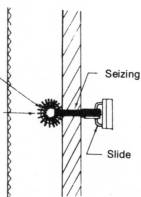

27

The Instant Whisker-spinnaker Pole

When you're 4 foot 10 and slightly uncoordinated, gybing a sail set on a 16-foot whisker pole in a lumpy sea at night becomes a moral dilemma. "Should I wake him up?" "Maybe this wind will shift back soon; maybe I'll just sail by the lee until the change of watch." On days when I felt like going sailing alone, getting that formidable pole off its chocks on the bowsprit, hoisting it onto its mast front ring, then rigging up its uphaul, hoisting its outboard end, and pulling the genoa across was more than I really cared to do. So I sometimes ran along with the genoa cracking and slatting behind the blanketing mainsail.

After seven years of cruising on *Seraffyn*, Larry finally got tired of having to help me set or take down the pole almost every time we used it. He decided to copy Dan Bowen, an English sailor we'd met on a 30-foot sloop called *Romadi*. Dan had used what he called his "instant pole." I must admit I fought Larry with my usual conservative attitude. "What if it doesn't work? We'll have ruined our beautiful varnished mast. What about windage?" But Larry had actually been sailing on *Romadi*. He knew some facts I only came to believe after I used our own pole for one day. Then I became a little perturbed that Larry had waited two years from when he met and sailed with Dan until the day he gave me the wonderful sailing freedom of an instant pole.

In order to change over to an instant pole, you'll need strong, external genoa slide-type track up the center front of your mast extending from a point 4 feet above the deck to a height that is 2 feet longer than your whisker-spinnaker pole when its end is sitting on deck. In our case we already had 4 feet of 1½-inch wide bronze track on the mast for normal spinnaker use. So we had to add 9 feet more. We couldn't buy identical track so we made our own from flat bronze bar stock ³⁄₁₆-inch thick and 1¼ inches wide which Larry

The upper end of the pole showing the
uphaul, downhaul block.

placed on a teak riser. Since this track will take a lot of torque pressure when it is in use, Larry secured it in place with a 1½-inch No. 14 bronze wood screw staggered every 4 inches. If you have an aluminum spar, use a track section that is as strong as that normally used for the spinnaker pole track on a racing boat of your size.

At the top end of the track, Larry fastened a small check block. Three feet below the track he put two small fairleads for ¼-inch line. Our pole has a clip-type end fitting which attaches to a normal spinnaker pole car. After adding the track, block, and fairleads, we used the same pole and fittings but attached a ¼-inch line to the bottom of the slider, ran it through the fairleads, up the front of the mast, through the block, and back to the top edge of the slider where it was lashed snugly with the use of a lanyard—sort of like an endless clothesline.

Fairleads for the lower end of the hauling line.

When you pull on one side of this line, the inboard end of the pole slides up the mast. Pull on the other side and the pole comes down. Now to make this simple uphaul/downhaul into a bit of magic, secure your staysail halyard to the outboard end fitting of your pole. Adjust your halyard so that when the pole has its inboard end a foot from the top of the track, the other end clears the deck by at least a foot. Now swing the pole end over your lifelines, haul on the pole downhaul and watch it swing right into place. If you don't have a staysail halyard, use your jib halyard to test the pole before you install a spinnaker pole topping lift block a few feet above the upper end of the whisker pole track. Prestretched Dacron line is perfect for the halyard. We did eventually install a separate topping lift when we started to race *Seraffyn* and found we needed to set the staysail at the same time as our pole was in use. But we sailed with

Our pole stored on its shroud ring.

the staysail halyard as the topping lift for three years and 17,000 miles.

Once the pole had its topping lift length determined, Larry swung its lower end over until it touched the forward shroud. He marked that spot and lashed a ½-inch rope thimble both port and starboard.

These three photos show the sequence for setting our instant whisker pole.

When we are finished using the pole we just snap it into whichever ring is closest. This leaves the deck completely clear of obstacles. Since the pole is almost in line with the lower shroud, it doesn't interfere with fore-and-aft traffic. And it's ready right at hand when it's time to use it. We found the pole end a good place to store the staysail halyard when it wasn't in use.

Now setting the pole or gybing is so simple we'll often use it just for the short run down the jetty. All you do is walk forward, unclip the pole from its shroud ring, put the proper jib sheet in the clip, swing the end of the pole clear of the lifelines, and pull the downhaul line. Then stroll aft and sheet in the jib.

For a gybe, let the windward sheet go, walk forward, and pull the pole uphaul. The pole will swing down to where you can reach its lower end. Unclip the jib sheet, guide the pole across the foredeck and clip it to the leeward sheet. Pull the pole downhaul and go aft to sheet in. Then take the mainsail across at your leisure.

You never have to handle the weight of the pole. It never has two ends free at the same time. Because of the friction of the running uphaul/downhaul line, it has never slid up or down the mast by itself.

There are only four small ways this system can give you trouble. If the track or slider are sticky, hauling the pole up and down will be difficult. We use a shot of spray beeswax or silicon lubricant on the slider or track when this happens. If there is any tension on the jib sheet, the pole will be almost impossible to set or lower. When you cast off the windward jib sheet and go forward to lower the pole, you'll learn just how many wraps on the sheet winch keep the sail from going forward and wrapping around the headstay but still keep the tension off the end of the pole. Third, you must watch the pole as you haul on the uphaul line and it swings down toward you. Ninety-nine times out of hundred the pole will come to rest against the lifelines, but the one time it doesn't because it sneaks down along the headstay where the lifelines dip, it could give you a nasty thump if you aren't watching. Finally, you must be sure the topping lift is lead properly when you gybe. If you accidently twist the pole so the topping lift turns around the pole's outer end, it may go up fine but the inner end can turn on its ring and jam aloft. If the wind is strong and you pull hard to try and force the slider down when it is twisted like this, the leverage could bend your track. This has happened to each of us once. Then we relearned the lesson about what should be done every time we handle a piece of sailing gear—check the leads and make sure they run clear and fair before you pull anything aloft.

All of the maneuvers I'm describing are planned for one person on watch with a windvane steering. This is where the instant pole really shines. But with two people it's just as great. And it's forever amazing everyone who sees us use it. Our favorite racing crew, Tom Linsky, a world-class champion dinghy sailor, claims gybing our spinnaker pole with this arrangement is just as fast as any way he's tried. It's also efficient since only one person has to be on the foredeck to detach the weather sheet and set the leeward one. A second person can stand almost completely still right at the mast to pull the uphaul and downhaul, so there's less movement to disturb the boat's progress through the water.

But windage aloft is a problem for racing and it's one disadvantage of the instant pole. We've eliminated much of the windage associated with cruising boats by using plastic-covered shrouds instead of baggy-wrinkly, so we're willing to give up the ½ to 1 percent efficency lost going to windward. On the other hand, we've made sure the pole can be easily lowered and removed so we can lash it on deck in case of an ultimate storm. If we had to ride out a hurricane in a tight anchorage, we'd want every bit of windage off the mast and deck including bagged sails, the instant pole, and even the spare halyards. On the other hand, we've carried the pole stored on its lifeline holder and track through a twelve-hour 75-knot-plus typhoon in the Bay of Bengal, plus four gales and two storms in the North China Sea and North Pacific. It's never once been a nuisance.

I've come to enjoy downwind sailing alone or with Larry twice as much since we have that instant pole arrangement. Even the thought of a 20-foot-long spinnaker-whisker pole on the new 29-foot-9-inch cutter Larry is bolting together right now 200 feet from my desk, doesn't worry me a bit. With the instant pole and a dozen other easy sail-handling devices I know Larry will rig for me, I'll be able to handle that 16,000-pound boat like the Mighty Mouse Larry always says I am.

28

The Indispensables

It took us eight-and-a-half years and 30,000 miles of cruising to find we already were carrying the perfect rain catcher. My mother gave us the perfect stove lighter as a farewell gift. We read about the handiest piece of canvas on board in one of the Hiscock books. We finally found the perfect crab and lobster boiling pot, after three years of frustration. And so it goes, year in, year out, as you live and cruise on your floating home. Simple ideas appear that make your life easier, more comfortable, safer, or more fun. We got a big kick out of finding solutions to these minor problems and adding the solutions to our list we call "the indispensables."

THE HISCOCK CANVAS SQUARE

Eric and Susan Hiscock wrote about an indispensable 3-foot-by-4-foot square of heavy water-resistant canvas they carried on *Wanderer III*. It had strong grommets sewn in each corner. We made two slight alterations. We added a center patch with a lifting eye and spliced a piece of ¼-inch line 5 feet long into each corner (Figure 28.1). That canvas is one of the most useful items on board. When it is raining and hot, we tie it across the forehatch, hoist its center lifting eye on a halyard, then open the forehatch for ventilation without getting any rain below.

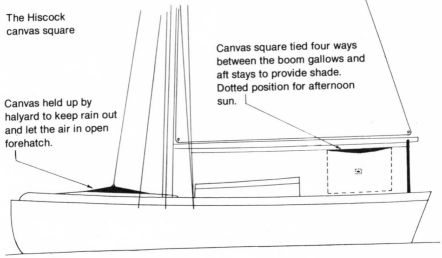

The Hiscock
canvas square

Canvas square tied four ways
between the boom gallows and
aft stays to provide shade.
Dotted position for afternoon
sun.

Canvas held up by
halyard to keep rain out
and let the air in open
forehatch.

FIGURE 28.1

If we need to protect the decks or bulwarks while we shift stores on board, the canvas does the job. If Larry is doing woodwork or metalwork jobs below, we tie the canvas in place to catch the shavings. If a squall comes up and there is something on deck that has just been varnished or painted, we can lash the cover in place quickly to keep the rain off. It serves as an instant spray dodger, ice carrier, and companionway cover. When we are sailing, it is small enough to be rigged overhead to provide shade without getting in the way of handling the sails. When the sun starts to sneak below the edge of our cockpit awning, that square can be easily attached as a shade. It never cuts down on the cooling breezes nor is it permanently in the way like a doghouse or permanent canvas enclosure would be. And, until we discovered our new secret rain catcher, we used the Hiscock square to catch tropical rain water.

PARDEY'S UNPATENTED NEARLY-PERFECT-PASSAGE-MAKING RAIN CATCHER

We're not sure why it took us eight-and-a-half years of playing with all sorts of crazy rigs before we came up with this one. But somewhere in the Strait of Malacca we hit a lovely squall full of sweet cool rain. Larry turned to me with a bright-eyed look and said, "Why didn't we think of it before? We've been carrying the perfect rain catcher all along." Much to my amazement he pulled in the main boom, tied our plastic-coated nylon mainsail cover upside down like a gutter under the main boom, eased the mainsheet and rain water started pouring off the mainsail, into the upside-down cover and out the end near the gooseneck. The large part of the cover that usually shielded the head of the mainsail made a reservoir area. A few clothes pins channeled the water where we wanted it. Larry sewed a rope grommet into the lowest point so that a garden hose jams in easily. During the average rainfall, the water flows through that hose just like it was under pressure. Since the rain catcher can be left in place most of the time, we even caught as much as 2 gallons of water every twenty-four hours in the heavy fog we found on our North Pacific crossing. During a twenty-minute tropical downpour we can collect 40 gallons or more. During real heavy weather we do have to remove the rain catcher because it makes reefing the mainsail more difficult.

Like most ideas, this one is probably far from original. But we are glad we thought of some way to make that nuisance of a sail cover serve a second purpose.

TWO-PART UNDERWATER PUTTY

Years ago, when epoxies first came into being, commercial divers dreamed up underwater putty. It was used to seal leaks on underwater construction jobs. It is wonderful stuff since its most important characteristics are that it sticks only to wet surfaces, it cures underwater to a hard-as-rock finish, and it sticks to wood, fiberglass, or steel.

The main reason we carry underwater putty on *Seraffyn* is to cover gouges in the underwater planking after we've hit a chunk of driftwood. Larry waits until the next calm day, dives overboard to inspect the scrapes and scratches, then waits while I mix up the prescribed amount of putty on a thick piece of cardboard. He then uses his finger to rub underwater putty on the scrapes. That way we don't have to worry about worms getting into the bare wood because there is a gouge in the hull.

We've used the same putty to help patch a hole in a steel hull that was the victim of electrolysis in Port Said, Egypt. A diver slathered putty on a piece of plywood that was larger than the hole in the steel, dove under and held the plywood and putty patch in place while the crew threaded some self-tapping screws through the sound steel around the hole and into the plywood. The putty set up hard as steel and worked perfectly.

We've heard of delivery crews depending on the two-part wonder product to keep glass boats with damaged hulls from leaking. There was even a case where the delivery crew made a one-foot-square patch under the counter of an old racing yacht with underwater putty, plywood, and some nails, and then sailed the boat 3,000 miles to get it to its home shipyard.

We carry underwater putty in our fiberglass dinghy's emergency abandon-ship kit. The putty could seal damage caused by launching the dinghy in a hurry.

THE HANDY DANDY PIPE LIGHTER

When my mother gave us two Ronson pipe lighters as a farewell gift, both of us were quite surprised because neither of us smokes. But Mom was a camper from way back. She knew that matches are never willing to light when you need them most, nor is their flame long enough to reach where you want without burning a finger or knuckle.

Now we have three Ronson butane lighters on board. One is in Larry's rigging kit for burning the ends of Dacron seizing thread or sail sewing twine. The other two live in easy-to-reach spots in the galley and forepeak. They work much better than a striker for lighting the burners on our propane stove and oven because we can see and direct the flame. The lighter flame stays on as long as you need it for reluctant oil lamp burners. There are wind-resistant models that work even in 8 or 10 knots of breeze if you want to melt and seal the end of a frayed line on deck. There is never a hot-tipped match to dispose of.

These lighters are really rugged. We dropped one off a dock in Panama. Larry dove down and found it. Then we soaked the lighter in fresh water for a few minutes, disassembled the striking mechanism, and baked the whole lot in a 150-degree oven for twenty minutes. That lighter is still working eight years later.

THE NO-HANDED FLASHLIGHT.

We've finally found the perfect gift for friends setting off on a cruise. It is small. It costs less than $3 plus twenty minutes of work to build. It makes everyone laugh when they see it. And, without exception, recipients of our no-handed flashlights all write letters of thanks describing how useful that silly looking gadget is.

We take a soft-bodied, lightweight, water-resistant flashlight such as the ones made in Red China with a flying goose on their side (they are sold in most Chinatown hardware stores). Then Larry cuts a strip of strong, stiff plastic about ⅛ inch by 1½ inches wide and 4 inches long and uses fiber-glass reinforced tape to attach it to the end of the flashlight (Figure 28.2). Presto—a flashlight you hold with a mouth grip. Now both of your hands are free to search for that wrench you dropped in the bilge. You can use two hands to disassemble that bilge pump that is hiding under the cockpit. If you are untangling a fouled-up traffrail log line, working on the foredeck, changing sails, or trying to clean out a dinghy at night, you can use two hands and still have light where you need it. An added bonus is that the plastic mouth grip stops the flashlight from rolling around when you set it down on deck.

These are just five of the indispensables we have on *Seraffyn*. The list keeps on growing. Only last week we were out sailing with Pete Nuteboom on his 28-foot Bristol Channel Cutter *Capriccio*. When lunch time came, he reached under a locker and pulled out a small companionway drop board with a glass and condiment tray attached to the back (Figure 28.3). Everyone's glasses stayed upright in the holes in the tray as we reached along on a 12-knot breeze. The salt and pepper were within easy reach.

And so we've added another item to our work list. As Larry started working out the sketch to go with this last item, he came up with an idea that will make it even more versatile for our use. So that is the way it goes. What was once Pete's idea for an indispensable on board *Capriccio* will become part of the collection of details that make *Seraffyn* more than just a boat to go sailing on. She's a hassle-free home, bound for adventure.

FIGURE 28.2 The no handed flash light

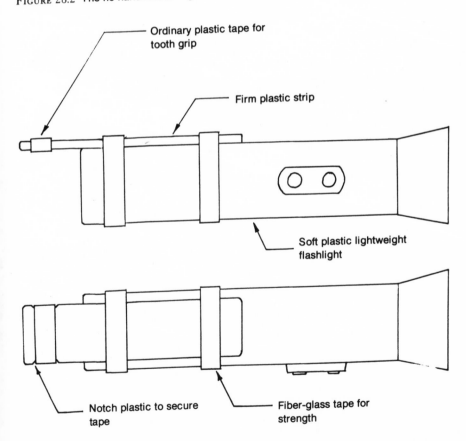

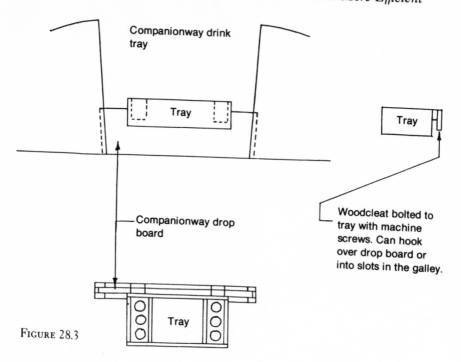

Companionway drink tray

Tray

Tray

Companionway drop board

Woodcleat bolted to tray with machine screws. Can hook over drop board or into slots in the galley.

Tray

FIGURE 28.3

29

Some Simple
Maintenance Tips

SPREADER MAINTENANCE

Keeping varnish on the tops of spreaders is a job for Sisyphus. Three years in the corrosive sun of the tropics proved this to us. The rest of the varnish on the mast and boom was relatively easy to maintain, but the tops of the spreaders just kept depreciating.

If you have wooden spreaders, they should be varnished so the condition of the wood can easily be inspected. Suspect any changes in the color of the wood as it might prove to be rot. With painted spreaders, rot can develop under the paint without visual knowledge. Sound spreaders are imperative, as one of the most common causes of dismasting is spreader failure.

Rather than worrying about this, we made *Seraffyn's* spreaders easier to maintain. We covered the tops and inboard edges with 1/32-inch, (0.794-millimeter) copper sheet and fastened it with escutcheon pins (round head brass tacks) and bedded it in a flexible fungicidal bedding compound (Figure 29.1). The whole job costs about $5 for materials and took four hours of labor. In the last year it has saved us much concern, varnish, and sandpapering.

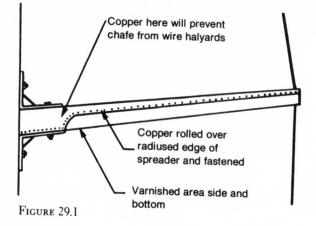

Copper here will prevent
chafe from wire halyards

Copper rolled over
radiused edge of
spreader and fastened

Varnished area side and
bottom

FIGURE 29.1

RADAR REFLECTOR

If you are building a hollow wood or fiber-glass spar (sorry, aluminum masts won't work), you can be much more obvious to another vessel's radar by putting wrinkled aluminum foil inside your mast.

Aluminum is the ideal radar-reflecting material, but it must have surfaces at right angles to the radar beam to return a good signal. An aluminum spar doesn't cause a good signal because it is usually round or oval. An internal reflector won't work inside the aluminum spar because the spar itself intercepts the signal.

If aluminum foil is wrinkled and then rolled loosely and put inside all the hollow areas of the wooden or fiberglass spar under construction, you will have a large, permanent reflecting surface without the windage, weight, or nuisance of an external radar reflector.

We have tested this system and it has given *Seraffyn* a larger blip on the radar screen than a vessel three times our size.

WHITER THAN WHITE

During our travels many people have asked, "How do you keep your paintwork so white and clean-looking?" Even the overhead in the main cabin has never been repainted in 11 years and still looks white and new, not yellow or grey.

The explanation is very simple, we don't use white paint. We put ½ teaspoon or 1/12 ounce (2.36 grams) of royal blue paint into every new quart of white paint and stir completely. This acts just like bluing in the weekly wash, giving the paint a lasting whiter-than-white appearance.

LIFETIME BRUSHES

Varnish and paint brushes can be a large and very worthwhile investment. Good brushes make a job easier and faster and give a smoother finish. Naturally the difficult part is servicing your brushes as soon as each job is finished. Brushes left for later will never get cleaned. Once this hurdle is overcome in your mind, the rest is easy.

I was taught this trick by a professional painter and some of my good-quality brushes are as good as new eleven years later.

After using your brushes, rinse them with kerosene or thinners until the paint ceases to work out of the bristles in the heel. This usually takes about four rinses for white paint and varnish, more for colored paint. Shake out the excess kerosene and work clean, inexpensive 30-weight engine oil into the bristles and particularly the heel of the brush. Then wrap each one in aluminum foil, up to but not including the handle. The oil stops any residual paint from hardening or sticking to the bristles, therefore the heel doesn't swell up with paint. The aluminum foil will contain the oil and stop the bristles from being bent, distorted, or separated. For storage in your boat or garage, roll all brushes up together in a heavy plastic bag and they will take up little space and not get lost or separated. When needed again, one rinse with kerosene will remove the oil and any residual paint. It will leave the brushes clean, supple, and free from the annoying flecks of dried paint or varnish that would transfer onto your next work of art.

TOUCHING UP VARNISH EASILY

Shiny varnish is admired and desired by every yachtsman and a simple trick we use on our boat makes it easy.

No matter how many coats of varnish you apply, a scratch which breaks the varnish surface will allow water to stain your wood and lift the finish. Consequently, frequent touch-up is necessary. But opening a can of varnish, cleaning a brush, and finding sandpaper takes time and makes a mess, so a varnish touch-up kit is a must. We have cleaned out a paste bottle—the kind with a brush attached to the inside of the screw-on top—and filled it with varnish. A rubber band secures a piece of sandpaper to the bottle, and the varnish kit is kept close at hand.

Once a week during the season we wander around with this kit, sanding and feathering any damaged spots on our varnished hatches and spars, and brushing on fresh varnish. We try to remember to put three or four coats of touch-up on each spot. Then, when it is time for a complete revarnishing, one good coat over the whole surface and the hatch or spar looks perfect.

When we're finished touching up, we just put the brush back into the varnish, and it needs no cleaning!

Update

On board *Taleisin,* we have created a combined paint-and-varnish touch-up kit. Now we have a varnish touch-up bottle and a white paint touch-up bottle in a small Tupperware container. We keep a few small pieces of 100-grit and 180-grit sandpaper plus a small rag in the box and store it in a cockpit locker. Then when one of us has a few minutes to spare, we can look around for any touch-up spots and take care of them before they start to peel or the wood beneath turns gray.

30
Mechanical Pumps for Bilge or Fire

An elderly cutter with badly leaking garboards is hove-to in a gale. On board, two young men have been handpumping two hours on and two hours off but they are tiring after thirty-six hours of gale winds. The water is slowly increasing. Their electric bilge-pump motor is burned out, but the diesel auxiliary is in good order.

Any vessel can be damaged or spring a leak. Why not take advantage of your engine to rig the most efficient, dependable type of bilge pump? As long as your engine is working, a mechanical bilge pump along, with a good hand pump, is the best insurance against foundering at sea. Since *Seraffyn* has no engine, I have often wondered what would happen if I ran into an object at night and developed a leak in my hand pump and I couldn't cope with it. How could I keep her afloat?

People have said to me, "Modern boats don't leak like old wood boats used to." This is rubbish. Any vessel, no matter what her age or material, can leak. Fiberglass boats are famous for leaking at the hull-to-deck connection. Steel hulls can be holed by corrosion or electrolysis. A wood boat can lose her caulking. Through-hull fittings can give way, and there is always the possibility of a collision at sea, be it with flotsam, a whale, or another vessel. All types of material have

their problems, but good strong initial construction and maintenance can lessen the possibility of a leak.

Any yacht with an engine can be fitted with a mechanical pump.
It will run off the flywheel pulley with a V-belt. A disengaging clutch
which allows the belt to freewheel when the pump is not being used
should be fitted (Figure 30.1).

A pump run off the main engine will not get tired and can pump a
hell of a lot of water. Most commercial vessels and fishing boats have
mechanical pumps as regular equipment and some better marine
engines come complete with the bilge pump built on as standard.

The main types of mechanical pumps I have used are the rubber
impellor type, geared type, and vane type. All of them have their
advantages and disadvantages, but studying the manufacturer's bro-
chures can help you take the steps necessary to insure a pump's
reliability.

Since a mechanical bilge pump develops a lot of pressure on the
outlet side, it can be plumbed up to a deck outlet (see Figure 30.2)
using two-way valves. These valves allow you to choose between
pumping the bilge or pumping fresh salt water up onto the deck.
The deck outlet can be used for many purposes. It makes a handy
fire hose. Hosing off a muddy anchor chain and anchor before it

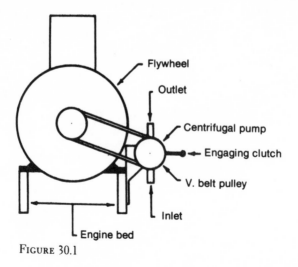

FIGURE 30.1

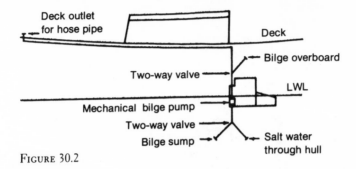

FIGURE 30.2

comes on deck is very desirable. Washing down the decks is a simple matter also, with the hose and pump easily ready to use. By installing and using a deck outlet for your bilge pump, you will be assured that your pump is always working since you will be checking it each time you turn on the deck outlet.

Naturally any pump has its limitations and can only control a leak of the same volume as the pump, but a mechanical pump won't tire as a man would, won't stop when the battery runs down, and will run as long as the engine has fuel. You double the convenience of having an engine this way by being much better prepared for ill luck in the form of a bad leak.

We managed to bring the cutter mentioned earlier in this article into port three days later. We'd fashioned a mechanical bilge pump by sticking the salt water cooling inlet hose into the bilge with a porthole flyscreen wrapped around the end of the hose as a rough but effective filter. This utilized the salt water cooling pump to cool the engine and pump the bilges at the same time. By this means we were able to keep the water in the bilge constant with only occasional additional pumping with the hand pump.

31

The Truth about Windvanes

During our years of cruising, I have talked to a lot of sailors who have had difficulties with their windvanes. I have also experienced the technical problems of building, fitting, and using my own gear, so I'd like to share some practical ideas to make your vane more successful.

To fit an efficient vane you first have to look at your boat's balance. Then you have to consider the problems of customizing a vane to your own yacht. You have to understand the limitations of vanes and finally you have to learn the practical tricks you can use to improve their performance.

The very first, most important step before you buy, design, or build anything is to get your boat perfectly balanced.

If she carries excessive weather or lee helm even the best-designed vane gear will not steer well. In medium winds (10 to 15 knots), you should be able to trim your boat out so that you can hold the tiller easily with your thumb and forefinger only and not get armstrain.

The tiller should be almost in line with the centerline of the boat. If it is constantly 10 or 15 degrees to one side, you have a difficult helm.

Raking your mast aft can eliminate some lee helm. Moving the mast forward can help a weather helm. Don't be afraid to experiment.

Try to get your boat perfectly trimmed so that she has a slight and constant tendency to head into the wind. This weather helm should become so insistent in a decks-awash squall that it will overpower the steering vane and automatically head your boat safely into the wind.

Some people install a wheel to overcome a bad weather helm. This doesn't cure the problem; it just hides the imbalance. It leaves the rudder at an acute angle to the centerline which causes extra drag and also puts unnecessary strains on the steering apparatus and the rudder itself. The wheel and its machinery will just add extra friction for the steering vane to overcome. This usually causes poor steering performance in the medium to light winds, especially downwind. When you are installing a windvane it is best to have the most frictionless system possible for turning your rudder—a tiller.

Before fitting your vane, your yacht should be on her lines, not way down fore or aft but within 1 inch (25 millimeters) of her designed load waterline. Being out of trim can make her hard to steer. If she is off her marks, put her on a diet. Throw out all that junk you might need "someday."

If you still have steering problems you might have to resort to hull changes. Maybe a larger rudder or an increased skeg aft. But you should get advice from a yacht designer before trying expensive surgery.

Once you achieve good hull and sail plan balance, you are ready to start thinking about your self-steering device. Most people who have tried windvanes and were not satisfied, skipped this most important first step—an easy steering yacht.

It takes time and patience to get a vane to work well. When I first installed the vane on *Seraffyn* it worked about 70 percent of the time. It took me a year of fiddling and changing to improve it to 90 percent. In the next three years I modified every moving part.

Helmer, as I call our self-steerer, will now steer in all conditions, including downwind under bare poles or running with the spinnaker if we have enough apparent wind to actuate the vane. It took a lot of headscratching, cursing, and persistence.

Seraffyn has a transom-hung rudder with a tiller and is one of the easiest and least expensive types of boats to fit a windvane to. You can simply add a small rudder (trimtab) to the trailing edge of the main rudder. This tiny rudder controls the main rudder exactly the same way the main rudder controls the ship (Figure 31.3).

When I built the vane I especially wanted good performance in the light-wind conditions of Southern California. Since friction is the main enemy of light-wind performance, I used teflon bushings on all moving parts of the vane, and I eventually installed teflon bushings on the main rudder's gudgeons and pintles.

To get a more sensitive vane I used thin-wall stainless-steel tubing as a framework and covered it with Dacron. This weighs about one-quarter of what a plywood vane with its counterweight does. I have found my vane of 6 square feet works just as well without a counterweight. Its total weight is only 6 pounds.

My trimtab is 4 feet deep and 4 inches wide with 20 percent of its area forward of the pintle centerline. This balanced effect makes it easier for the windvane to turn the trimtab in light winds. On this

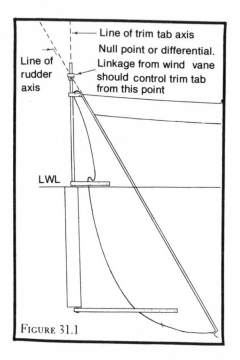

FIGURE 31.1

type of installation you should make the tab narrow and as deep as possible, similar to an aircraft's aileron. It should be about 4 inches from the bottom of the rudder to prevent damage when hauling or grounding.

The most subtle design feature on the trimtab-type vane is rigging the control linkage from the windvane to the trimtab with a null point connection or zero movement point. This can also be called a differential. It should allow the main rudder to move independent of the trimtab and vice versa.

In other words, when the trimtab is moved by the windvane and it in turn swings the main rudder, the trimtab and its linkage should be unaffected by the main rudder's movement (Figure 31.1).

I prefer the trimtab-type of vane with an outboard rudder because it is usually cheaper and simpler to build and because it can't foul lines, driftwood, or flotsam. I can remove our tiller to clear the cockpit, and the vane steers the rudder just as happily. But most trimtab installations on outboard rudders have to be at least partially custom-made and designed so few people rig them themselves.

If your yacht is well balanced the storebought gear is usually the easiest and maybe the cheapest way to go.

When you're testing your new windvane, go offshore 5 or 10 miles to get away from the erratic coastal winds. If the wind is changing quickly, it is hard to know if your vane is holding course or following a wind shift.

A vane gear will work your boat to windward much better than the best helmsman, especially at night. It will pick up every windshift and immediately adjust your course to the ideal sailing angle without tiring or getting bored.

When you are tacking in shifting winds, note the compass course regularly. If in your three-hour watch you observe a gradual lift from due north to 50 degrees magnetic, you can safely plot your course on the chart at the end of your watch as an average made good of 25 degrees. This works just the same if you are being headed and will give a reliable dead reckoning (DR) position.

If you are being headed and cannot lay about 45 or 50 degrees to your rhumb line course, you should note your log reading and time on your chart, then come about. This will put you on the more favorable tack with the wind lifting you closer to your rhumb line instead of slanting away from your desired course. This is a very basic racing tactic. Your windvane will show you the wind shifts. It is up to you to take advantage of them.

Windvanes have their limitations. They need apparent wind to steer your boat. When you are sailing with the wind aft you must subtract the boat's speed from the actual wind speed. In 6 knots of wind with your boat moving 3 knots, the effective or apparent vane-actuating wind velocity is only 3 knots. This is why sailing downwind in light winds is a windvane's weakest area.

Reaching or running, you can expect your windvane to zigzag 5 or 8 degrees either side of your plotted course. Your course made good will average out at the middle figure of the zigzag course. Broad reaching, 7 or 10 degrees wandering can be expected. Dead downwind 5-degree wander either side is standard. This wander depends greatly on sea conditions and wind strength. When broad reaching before a large sea, most boats tend to head up as they accelerate over a wave and down its face. You can help your vane in these conditions by sheeting the jib in 5 or 10 degrees flatter than normal and trimming the mainsail so it luffs as soon as the boat starts to round up. Because the jib is sheeted flatter than normal, it holds the bow down long enough to give the vane time to react and put you back on course.

In stronger conditions you might put a reef in the main or drop it and broadreach under jib alone.

Sailing downwind wing-and-wind I like to split the sail area so it is more or less equal each side. In strong winds and big seas the windvane works well if I put all of my area forward by using the jib or staysail alone. This area all the way forward tends to pull the boat by its nose and assist the vane to keep a good course.

When I raced around Britain on a Sparksman & Stephens fin-and-skeg 30-foot sloop, we had a Hasler pendulum servo-type gear and it worked well until we pushed the boat over 7 knots. At this stage the boat began to wander quickly side to side and we had to hand steer.

The solution when you are not racing is to shorten sail to a more comfortable cruising speed.

Shock cord on the tiller is another way to reduce wander. By tying some tension on one side of the tiller you can eliminate some moderate weather or lee helm. With two shock cords, one port and one starboard, you can limit overcorrecting caused by too strong an apparent wind. With the shock cords, the vane doesn't force the tiller hard aport then hard astarboard. Trial and error will teach you how much tension you need in any given condition.

Remember when adjusting your vane to various conditions, it is only mechanical and cannot anticipate the sea conditions. It can only react after the boat has moved off course.

Like all gear on a boat, a windvane has its disadvantages. The vane is hung over the transom and is susceptible to damage. When you are tied stern-to Mediterranean-style, it is harder to rig a boarding ladder. It is not safe to use the vane approaching harbors or within 3 or 4 miles of the coast especially at night. With only one person on watch and the other asleep, the watchkeeper could nod off or black out. A wind shift could put your vessel, steered by your own vane, on the rocks. Don't laugh—this has happened. To be safe, hand steer within 3 or 4 miles of the coast or stay well off.

On our boat we always keep a watch even if the windvane is working. We recently heard of a vessel using a windvane while approaching the Azores. The skipper reckoned he was 40 miles off the islands and let the crew all go down for a good night's sleep. They were awakened when they hit. The yacht was a total loss. Even though the navigation was in error, a man on watch probably would have seen the islands or heard the surf and saved the ship.

It doesn't pay to fall overboard with an efficient windvane connected. The boat will carry on quietly, leaving your crew sleeping in their bunks. A good friend of ours rigged an interesting safety line. He connected a 100-foot line to his trimtab and knotted the trailing end. He rigged some shock cord to take the initial drag of the line. Whenever he left the cockpit, he threw the safety line overboard. If he happened to fall off the boat while he was trying to work on deck, he figured he could grab the line with its knotted end. The extra drag of his weight would stretch the shock cord. The safety line would turn the trimtab and head the boat into the wind. With the boat's forward motion stopped, he could work up to his boat and climb back on board. But the safest way is to stay on board.

Persist in balancing your hull and rig. Fit your own home-built windvane or install a storebought model. Learn how to help the vane do its job better. Having a full-time efficient windvane is a godsend, as it reduces the number of crew needed. What is more, you can spend your time on watch being extra careful with navigation and sail trim. You can even read a book or study the star charts.

In short, an efficient windvane is the most valuable and most enjoyable piece of cruising gear a yacht can carry.

Update

Off-the-shelf windvanes we have seen used include the Aries, Monitor, and Clearway Auto Steer. The Monitor vane is sold by Scanmar Marine (432 S. 1st St., Richmond, CA 94804-2107; tel. 510-215-2010, fax 510-215-5005, selfsteer@aol.com), which also sells and services other vane gear.

Auto Steer is available from Clearway Design (3 Chough Close, Tregoniggie Ind. Est., Falmouth, Cornwall, TR11 4SN, England; tel. 01-326-376048, fax 01-326-376164).

The Aries windvane, originally produced by Nick Franklin on the Isle of Wight, England, was out of production for a few years but is now being built in Denmark using metric nuts and bolts. It is available from Peter Matthiesen (Ruglokke 30A, 6430 Nordborg, Denmark; tel 7445-0760, fax 4574-459519). Spare parts, using the original nuts and bolts sizes, are now available from Aries Spares (48 St. Thomas St., Penryn, Cornwall, TR10 8JW, England; tel. 01-326-377467).

32

Handy Headsail Dowsing

For easier headsail handling when cruising, try using a jib downhaul. With or without a bowsprit, this is a good piece of gear for single or shorthanded sailing.

I first used a jib downhaul on a 120-ton gaff-rigged schooner I was sailing aboard as we ran from Los Angeles to Honolulu (and back). One crewman could ease the jib sheets, then with the halyard tail secured, he could haul the jib down the forestay without going forward of the mast area. Going forward alone to pull the luff down the headstay on a boat that size could be dangerous.

Then, when the sail was down, he could muzzle the large headsail into the jib net and work out on the bowsprit to secure the sail with gaskets (sail-stops) that were permanently attached to the top of the spar.

A jib downhaul can be just as useful on any shorthanded cruising yacht no matter what size. To rig a jib downhaul, you splice a light line through the eye of the halyard shackle (Figure 32.1). This line should be a small diameter, soft lay, three-strand nylon or Dacron so that it will not jam or kink when hoisting the sail. It should lead down to and through a single block at the tack, then back along the deck to a handy open cleat near the mast.

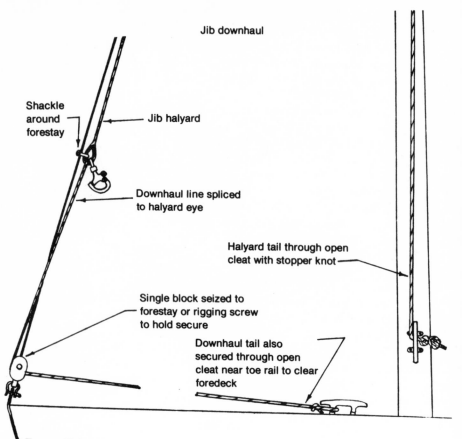

Jib downhaul

Shackle around forestay

Jib halyard

Downhaul line spliced to halyard eye

Halyard tail through open cleat with stopper knot

Single block seized to forestay or rigging screw to hold secure

Downhaul tail also secured through open cleat near toe rail to clear foredeck

FIGURE 32.1

The bitter end of the downhaul line should be secured through the open cleat with a figure-eight knot or a bow line tied around a leg of the cleat. The end of the jib halyard should also be secured in this way.

A shackle put through the eye-splice of the halyard and around the forestay permits you to leave the downhaul and halyard snap shackle in position at the lower end of the forestay. If you have a rod head-stay you might have to modify the snap-shackle arrangement somewhat because of the nicking problems. Check with the headstay manufacturer to be sure your rig is satisfactory.

When the downhaul line is tightened and secured, it holds the sail down and keeps the head of the jib, with its heavy shackle, from swinging around and whacking you on the head while you are working on the foredeck.

When you are ready to hoist your jib, uncleat the downhaul line and coil it on deck ahead of time so it runs free. It may take a bit of time to work all the kinks out of a new piece of line so be patient and watch it carefully when you are pulling on the halyard. If your jib has a wire luff and the hanks are of minimum size, the bending of the luff wire can cause the hanks to twist and jam on the headstay. Larger hanks will usually solve this hang-up. Rope luff or stretchy luff sails are better and downhaul like a dream.

Other advantages of the downhaul shackled to the forestay are that the halyard cannot be lost accidentally halfway up the mast; you simply pull it back with the downhaul line. Your downhaul also can double as a stowing pennant to keep the halyard from banging against the mast. Finally, this inexpensive piece of gear also allows you to send the anchor light aloft easily and quickly. And you can get it down again as well.

The next time you take your jib down alone, think about how much safer and more convenient it might be if you eased the halyard, then pulled the jib down to the deck or jib net while you stood safely back near the mast.

33

Idle Boats Make Rotten Hulls

We got a written reply from the retired Admiral of the British Navy, head of the Cutty Sark Preservation Society, "Twenty years ago we decided to keep *Cutty Sark* in dry dock. As you know, good timber will keep indefinitely if either completely dry or completely wet. We chose to keep her dry."

The finest surviving example of a wooden clipper ship is sitting out in the English rain, neither completely wet nor completely dry, rotting and shrinking, costing the Cutty Sark Society thousands of pounds each year for repairs mainly for the lack of the *Cutty Sark's* natural element, salt water. It is only 100 yards away in the tidal Thames.

Don't give your wooden vessel a steady diet of rain water and twenty lashes with the fresh water hose. Salt her down! This, along with good ventilation will probably make her last as long as the Falmouth Oyster cutters. These beautiful sailing smacks, built of pitch pine on oak and fastened with iron, are almost all "three score and ten." One regularly working cutter is actually 160 years old! They dredge for oysters eight months in the winter. In the summer they race in local regattas as the working boat class. Arfie Trenier, who owns and fishes the very fast *Magdalena*, observed, "The boats that sit on the mooring all winter have much more problem with rot than the boats that work dragging oyster trawls."

The cutters that are dredging are constantly being washed down with salt water. The unused ones, hanging on their moorings, get only rain water.

Keep your boat swollen up tight and free from rot by washing her down at dusk so the salt water will have all night to seep down into the nooks and crannies. Salt water put on during the day evaporates before it has time to do its work. With rot the prevention can be much easier than the cure!

Along with salt water baths at dusk, the old working vessels that were fitted with ceiling used to have boxes between their frame heads. These containers had small holes in the bottom and held lumps of rock salt. Moisture collected by the salt kept a steady drip of brine running under the ceiling to pickle the hull right down to the bilges. I have seen these boxes on a Baltic trader that was cruising in Mexico, and after eighty years the unpainted oak of the 90-foot long vessel was still hard and sound.

Good air circulation is as important to your boat as clean air is to your lungs. A lot of potential rot spots are built into wooden hulls and I would suspect rot in any area of a boat that has restricted air flow—closed-in bulwark rails, narrow counter sterns, or behind permanent closed ceilings. These pockets of still warm air are breeding grounds for mold and rot spores.

The cure?

Create ventilation. Drill holes in any enclosed space. Don't use wall-to-wall carpets that will trap the air in the bilge. Make floorboards removable with 1-inch fingerholes. Rather than fit the floorboards tight to the frames and planking (a difficult and time-consuming job) have kickboards fastened to the frames (Figure 33.1). These kickboards will allow free air circulation between the frames and down into the bilge.

A tongue-and-groove or tight-fitted ceiling permanently fastened from stem to stern hides a multitude of problems. You can't clean or paint behind it. The ventilation is restricted, and you can't inspect for bad fastenings, fresh water pockets, or rot.

Internal ceiling was originally used in large working sailing boats

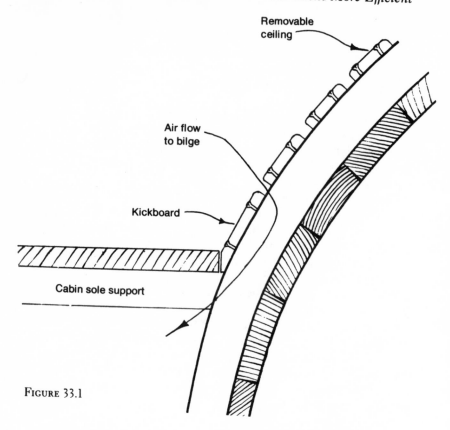

Removable ceiling

Air flow to bilge

Kickboard

Cabin sole support

FIGURE 33.1

for extra structural strength and protection. If cargo was mistakenly dropped in the hold, it didn't spring the planks. Since you are not carrying cargo in most yachts, even open ceiling should only be used where necessary, next to bunks or for esthetic reasons. This ceiling should be made of fore-and-aft slats with ¼-inch gaps between each one, fastened down with oval or raised head screws (Figure 33.1). The screws, instead of nails, allow easy removal for inspection, maintenance or emergency repairs at sea. The gap allows adequate air flow.

Sheer clamps (called a beam shelf in England) fitted up tight to the deck restrict air flow. Ideally the deck beams should rest on the top of the sheer clamp and allow air movement around the clamp and between the deck and planking (Figure 33.2).

Open slat partitions are better for storage lockers used to hold damp things such as line, warps, anchors, and sails. Lightweight, easy-to-build, well-ventilated sail bins can be made with nylon fish nets.

Lin recently complained, "My onions and potatoes are spoiling in their locker." The drain holes to the bilge were not enough ventilation. So I bored several 1-inch holes in an inconspicuous side of the locker and—presto, no rotten spuds. If the potatoes were rotting, so in time could our wooden hull.

Be extra careful of fresh water pockets, especially leaks from your icebox and sink. Make sure butt blocks on your planking have ¼-inch gaps on either side or bevelled tops so water does not get trapped.

Frame heads should be sawn off with an inboard slant so water will run off (Figure 33.2). The bottom of the mast step mortice should have a hole for drainage. (A copper coin under the mast was not just for luck but had practical reasons. The coin gave off copper sulphate, the basis of most anti-rot preparations.)

I would sooner sell my little cutter and buy a farm than paint out my varnished spars. The mast is the crankshaft of the sailing vessel. Engineers would love to have a little X-ray window to look at the condition of the bearing inserts or crankshafts of their engines. With

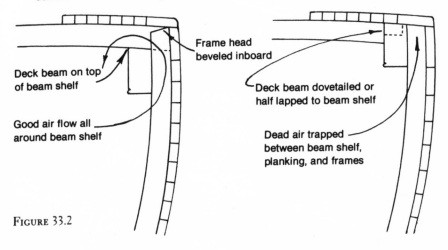

Frame head
beveled inboard

Deck beam on top
of beam shelf

Deck beam dovetailed or
half lapped to beam shelf

Good air flow all
around beam shelf

Dead air trapped
between beam shelf,
planking, and frames

FIGURE 33.2

varnished spars you have that window and can see the darkening caused by fresh water seeping into the wood, under tangs and around fittings, before it becomes rot. You can observe the condition of your glue joints.

Going aloft every six months to inspect your spar and rigging is a must, and so it is not much extra work to sand the spar as you do your inspecting on the way up, then varnish on the way down. On a 40-foot spar it can usually be done in about six hours. Paint out your spar and you still have to go aloft to inspect twice a year, but you won't be able to see the actual condition of your mast.

A wooden spar has all the ventilation it needs, but must be protected from fresh water. (I hope you rarely get good old salt water at the masthead.) I use 1/16-inch copper sheet to line my halyard sheave box. It protects against the chafe of halyards. Wood chafed bare at the masthead can absorb fresh water, causing rot. Thin copper sheet covering the top and rolled over the radiused edge of your spreader, bedded in with mastic, will eliminate rot and the need to paint or varnish the top of your spreader. Spreader failure is the most common cause of mast failure.

Removing the rot caused by a thin layer of fiber-glass and polyester resin laid over one lamination of fir plywood on decks and cabins is the most common repair job I have done. The flexing of the boat causes the butt joints of the plywood, which are usually landed on the relatively narrow top of a deck beam, to work and crack the single layer of nonflexible glass. The minute cracks allow fresh water into the end grain of the plywood and cause rot that spreads very quickly.

One solution to this problem is to glue the butt joints with resorcinol glue, apply wood preservatives, then paint and apply nonskid right on the plywood. This allows the wood to breathe from both sides. Water can't be trapped under a layer of glass.

Another solution is to buy good quality mahogany plywood which is much more resistant to rot than fir, and instead of using a single 1/2-inch layer, use two layers of 1/4-inch plywood. Stagger the butt joints and glue both layers of ply together with resorcinol glue. This will stop any movement and give a stronger deck. Now apply your resin glass to the bare plywood. Two or three layers will resist cracking better than one.

If your fore and aft decks are laid tongue and groove, a flexible canvas covering is better than resin glass as you are almost certain to get cracks caused by the movement of the many seams. Epoxy resin is supposed to be more flexible than polyester resins and could be used in place of canvas and paint, but the two-part epoxy resins are hard to work as you can't control curing time.

If you add a layer of teak over plywood, bed the teak in resorcinol glue (Figure 33.3). I didn't realize how great the rot-preventive and waterproofing characteristics of resorcinol glue were until I had the job of modifying the afterdeck and cockpit of a fourteen-year-old 40-foot cutter in Poole, England. One side of the deck had been damaged in a collision and the repair had been done by substituting white lead between the teak and the mahogany plywood. The rest of the teak was still bedded in resorcinol, the work of the original builder. As I ripped up the whole 15 feet of afterdeck, all the areas of plywood under the white lead were rotten. But just like night and day, the plywood under the waterproof resorcinol glue was perfectly sound.

One word of warning about plywood. I was talking to a boat-building friend from Canada's West Coast. He said he now had to order special plywood with all laminations solid fir because lately even the marine grade fir plywood was being produced with a hemlock core. Hemlock has a very *low* resistance to rot. To avoid the problem, solid Bruynzeel mahogany plywood to British standard 1066 is the best bet.

All jointed surfaces such as the edges of plywood bulkheads, where planking fits to frames, or where fittings are fastened to the hull, deck, or spars, should be sealed in some way. The very best product I

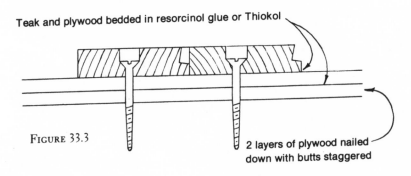

Teak and plywood bedded in resorcinol glue or Thiokol

FIGURE 33.3

2 layers of plywood nailed down with butts staggered

know of for this job is fungicidal Dolphinite. I have removed two bulwark strakes from a wood stanchion on a five-year-old boat. The lower strake was bedded in Dolphinite and the jointed surfaces of both the mahogany bulwark strake and the oak stanchion were in perfect condition. The other strake, not sealed with Dolphinite, had fresh water in the joint and had started to rot. The rot stopped right where the Dolphinite began.

Wooden boats don't have to rot. The more you use them the better. Each time you open the companionway you'll increase the ventilation. Each time you head out to sea you can't help but get salt water on the boat. With proper open construction, lots of salt water, and lots of use, a wooden boat will last longer than its builder.

34

A Near-fatal Bit of Carelessness

This article was written six years ago and it tells of the closest call we had during our ten-and-a-half-year circumnavigation.

For four-and-a-half years we'd cruised half the world aboard our 24-foot cutter *Seraffyn*. All that time we kept reminding ourselves that the sea watches for the unwary. As a result, until yesterday even our worst mistake resulted in no more than some scraped paint when the tide swept us against a fairway buoy.

Yesterday, however, we were almost killed by a very simple bit of carelessness while lying peacefully moored in front of the Royal Norfolk and Suffolk Yacht Club.

We had had a nice dinner aboard in the evening. Since it was cold and drizzly, we turned on our heater, lit the oil lamps, and played a game of gin rummy. A heavy rain set in, so we closed our skylight hatch and at 2200 got ready for bed.

I climbed in first; Larry blew out the lamps and joined me. It was much cooler in the forward cabin, since we have a 3-inch ventilator in the chain locker. So we left the propane heater on, as we had on other nights, and went to sleep, cozy and secure in our double bunk.

At 0600 we both woke up with headaches. Larry got us two aspirins each, then I went into the main cabin to use the head. That is the last thing I remember.

Larry said the sound of my falling woke him. He rushed from the bunk and found me unconscious on the cabin sole, deathly white. He pulled me up onto the settee but I was still out, so he opened the sliding hatch to let in some cold air. Slowly I came to. I was hysterical and possibly delirious, and I can still remember a horrible sense of fear as I lay on the forward bunk recovering.

Gradually it dawned on us that our watertight boat was airtight also, and we had both been slowly suffocating from carbon monoxide. More fresh air had us feeling better, but it took most of the day to get over the nauseous feeling.

One open ventilator obviously wasn't enough for the whole boat. We had had only headaches while in the forward bunk within 5 feet of the air scoop. Only when I went aft and sat down in the main cabin was I overcome—because we had shut the main skylight.

Today, one of the members of the yacht club told us about the worst tragedy of the season on the Norfolk Broads. Two couples were found dead, sitting around an uneaten dinner on board their small cruiser. The wailing of a small baby attracted the attention of some people strolling on the pier. They found the child in the forepeak of the boat, near the chain locker with its open chain pipe. Its parents had died 10 feet away in the main cabin, warm and secure against the cold night, suffocated by their charcoal stove.

Carbon-monoxide suffocation is painless. The only signs are a tired feeling and maybe a headache. Fortunately preventive ventilation is easy to achieve. One opening forward is not enough, since it doesn't create a flow of air. But a large ventilator, hatch, or port light open forward *and* one aft provides good through-ventilation. Without this flow of oxygen, we found, death waits in the cheery glow of a cabin heater.

A WORD OF WARNING

For safety, any heater that burns solid or liquid fuel (as opposed to passive heaters, such as electrical or water-circulating heaters) should have a smoke stack and smoke head designed to vent the CO_2 gases. This must be used in tandem with adequate airflow to prevent suffocation. Boats are amazingly airtight structures, and dorade vents, plus one other air source, are best for any boat with a heater.

35

Winter Projects for a Cool Summer

Most sailors consider sun awnings and windscoops specialized equipment for cruising boats on their way south to the tropics. Yet even in northern climates like the Puget Sound and Great Lakes, a two-week summer cruise can be less than fun when long hot days and constant sun glare turn your boat into an oven. Headaches, eyestrain, sweaty sleepless nights, restless overheated children and sunburned shoulders can all be prevented by building some summer sailing gear now.

Even racing sailors should be able to carry the lightweight items that help you cool your boat. This in fact is one of the keys to the best boat air-conditioning devices. They must be lightweight. They also must be easy to store, simple to make, and inexpensive, since they could need replacing every two or three seasons. To make sure you use sun covers, windscoops, and port light coolers, they must be very easy to put in place. But even more important, they must be easy and fast to remove. In the calmest, most sheltered anchorage, summer squalls can come up without warning. The strong gusts of wind could threaten the strongest sun cover. Your boat could start to drag or your neighbor could start to drag into you. That's when you'll want your sun cover and wind scoop out of the way quickly so you can handle the ground tackle and maneuver with clear decks and full visibility.

SUN COVERS

We carry two separate sun covers on *Seraffyn*. One is a simple 3 foot by 4 foot piece of heavyweight, waterproof canvas, strongly reinforced at each edge. There is a 5 foot long, ¼-inch diameter line spliced into each of its corners. At sea this little shade patch can be set up in all sorts of ways to provide a cool spot for the watchkeeper. Since it is strong and small it can be left up in winds up to 25 knots. It can be strung between the boom gallows frame and a shroud to provide cocktail hour protection from a glaring late day sun. It also works as a side curtain when our full sun awning is in place at anchor.

After experimenting with dozens of sun cover ideas, we've come up with several don'ts. Don't use Dacron sail cloth; it is noisy and won't last more than two seasons. Avoid wooden battens; they break too easy. Don't build a cover that goes forward of the mast; it is too difficult to put up, so you probably won't use it unless you've anchored for a long stay. Worse yet, once you have it up, you'll be reluctant to sail to a new spot because disassembling the cover will take too much time. Don't build side curtains directly onto the cover; they'll make it too bulky and cut off stray breezes so your cockpit becomes like the inside of a tent.

We've found white acrilon (synthetic canvas) is best for long-lasting sun covers. It is strong and quiet in a breeze. On hot drizzly days, acrilon is water-resistant enough to serve as a rain shelter. This way you can leave your sliding hatch open for ventilation and arriving guests will have a semi-dry place to shed their boots and foul weather gear before climbing below decks. For added luxury, a layer of ¾-ounce blue nylon (spinnaker cloth) on the bottom side of the cover will cut down glare and make you feel even cooler.

For poles we use two-part aluminum tubes that socket together. Wooden knobs with holes drilled through them make end fittings that don't chafe the hold-down lines. We've placed tennis balls over the ends of each pole so nothing gets scratched when we're storing the cover away.

Measuring for a sun cover

The most convenient size is as shown, with one end secured to the mast, the other to the back stay

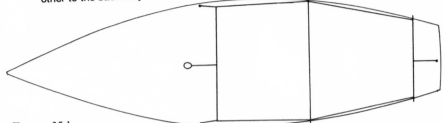

FIGURE 35.1

We've found that a cover reaching from the backstay to 1 foot aft of the mast and measuring the same width as the boat works well. By placing grommets between each tie-down, we can secure our small sun shade to cut glare when the sun gets near the horizon.

A strip of velcro running along the top edge of your cover could be used to attach a mosquito netting if this is a problem where you sail. Sandbag weights on the bottom of the net will hold it in place. I'd make sure this additional netting could be quickly removed or the weights will become a flying menace when a squall comes up.

We set our cover above the boom, one end tied to the backstay, the other to the mast. Three tie-downs per side seem to be sufficient. We secure them with a running hitch so that getting the cover down is quite easy. If we are in a real hurry, both of us get right aft of the cover, untie one line at a time and roll the cover into the wind.

Once each edge of your sun cover is turned over and reinforced, fold the cover in half and secure a ⅜ inch Dacron line along the center.

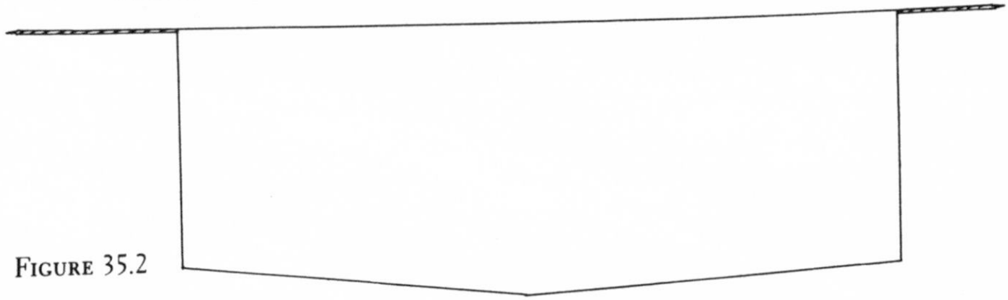

FIGURE 35.2

To stretch the canvas along the poles, secure a line to the reinforced grommets on the cover and run the line through the holes in the wooden end fittings. This same line then runs down to a handy tie down spot such as your lifelines.

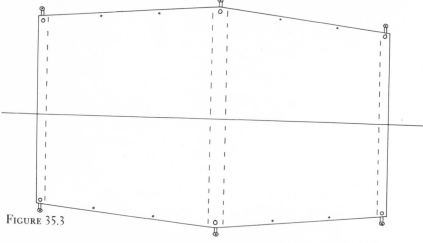

FIGURE 35.3

We've been able to do this in up to 50-knot squalls. Rolled this way the cover makes a 9-foot-long package that is difficult to store away completely. So for passages we disassemble the aluminum poles, fold the cover in half, and roll it tightly. Our 9-foot-by-12-foot cover stores in a space 4$\frac{1}{2}$ feet by 7 inches and weighs about 9 pounds complete.*

WIND SCOOPS

Probably the most effective piece of boat-cooling equipment you can carry is a galley sail or wind scoop. This fabric contraption catches each breeze and directs it through your hatch into the cabin.

There are several commercially made winds scoops available, but most of them are too large and too complicated. They also have wood or metal spreaders and positioners which knock and beat against hatch coamings in a 10-knot breeze. The scoop we've come to depend on has no solid parts and folds to the size of a T-shirt.

We make a 4-foot-tall, semi-flat spinnaker out of unbleached muslin or very soft, lightweight nylon. At the head and 1 foot down each luff of the wind scoop, there are small grommets with 6 feet of

*See the update at the end of this chapter.

Cutting out a simplified wind scoop

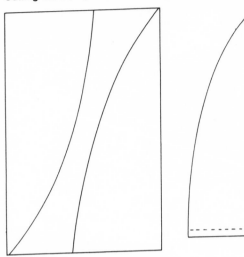

A piece of fabric 1½ yards long by 36 inches wide will yield a four-foot tall wind scoop

To finish the wind scoop, seam up the center, turn up the bottom edge and insert shock cord, tie six-foot lines to each grommet. There is no need to turn over the luffs of the scoop if they are formed by the selvage of the fabric.

FIGURE 35.4

Dacron line permanently spliced in place. These lines are tied to the forestay and two shrouds. They can be switched to adjust the mouth of the scoop directly into the wind. The bottom of the scoop has a ¼-inch shock cord run through a strong hem. This snaps over the hatch coamings. We have a snap at each corner of our coaming for a hatch cover. This is enough to keep the scoop in place. Four small hooks at the corners of your hatch will serve this same purpose.

This simple scoop sends an amazing amount of air into the cabin. Even in the deep tropics we found the bunk in the forepeak, directly under the wind scoop, cooler at night than the bunk out on deck. During our summer time run down the Red Sea, we found we could keep the wind scoop in place even while we sailed. Since we were running, we oriented the mouth aft. It didn't interfere with sail changes at all. Even in 110-degree temperatures the wind scoop breeze made cooking below possible.

In harbor you'll get the best out of your scoop if you lay at anchor where cooling breezes can reach you unobstructed by other boats and buildings. Since sailboats will usually lay bow into the wind you won't have to adjust your scoop for each wind shift.

Best of all, if you secure the scoop holding lines with a round turn, two half-hitches and a running bight, getting it down and out of the way is simple. Just jerk on three lines, unsnap the shock cord and toss the wind scoop down the hatch. It won't scratch or mar anything.

PORT SCOOPS

Another way to direct cooling air into your cabin is with plastic port scoops. You'll see these in the portholes of large commercial ships, usually in the form of cut-out buckets. If you have round port lights, your job is easy. Find a deep plastic container that will just jam into the openings. Cut away most of the part that faces forward but leave the bottom of the container intact. For square or rectangular ports you'll have to try plastic bread loaf containers or other types of storage boxes.

What is especially nice about these scoops is that they can be left in place when it rains. They'll deflect water away from your port light but invite the cooling breeze in. In the Puget Sound where night time rains and hot weather come at the same time, the breeze these scoops provide will help you avoid that muggy, closed-in feeling.

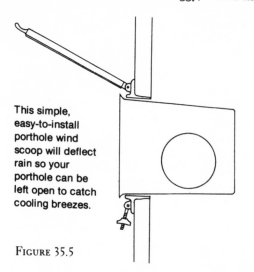

This simple, easy-to-install porthole wind scoop will deflect rain so your porthole can be left open to catch cooling breezes.

FIGURE 35.5

SUMMER SLIPCOVERS

A final summer-cooling idea we discovered, due to necessity in Malaysia's hot sticky climate, was simple cotton slipcovers for all of our cushions. These are tailored sacks of soft, dark-colored, pure cotton which slide snugly over the cushions we use most. They secure in place with a drawstring.

We have two sets so we feel free to use them on our cockpit cushions. The slipcovers turn the stickiest plastic-covered cushion into a luxurious seat or mattress. They are easy to wash, so salt-water bathing suits are no problem.

With these slipcovers we can have the maintenance advantages of naugahyde-covered, waterproof, long-lasting, stain-resistant cushions throughout the boat for deep-sea passages plus the luxury of nonsticky, nonsweaty fabrics for hot days in port.

Update

From page 266: Andy, an American sailmaker cruising on his large sloop, *Jakaranda,* added a fine water-collection system to our sun awning with only about two hours' work. He sewed four fabric udders to the cover, 3 inches in from the edges at the middle of each section. We lash lengths of hose to each udder and lead them to various watertanks. During a 20-minute squall we have sometimes collected 60 or 70 gallons of water with his system. When we do not need to collect rain water, the udders can be rolled up and kept out of the way with tiny straps that Andy has placed right next to the collection holes.

Cruising Isn't Easy

Many sailors dream of setting off into the perfect world of ocean voyaging. "Once this boat is complete, outfitted, and I've got cruising funds set aside for three years, my problems will be over," they tell themselves. It's these sailors who return to the safety offered by the regularity of a shoreside life within five or six months.

A cruising life is challenging, interesting, full of variety, sometimes exciting, sometimes frightening, but it's rarely easy. The most difficult problems come about because services you took for granted when you lived in a shoreside community are now luxuries or a frustrating maze of unfamiliarity.

The following chapters will give you an idea of some of the problems you may encounter. Set out prepared for language difficulties, business problems, and shoreside confusion caused by new customs, and you may find it's all a challenge that makes cruising even more interesting. But don't expect frustrations, delays, decisions, and confusion to end when you wave good-bye to your old friends and finally head out to sea.

36

The Curse of Cruising

"It must be wonderful to wander about like you do—no cares, no worries." I guess our cruising life must look that way to outsiders, but sometimes I think we've exchanged the complex problems of shore life for a whole new set of nuisances that are all the more frustrating for their outwardly simple appearance. Our mail gets lost; it's always a hassle to get money transferred from our account in one country to the country we're in; and just like a shore-based family, once a week we end up with a great big bag of dirty clothes. But unlike most homes, ours doesn't have a washing machine. Not only that, but we haven't running water and since each gallon of water we use must be carried or transferred from shore, we can't easily do our washing by hand on board and just hang it out to dry. The corner launderette would be the most obvious solution, but in 60 percent of the ports and harbors we visit, they don't exist. That's why we've come to call our laundry the curse of cruising.

Salt water just doesn't do the trick. Soap doesn't foam up. Clothes washed in salt don't dry well and the minute they get near water again they feel damp. Underwear washed in salt water soon creates a rash on sensitive skin. So even on longer ocean passages we save our laundry until we get ashore.

As we enter each new harbor we sail by any yachts we recognize. After the usual happy greetings someone almost always shouts something like, "There's a lady in the green house next to the post

For us on a
cruising budget,
it was devastating

office who does laundry." I used to grab at the chance to have the "lady in the green house" scrub my dirty clothes, but a few odd experiences have made me less enthusiastic.

In Cabo San Lucas the crews of several large sportfishing charter boats suggested a washing woman I'll call Anna. "Is she expensive?" I asked. They assured me she wasn't. I asked Anna how much my 20-pound bag of laundry would cost. "Not very much, I only charge for the time your laundry takes." Two days later I had the scrubbed, dried, ironed, and folded clothes back with a bill for $12 (5 pounds sterling). That might not have seemed high for a charter boat that charged $1,000 (400 pounds sterling) a week, but for us on a cruising budget it was devastating.

I learned from that. I asked for an exact price before I turned any more laundry over.

In Guaymas, Mexico, it rained twice each day. I finally gave up my attempts to dry my laundry and asked a taxi driver if he knew a lady for me. "Yes, I do. My sister. Come with me." I rode through the hills of Guaymas, over rutted roads full of puddles, chickens, and children. "This taxi ride alone is going to cost me a fortune," I said to myself. My taxi driver spoke with his sister and then told me, "For 20 pesos your laundry will be done and I'll deliver it to you." I agreed

This taxi ride alone is going to cost me a fortune

immediately, for $1.60 (62 pence) seemed a very fair price. Sure enough, the next day my laundry arrived on the quay. "My sister had to hang your things around her fire to dry." I could tell. Everything smelled of smoke. For the next few weeks we walked around perfumed with the aroma of pine smoke.

Not all of our laundry experiences have been unusual, but our average seems rather poor—overcharges, missing socks and bikini tops, clothes pounded on rocks till the colors came out, voyages delayed for a day or two while the lady finally finishes washing the last towels. Then you figure the time it takes to carry your laundry to town, find a washing lady, return to pick it all up, pay the lady, and then carry it back to the boat again. After eleven years of cruising we came to the conclusion that unless there is a coin laundry within walking distance, it's easier financially and timewise to find a local water tap and do our own.

To get really clean clothes, I separate my colors and whites. I put the white clothes in a bucket of fresh water with soap and a bit of bleach and let the bucket sit in the sun for a full day. The next day I take everything ashore along with a soft bristle brush, liquid soap, and two buckets. I scrub a rock or plank clean and then proceed to scrub each piece of laundry with the brush, adding water, and liquid soap to my heart's content. Even my husband usually pitches in, rinsing each piece five or six times and then wringing it dry. Clad in a bikini, sun beating on my back, even this chore becomes fun. We return to *Seraffyn* and string our laundry from the lifelines, putting on extra clothespins if there is any breeze at all.

A friend of ours with a larger yacht and two nap-aged children, has a 20-gallon pail with a secure top. She fills her pail halfway with clothes, soap, and water and then lashes it on the stern deck as she heads out to sea. The motion of the boat agitates the clothes for twelve or twenty-four hours and a quick rinse in the next port finishes the laundry off. But, if she is harborbound for a week, she too is reduced to handwashing.

Most of our cruising friends agree with us about sheets and towels. It is impossible to keep white things white without the aid of a good washing machine and hot water. They soon look grey. So most of us use light blue or green linens. They may not be as sparkly as they would look if they were washed ashore properly, but at least they don't look dingy.

We try to show a bit of extra respect when we are moored at a yacht club by not flying our laundry after noon. We do this since many of the clubs who so kindly offer their facilities to us serve lunches to their members. A yacht dressed with flags presents a beautiful sight, but my undies and dish towels aren't quite so elegant.

Taking care of laundry on a cruise is a real nuisance. Even in the tropics where only a bikini is necessary, dish towels, sheets, and pillow cases constantly fill the laundry bag. But it's a small price to pay for the thrill of new landfalls, sunny shores, and a fine sailing breeze.

Many of the clubs who so kindly offer their facilities to us, serve lunch to their members

37

Cruising, Guns, Pirates, and Thieves

Should cruising sailors have guns on board? Will firearms protect you from pirates? Will they prevent thieves from taking your boat's equipment?

We've put a lot of thought into these problems. When we set off eleven years ago on *Seraffyn*, we carried a Lee Enfield .303 and a .22-caliber revolver. Larry's father had suggested we carry his old .303 for protection and a boat-building friend insisted we take the handgun as a gift to protect ourselves in the wilds of Mexico. As we wandered through the Sea of Cortez and along the western coast of Mexico we only once made use of the rifle for target practice. A year into our cruise we arrived in Acapulco to hear a distressing story.

A cruising couple had anchored for the day near Chamela, a secluded bay in an area know as "Mexico's Wild West" halfway between Mazatlan and Acapulco. When some fishermen came alongside for a chat the conversation turned to hunting and soon the couple were ashore with their .22 rifle. As evening fell, the local fishermen, who had no firearms of their own, built a campfire and the cruising couple joined in, drinking Mexican beer. The wife, who understood Spanish quite well, heard one of the fishermen suggest taking the rifle, then holding her and her husband while the Mexicans robbed their yacht. She whispered to her husband and when they stood up to leave, the Mexicans jumped her husband while she ran into the bush. Somehow in the ensuing struggle, the rifle went off and the American man was shot through the neck. The bullet lodged against his spine. The woman somehow dragged her husband to the dinghy and got him on board, then sailed to Acapulco for medical help. He survived after three weeks of intensive care. Meanwhile the Mexican authorities relentlessly hunted down the Mexican fishermen and quickly had them in jail for a long term. The authorities explained that they wouldn't put up with the publicity from events such as this which could hurt their vital tourist industry. The port captain made a point of telling each new cruising arrival, "Do not carry a gun among people you don't know. Don't drink with people you've just met and can't communicate with." This incident started us rethinking the whole idea of guns on board. Could our own weapon be turned against us to rob, wound, or kill us?

Two years later in Cartegena, Colombia, where over 74 percent of the work force was unemployed and burglary was therefore rampant, we met the chief of police who took a real fancy to *Seraffyn*. While we lay at anchor in the beautiful, secluded lagoon behind his office, we asked him about defending ourselves with our rifle. His comments gave us more food for thought, "If you confront an armed burglar with your rifle, he's got to shoot you because you may kill him. So if he kills you you've wasted your life for some material possessions. If on the other hand you kill him, you'll spend months straightening out the bureaucratic problems which could include spending time in jail yourself and going to court. Then you might find you've killed the father of four children who were close to starvation—a man who was looking for any possible way to feed them. It's better to lock up your valuables or tie near a guard or stand anchor watch if you are worried."

We left Cartegena bound for Jamaica and there our rifle debate was settled. The customs and immigration officials were warm and welcoming until they asked us, "Do you have any firearms on board?" We showed them our rifle and their attitude toward us changed immediately. They insisted on placing the rifle in a locker they could seal. Then we had to fill out special forms relating to the purpose of our firearms and stating we would forfeit our vessel if we sold the rifle in Jamaica. Two weeks later when we wanted to repair the chronometer which was sealed in the same locker, the officials resented the inconvenience of having to come out and open the sealed locker, then reseal it again. We also had to have them on board at our departure to prove we had not broken the seals. That is the only time in eleven years of voyaging and delivering yachts that we have been the victims of obvious resentment from customs officials. Our rifle was a threat to their country and a nuisance to them. It was a nuisance to us and when we reached the United States, we sold it.

Since then we've cruised about twenty-six more countries from Scandinavia, through Europe to the Far East. We've sailed down the Red Sea, where most pirate stories originate, and to the Philippines without any firearms on board.

Then in March of 1978, Peer Tangvald sailed into Manila harbor and moored his 50-foot engineless gaff-schooner, *L'Aretmis de Pytheas*, 100 yards away from *Seraffyn*. Since we had been influenced by Peer's book *Sea Gypsy* and chose to voyage without an engine also, we quickly became friends. Within a few days, Peer's wife Lydia, a spunky attractive twenty-six-year-old French girl and I were out shopping together. Somehow our conversation turned to pickpockets. Lydia opened her purse and showed me the revolver she kept with her at all times.

Less than eleven months later, we heard a shocking report. Lydia was dead, the indirect victim of her own weapon. These first reports which were broadcast by Jane DeRidder from her ham radio on *Magic Dragon*, were later confirmed by Peer in a letter to the Seven Seas Cruising Association.

Peer and Lydia, with their three-year-old son Tomas, were sailing south through the Sulu Sea bound from the Philippines to Borneo when a motor vessel approached. Lydia wanted to fire a warning shot, but Peer told her not to get the revolver since the approaching vessel might be manned by fishermen who wanted to trade for some whiskey. Besides, Peer believed that if they happened to be pirates, compliance would be the best tactic.

Unknown to Peer, Lydia went below, got her gun, and climbed out the forehatch. When the motorboat came alongside, Lydia shouted, then shot off her gun. A shot was immediately returned from the wheelhouse. Lydia fell overboard dead. After that, the Philippinos did board *L'Aretmis de Pytheas*, took Lydia's gun which lay on the deck plus the cash Peer had on board. They left Peer to sail on in the light breeze.

When we read Peer's story, we were left wondering if the boarders had been innocent fishermen startled into their murderous act by Lydia's aggression. We've become even more convinced that carrying firearms might have gotten us into serious trouble if we had used poor judgment in a tense situation. *We know that in our eleven years of cruising we have never heard of one instance when a gun got any sailor out of a tight situation.*

No other kind of tourist carries weapons when he goes to visit a foreign country. So the yachtsman who sails in with weapons projects distrust and fear. How are locals to know you are friendly and not pirates yourselves if your weapons are in view or the officials let it be known that you have weapons on board? The people you meet might be less likely to invite you into their lives. How would you feel if a foreign yacht came into your home port, bristling with weapons?

Someone will say the answer is to hide your guns. Gordon Yates, who has sailed his 28-foot Great Dane sloop *Amøbel* from Denmark to California, gave this some careful thought, then wrote, "If you give your gun to the officials when you enter port, pirates or thieves will know for sure you are unarmed. If you hide your gun and deny having one on board and the officials search and find it, kiss your boat good-bye."

There are very few countries where it is legal to enter without declaring your weapons, yet there is a fifty-fifty chance that the customs officials will not remember to ask if you have one on board. We were arrested in Tunisia for anchoring next to the country's main ammunition dump. We'd done so in complete innocence, choosing the calmest spot to anchor during a blow. When we were taken into custody, seventeen different officials searched through *Seraffyn* looking for firearms. They even unrolled our sun cover and sleeping bags to check. If they'd have found any guns, we'd have been in a real mess, even though no customs officials had asked about weapons or even looked inside *Seraffyn* when we entered the country. As it was we were released four hours later when the Tunisian officials were satisfied with our identification and innocence.

Pirates are the main reason cruising people give for carrying weapons. They do exist in some parts of the world, but stories of the number of attacks on yachts and the results of attacks have been vastly exaggerated.

For two years after Suez Canal reopened, we were cruising in the Mediterranean and heard stories of ferocious pirates attacking every yacht that sailed past Socotra Island at the entrance to the Gulf of Aden. Stripped yachts, maimed sailors, blood from waterline to masthead—the stories were each more wild and frightening. After a while we realized that every report mentioned either a retired Swedish-American cruising man or a 41-foot Taiwan-built ketch. Finally, just before we were ready to sail down the Red Sea we met Gus, the 65-year-old Swedish-American cruising sailor who had hove to in his 41-foot Taiwan-built ketch just 3 miles off Socotra Island to get some rest and repair storm damage to his rigging. Fishermen from Socotra boarded his boat and did damage the toerails in doing so. They put him under tow and headed for an anchorage. When they didn't reach their goal by nightfall, the fisherman took most of Gus's food, then cast him free. There were no weapons involved. They did not threaten Gus's life and as Gus pointed out, even the *British Admiralty Sailing Directions* warn all seamen to avoid Socotra because of the inhabitants' bad reputation as pirates and thieves. It turned out that every story we'd heard had been a different version of the same incident.

When reports in the United States somehow stated that over three hundred yachts in the Caribbean had gone missing and were probably victims of pirates or drug runners, further research by a congressional committee found the true number of yachts unaccounted for was actually about thirty, and some of these later turned up. Evidence proved others had been lost due to sailing mishaps.

Prudent sailors can easily avoid those areas where recently confirmed evidence of pirating exists. Listen to people who have actually just voyaged through the area and use their up-to-date information to plan your route through areas like the Red Sea or South China Sea. We met five Australian sailors who'd come up the Red Sea while we were planning to sail south from Rhodes to the Indian Ocean. Their two-month-old information regarding which areas to avoid made our passage down the Red Sea uneventful. We did stop in Egypt, and had it been cooler we'd have visited the Sudan. We felt free to seek refuge in some offshore island groups owned by North Yemen and we were made welcome in Aden. But we did not sail within 50 miles of Eritrea or Ethiopia. We did not stop in Djibouti since the Australians confirmed news broadcasts that these countries were in a state of unrest.

Don't discount fair warning by local officials. All of us visiting Manila in 1978 were warned by the harbor master and immigration officials that there was deep unrest among the Moros of the Sulu Sea. We were advised against sailing in this area unless we requested and stayed with a Philippine military escort.

Don't rely on old information to plan your cruise since danger areas do change. Three years ago the Gulf of Thailand was considered a delightful place to cruise with exquisite offshore islands and the exotic city of Bangkok as a lure. Now with the Vietnamese and Cambodian refugees using rickety boats to seek freedom, these waters have become a bonanza for pirates who rob the boat poeple of their last valuables. Don Johnson, whom we also met in Manila on board 49-foot *Styx*, sailed toward Bangkok and was concerned when a motor vessel full of shouting people came toward him. When it drew closer women and children were lined alongside the bulwarks of the obviously sinking vessel. Don became involved in the rescue of forty-two Vietnamese who were out of water, food, and fuel. They told him of being harrassed by armed seagoing thieves in the local area and losing the last of their money.

Pirate situations change with the political climate. Places we avoided seven years ago are now a welcome haven for cruising. We chose to avoid the Caribbean islands during the early 1970s due to political unrest in several small island countries. When we delivered a boat through the same area in 1976 our reception was delightful.

One final thought on pirates and places to avoid is that some yachtsmen have added immensely to this problem with drug smuggling. All too often we have heard firsthand reports of cruisers getting down on their luck and accepting someone's proposition to smuggle drugs. The hapless and foolish cruising man sails somewhere, picks up 2 or 2,000 kilos of drugs, then heads to a rendezvous spot. Unfortunately the unscrupulous person who financed the venture may be the very same pirate who attacks, takes the drugs, sinks the vessel, and kills the crew. As long as some yachtsmen are willing to risk their lives and vessels by getting involved with drug smuggling, certain areas of the world such as the Gulf of Thailand will be unsafe for yachts.

Petty thieves are more of a problem by far than pirates, but here a gun is even less useful and current information from other cruising people and locals is the best protection. Just as I would always lock my car in New York City, yet leave the keys right in the ignition in the village where we now live, so local information has determined our attitude toward each anchorage we've visited. In harbors such as Tangiers and Cartagena where thievery is a way of life, we'd stand an anchor watch with a high-powered flashlight close at hand. In harbors where only occasional robberies have been known to take place, we'd clear movable items off the decks, leave a radio on, and burn an oil lamp below while we went ashore so would-be visitors would think someone was on board or returning shortly. In little villages where you don't know any locals to ask, lock your dinghy and oars to a tree or lamp post so they can't be borrowed. Don't flaunt large amounts of cash or fancy jewelry in places where the locals are especially poor.

It's usually the largest boat in any anchorage that attracts robbers. They are looking for items that are easy to disguise and easy to sell. Depth sounders, outboard motors, two-way radios, cameras, and hard-to-identify, easy-to-deflate rubber dinghies are favorites. So the man on a simple small yacht with a hard dinghy is less likely to be bothered by burglars. The same holds true for drug smugglers, who are looking for large, high-powered vessels, not under-powered 30-foot sailboats.

Finally we've found cruising to be surprisingly safe. In eleven years visiting over 200 ports we've only locked *Seraffyn's* cabin two dozen times. We've only had five thefts, three of which could have been avoided. The two we could do nothing about were when first a Mexican and later a Spanish fisherman cut the painter off our dinghy when we left it on the beach unattended. In Italy we lost two sailing jackets when we carelessly left them sitting in the dinghy on the fishing dock and went into town for over four hours. In Santa Cruz harbor, California, our dinghy was tied away from *Seraffyn* on another dock and some youngster borrowed it while we were below decks. We got it back an hour later. The final theft was the only real nuisance. We'd anchored in an out-of-the-way village on the south end of Penang, Malaysia, and gone ashore for two hours just at dark. We returned to find our own dinghy had been used to take $1,000 worth of cameras, $70 worth of jewelry, and two jackets. If we'd locked either *Seraffyn* or the dinghy this wouldn't have happened. (The police recovered the cameras and my jacket.) A gun would not have prevented this incident; a bit of care would have.

In our opinion it comes to this: If you are so worried about pirates and thieves that you feel you need a gun for protection, maybe you shouldn't be out cruising. On our return to the United States we heard more stories of burglaries, shooting incidents, even boat thefts than we did while we were out cruising. We feel that cruising is far safer than living on shore. Especially if you avoid disturbed areas, use a bit of caution, and present a warm, non-gun-toting attitude toward the people whose country you've come to visit.

Update

The customs officials we met in the South Pacific say one of five non-American yachtsmen carry firearms, while four out of five American yachtsmen carry firearms. One official told us, "If you want a formidable close-range weapon, your flare pistol will legally serve the purpose, especially if it looks just like a defense weapon."

A defense specialist with the Royal Canadian Mounted Police suggests: "Keep a can of pepper gas near your bunk. Then if you hear a burglar inside your boat you can immobilize him without endangering yourself or possibly killing another human being. In a scuffle in close confines, you are just as likely to get hurt by your own gun as the thief is. Worse yet, you could accidentally kill some friend who is playing a practical joke. The pepper gas would turn the joke without having permanent effects."

During our cruise on *Taleisin*, we have visited another 35 countries, including an 18-month stay in and around South Africa. We explored by vehicle into some of the most isolated parts of Namibia and Zimbabwe and never once felt a weapon would have been useful. In fact, the only time we have been threatened by a loaded weapon was in California outside our home while we were building *Taleisin*. So our views on guns and cruising outside U.S. waters remain the same.

38

Sailing through the Red Sea

Pirates; civil wars; political unrest; head winds; gales; sandstorms; heavy shipping; currents; reefs; poor navigational aids; refraction problems; heat; *baksheesh*.

As soon as we mentioned our plans to leave the Mediterranean by way of the Suez Canal and Red Sea, most sailors we met shook their heads and warned us to reconsider. "I wouldn't worry about you so much if you had an engine," Humphrey Barton said, and he has crossed the Atlantic twenty times under sail. By the time we reached Rhodes, Greece, bound eastward, and found more warnings from friends and family in our monthly mail package, we had almost considered turning and taking the more familiar Atlantic-Caribbean route, then beating north from Panama to reach our home port on the West Coast of the United States.

Then we tied between two Australian boats in Rhodes. Both *Shikama*, a 45-foot ketch designed and built by Max and Shirley Vanderbent, and *Girl Morgan*, a 31-foot ketch built by Ross and Margaret Irvine, had sailed up the Red Sea in the spring of 1977. They were eager to trade charts and information. Everyone on both boats agreed that they'd go south through the Red Sea again, but that once was enough to travel north. And Irvine even admitted that he envied us. He liked the Red Sea. After spending some delightful mornings poring over Red Sea charts in Rhodes and later in Tel Aviv, Israel, where we met four other yachts fresh from a northbound transit, most of our concerns were laid to rest.

Pirates were the most worrisome item on the list of Red Sea dangers. Joshua Slocum chose to go around Cape Horn rather than face the Red Sea pirates. But after questioning we found only two actual cases that could positively be construed as piracy involving yachts since the Suez Canal reopened in the spring of 1975. These two stories were being repeated with endless variations throughout the Mediterranean and Far East.

One concerned the single-handed sailor who came too close to Socotra Island, whose story we told in the last chapter.

Even big ships are warned to give Socotra a 40-mile berth, and not only because of the navigational and current problems. As the *British Admiralty Pilot for the Red Sea and Gulf of Aden*, states (page 495), "Being exposed to both monsoons and having no harbors in which vessels can anchor at all times with safety, coupled with the unfavorable character the natives have hitherto borne, it is but little visited."

The second case of piracy since the Suez Canal opened, luring yachtsmen from the Indian Ocean into the Red Sea, made headlines and news broadcasts worldwide. Four young people, two of whom held South African passports, were delivering a boat from the Seychelles Islands. They took refuge behind a reef next to the coast of Somalia one evening. When they prepared to leave the next morning, the tide was down and they ran aground. Natives saw them and they were hauled off to jail; the yacht was left to destroy itself on the reef when the tide came in. The four crew subsequently spent nine months in jail and were threatened with twenty-five years imprisonment as spies. The Somolian President finally pardoned the four after much political pressure from other countries. The captain of a ship that has plied the Gulf of Aden for ten years told us one more fact about this frightening case, a fact that wasn't brought out in the new reports. The four had had the bad fortune of choosing a reef anchorage within 1 mile of Somalia's first nuclear power plant.

There is no question about it. Much of the area around the Red Sea is politically disturbed. It is dangerous for sailors even to ap-

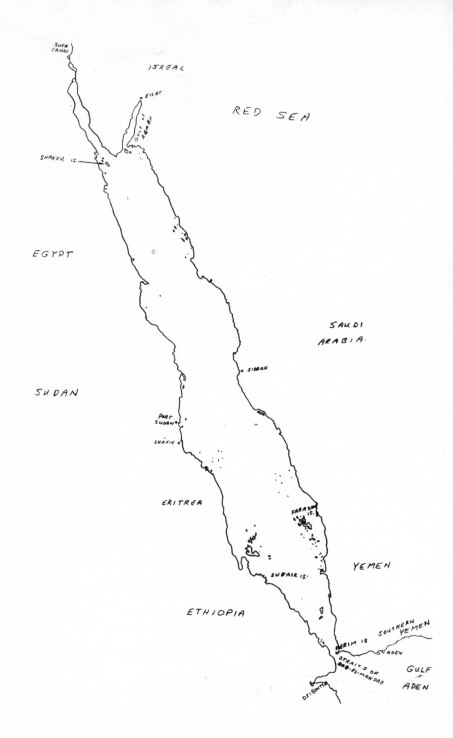

proach the coasts of Socotra, Somalia, or Ethiopia. Perim Island in the straits of Bab el Mandeb, the Farasan Islands off Saudi Arabia, and Shaker Island near Egypt have major military installations and are hostile to visitors. But the majority of ports and anchorages on the shores of the Red Sea are still usable for yachtsmen in transit. In almost every Egyptian anchorage, three or more soldiers will come on board and demand a crew list. They can be extremely annoying, as were the four who rowed out two hours after we had anchored behind a deserted-looking, sand-dune island just at the entrance to the Gulf of Suez. They were carrying two automatic rifles; the wind was at least Force 6 and their boat was an 8-foot plastic dinghy propelled by short paddles. The men spoke no English other than the word "passport." We wrote out a crew list and tried to fend off their crude oil-covered, prancing dinghy. Then they set off for shore, only to find they couldn't make headway in the choppy seas. They managed to work back to *Seraffyn's* side again and indicated they wanted us to turn on our engine and tow them closer to the shore. When we explained that we had no motor, they indicated they wished to be tied to *Seraffyn.* A few minutes later we couldn't believe our eyes when a fishing boat came past the island, and one of the soldiers tried to attract its crews' attention by firing his rifle straight at the fishing boat. Then the wind went to gale force and we spent the night with four Egyptian soldiers sleeping in our cockpit, their rifles in our quarterberth, while we lay awake listening to our anchor grumbling over the coral heads. In the morning the wind was lighter and the men left, but great gobs of crude oil from their shoes and clothes stained our decks, sheets, and topsides.

Ours was by no means an unusual encounter in Egypt. In several ports, antipersonnel bombs are thrown into the harbor every fifteen minutes throughout the night to discourage people from coming ashore. But it is a case of any port in the storm and we have heard of no major incident in an Egyptian port or anchorage. U.S. and British oil-rig supply boats in these ports are great hosts, welcoming the diversion of sailors and offering all sorts of assistance and technical advice.

All ports in Israel are available to yachtsmen and the reefs along the Sinai Peninsula offer some of the best skindiving in the world. But be sure that the Israelis don't stamp your passport. And remove all labels from any Israeli items you take on board. In all Arab ports we were asked if we'd visited Israel and before we were allowed to transit the Suez Canal we were asked to sign a release stating we had never been in Israel. No official ever inspected our stores, or even looked inside our boat, but it is wise to be prepared.

All of Sudan not only allows yachtsmen to visit, but welcomes them with open arms. Sailing behind the reefs along the coast of Sudan is one of the major joys of the Red Sea. The skindiving is fabulous and Suakin, an excellent protected harbor, is the marketplace for camel caravans that still ply the trade routes of northern Africa.

Saudi ports such as Jidda are open to yachtsmen, as are all of those on the coast of North Yemen. The Zubair Islands—with no people and no hassles—make a wonderful rest stop.

Aden and Djibouti are the only ports available in the Gulf of Aden. We chose Aden because Djibouti had just become independent and was suffering from sporadic incidents of guerrilla warfare. Aden proved friendly and safe. We did have to surrender our passports each time we went ashore, though we were given a receipt for them. And we found vegetables and eggs almost impossible to obtain. But as was true everywhere we have been, the British and U.S. employees of oil companies like British Petroleum did everything they could to help us and any other yachtsman.

Though rumor has it to the contrary, as of January, 1978, absolutely no visas were required by any of the countries bordering the Red Sea or its approaches. Sailors who have valid passports are issued landing passes when they arrive. These passes are good for an area within 5 miles of the port, and we know several yachtsmen who used their landing passes for two or three-day trips to Cairo or Alexandria with no problems at all. But if you wish to travel inland extensively, it is wise to obtain a tourist visa before you sail for Egypt.

You must have valid vaccination cards for yellow fever, cholera, and smallpox to enter Sudan or Egypt if you are coming from the east. But smallpox and yellow fever vaccinations will suffice if you are on a southbound transit from the Mediterranean.

Political situations can change quickly in this part of the world and ports welcoming us in 1977 could be closed to visitors in 1982. But information is readily available from an organized "yachtsmen's coconut telegraph." For those southbound, Ali, the helpful steward at the Port Said Yacht Club, Port Said, Egypt, maintains a scrapbook that all transiting sailors write in, giving nuggets from their Red Sea and Suez Canal experiences. Don Windsor runs a yachtsmen's reception center, 5 Closenberg Place, Magalle, Galle, Sri Lanka, and is himself a mine of information for sailors bound west and north. Both these men are receptive to questions and their mailing addresses are reliable.*

The Red Sea has an extremely regular wind pattern. Twelve months of the year, 90 percent of all winds from Port Suez to Port Sudan, the halfway mark of the red Sea, blow from the northerly quadrant. From Port Sudan south, 75 percent of all winds reported blow from the south during all months except June, July, and August, when they come from the north. But wind strength varies from month to month in the Red Sea. January is almost gale-free throughout the area and July has up to 5 percent chance of gales in the Gulf of Suez and Straits of Babel Mandeb, according to the British routing charts, *Ocean Passages for the World*, and the Red Sea pilot books. Wind records kept by oil rigs in the Gulf of Suez and compiled by Santa Fe International for an eight-year period showed the percentage of gales during July as almost double those recorded on the pilot charts. We spoke with fifteen different yachtsmen who had made the transit, north- and southbound and their experiences and ours on *Seraffyn* confirmed these wind reports. We had winds aft of the beam for all 1,300 miles of our southbound transit in late August. We did have three days of gale-force winds in the Gulf of Suez. *No Name*, a tiny engineless 24-foot U.S. trimaran sailed by Margo and Steve Wolf, needed only seventeen days to sail from Djibouti north to Port Suez during late December and early January. They never experienced winds over 25 knots and had lots of assistance from favorable currents mentioned in the pilot books. On the other hand, *Shikama*, the ketch we met in Rhodes, sailed north from

* The U.S. State Department and the British Foreign office are extremely cautious about the safety of traveling in these areas. Their information is often limited We were interviewed by one state department official seeking up-to-date reports on a troubled area. His normal sources could give him no answers. This same official told us that Yugoslavia, Poland, Turkey, and all of the Red Sea countries were on the state department's unsafe-for-tourists list in 1974 to 1977, yet we and other yachtsmen encountered no problems there.

Djibouti starting March 23, 1977, and encountered strong winds most of the way, spending three nights anchored behind a point in the Gulf of Suez while the winds blew from the north at up to 55 knots and heavy sand covered their decks to a depth of 3 inches.

One 40-foot trimaran beating up the Red Sea in early spring covered 4,400 miles to make good 1,300. Theirs was the most extreme case we heard of, but two other northbound yachts who did not use their engines reported recording 2,200 and 2,500 miles respectively on their traffrail logs to cover the distance required. Any way you slice it, a northbound trip is not easy. But choosing the right months to make the trip as *No Name* did can really help.

North- or southbound, the Red Sea can be a real test of your seamanship and navigation skills. Sandstorms can reduce visibility to less than 100 yards, though during the most favorable transit months sandstorms are not too common. Currents throughout the Red Sea are variable, especially so near the reefs. We experienced a 2-knot current setting us onto the reefs one day and none the next.

Because the Red Sea is flanked by hot deserts, a refraction phenomenon mentioned both in the pilot books and in Bowditch, *American Practical Navigator*, causes daytime sights to be in error up to 20 miles east or west. But as both books suggested, our early morning star shots proved to be right. Lights and navigation aids throughout the Red Sea, with the exception of those maintained by Sudan, are not dependable. In fact, one way to check your navigation is to use another special hazard of the Red Sea—the heavy shipping. We found that the big tankers stay right in the middle of deep water and rarely did we see less than three ships at a time during our entire thirteen-day voyage. Of course ships should serve to only confirm navigation as we saw the recently wrecked hulls of three different ships stranded on reefs along our route.

To a becalmed yacht or one beating in the confined areas of the Gulf of Suez, shipping can be a real problem. We were told second-hand of a ship that arrived in Jidda with the mast and rigging of a sailboat caught up in its bow anchor. The ship's captain was completely unaware that he'd hit a yacht until he let his anchor go and saw the wreckage.

As is always true, navigation among coral reefs must be by eyeball, with the sun behind you. So to avoid hitting newly grown coral heads or improperly charted reef spurs, you must have your anchor down two hours before dusk if you choose to go behind the reefs. This is especially important for those people who have done most of their cruising in European waters where there are no reefs and no chances to learn to judge water depth by color.

The navigational dangers of the Red Sea should not be under-rated. A beautiful 58-foot Herreshoff ketch went on a reef in the Gulf of Suez because of several of the factors we mentioned. They were northbound during March and April. It was night; winds were up to 40 knots from the north; visibility was poor; and shipping was very heavy with up to ten ships passing every hour. The owner felt he had a confirmed position because of the light he had passed and identified a few hours previously. He therefore decided to short-tack near shore, clear of the shipping lane. The ketch hit a reef and was carried onto it and stranded for over one week, suffering extensive damage. The lighthouse sequences had been changed and the ketch was really near a lighthouse 20 miles south of their assumed position.

Nowhere in the world is it so important to keep a good watch, yet the temperatures encountered during a Red Sea passage really make watchkeeping a chore. Southbound during August we had ten days of 100-plus degrees Fahrenheit, with humidity in excess of 90 percent. Even with a good breeze blowing, sleep was often difficult and during the day we were reluctant to move out of the tiny bit of shade our sun cover provided. Northbound yachts find the opposite problem. Most people who come up the Red Sea have spent a year or two at least cruising in tropical climates. As they sail north of Port Sudan, the temperatures drop to 45 degrees Fahrenheit at night. With a fresh headwind blowing, that feels darned cold. Several people we met in the Mediterranean after their northbound transit complained that after a long time in the tropics they just didn't have the heavy clothes they needed to cope with the low temperatures, especially when they were standing night watches.

Almost everyone we talked to about their Red Sea transit said that the most difficult part of it was the Suez Canal. We heard lurid stories of officials demanding *baksheesh* (bribes), tons of paperwork, overcharging, unscrupulous agents. We arrived at Port Said prepared to be calm, cool, and collected. And we found it difficult to keep our tempers, especially in the heat! Bargaining is a way of life in the eastern world and so is paperpushing. The agent suggested by the yacht club asked for $200 to arrange our transit though we knew the canal fees should have been about $50. After bargaining, we got him down to $130. But since we had to wait several days for a tow, we decided to try to clear our own papers, just as 20 percent of the other transiting yachts had done. Several had written hints and instructions for clearing in Ali's book at the Port Said Yacht Club. Judy Vaughan of *Currant Bun* had even drawn a map showing each office we'd have to visit. We walked 5 miles to visit seven different offices and the final fees came to $45 for one boat and two crew. (In 1977 if you asked permission to clear your own papers, the small-craft officer who is in charge of yacht transits would say, "You must get an agent." But if you ran around and got the proper papers, checks, and receipts, then walked into the small-craft office and announced, "I have cleared myself and want to transit tomorrow," the officials would accept the accomplished fact and would clear you through).

We saved $85 by doing our own paperwork. But we think we'd hire an agent next time around. As for baksheesh, each pilot asked us for a "gift." We gave each pilot five $1 bills, and they seemed unsatisfied but left us. There is one way to save 50 percent of the canal paperwork: clear directly for sea instead of stopping in Port Suez or Said after your canal transit. If you do stop you must go through a complete clearance procedure a second time.

The canal itself is well marked but because of constant dredging operations, the canal sides are often surprisingly steep-to. There is a shortage of pilots in the Suez Canal and, since it is unlikely that a grounded yacht will interfere with canal traffic, the authorities put fourth-grade pilots on most yachts. So it pays to have a recent chart of the canal and insist on sticking to the buoyed channel. Three yachts in convoy from the south were put aground and stuck for two days in the great Bitter Lakes in March, 1977. Their pilot had decided to take a short-cut!

Is a trip up or down the Red Sea dangerous? At the time we transited the canal, 130 yachts had been through since its reopening. Of those, only the two mentioned in our piracy section had had major people problems; two suffered major damage from going aground in the Red Sea; one was run down by a ship. A large percentage resented the hassles of dealing with Arabs because of their vastly different cultural backgrounds. Several reported annoying damage to topsides and deck work caused by Arab boathandlers who are used to big steel ships and by Arab officials wearing hard-soled, grease-covered shoes. So the Red Sea passage is definitely not to be taken lightly. But for a well-prepared yacht with sufficient crew, it is a short-cut to the Far East or Europe, depending on which way you are headed. It cuts off 8,000 miles of passagemaking around the storm- and current-ridden Cape of Good Hope, an area with few good harbors and much political unrest. For skindivers, the Red Sea holds the bonus of some of the world's finest unexplored coral reefs. The fishing throughout the Red Sea is fabulous (even *we* had good luck), and for people making the voyage in the cooler months, ports such as Suakin with its camel caravans and Jidda with its pilgrims bound for Mecca are fascinating places to visit and to explore.

Ross Irvine on *Girl Morgan* took two months to sail up the Red Sea with his wife and three young sons. Their engine didn't work from Suakin north. They anchored almost every night and wandered north behind the reefs of Sudan and Egypt, spending wonderful days with oil-rig crews from many countries. Irvine summed it up pretty well as far as a northbound passage goes: "We loved it, but you either need lots of time to sail, lots of patience, or a very big, dependable engine."

As for the southbound trip, we have heard of no yachts reporting serious difficulties, and we found it great sailing, though hot as hell. And the hassles of the canal seemed small and far away as we spent yet another day in Sri Lanka surrounded by palm trees, outrigger canoes, and beautiful sari- and sarong-wrapped people—enjoying the lowest-priced tastiest food we've ever eaten.

Update

No longer must you deny you have been to Israel in order to pass through the Suez Canal. Furthermore, clearance procedures have been simplified for canal clearance. Port facilities have improved on the Mediterranean side of the canal. The weather and navigation problems are still the same, according to reports of friends we correspond with. The Brothers Light, an important beacon near the top end of the Red Sea, is frequently off, as the United Nations no longer is fully responsible for its care. Political situations in the area are constantly changing, so check for safe ports with sources near the Red Sea when you actually get ready to make the passage.

39

Business and the Long-term Cruiser

It's a beautiful anchorage, surrounded by palm trees, fringed by coral reefs, and on shore is the largest city in the island group. In fact, the largest city within about 700 or 800 miles.

You've come here especially because you noticed your supply of traveler's checks and cash was getting low. The *Coast Pilot* for the area said this town had excellent external communications. What the pilot neglected to tell you was that the communications were excellent in 1944 but since have been completely neglected. You go ashore to the one bank in town and start a three-week ordeal of trying to get funds transferred from home.

This is no exaggeration. Jim, a friend cruising on a 40-foot yacht, spent five days sitting at the telephone exchange for hours at a stretch trying to call the United States from Horta in the Azores. Don and Heather spent four weeks waiting for the bank of Gilbralter to clear their check from Maine. Larry and I sat for seven hours at the phone exchange in Gydnia, Poland, to call Washington, D. C. Handling your financial and business matters when you are out cruising can be a real headache and should be carefully considered before you leave home.

One thing we are sure of is that you can't cruise enjoyably for long periods and still run your business back home. We've met people who try, and they are either nervous wrecks or have quit cruising prematurely.

We have met many people who close their business for a year, find a full-time manager on a profit-sharing basis, or lease the business with an option to buy. These people often enjoy cruising so much that they sell out and keep going. But if they find cruising isn't the fun they expected, they go home and build up again. One very successful sailing businessman we know put it this way; "Building a business is a full-time job. So is cruising. When I'm ready to cruise indefinitely, I'll sell out and put my money in the bank. If I want to go back into business, I'll start again. I made it once. I've learned a lot that I didn't know when I first started, so it will be easier the next time."

About half of the people we know who have been cruising for over a year own a home somewhere. Almost all of them have leased their homes through reputable agents who take a 10 or 15 percent fee for maintaining and managing the house. Other assets seem to be best put into bonds or high-interest-bearing accounts that can be handled by your bank. Speculative stocks and shares are impossible to combine with cruising. You can't have both worlds. You just have to accept the fact that long-term cruising is a way of getting out of the rat race completely or you won't enjoy it at all.

On the other hand, the other half of us who go cruising aren't fortunate enough to have these problems. We own our yachts and have some money in the bank. We earn our cruising funds as we go along. But even for us, handling business matters, mail, and money transfers can be a problem.

We've found that the very best formula for us is to outfit our boat completely and then take six months cruising funds and buy small denomination traveler's checks. I stress small denomination because we've been in places where no one in town had the money or inclination to cash a $20 traveler's check. We carry all $10 checks and don't find it much trouble to sign five at a time if necessary. We purchase half of our checks in Larry's name and the other half in mine.

That way if one or the other of us is ill or too lazy to go to town, the other can get money. Dollar checks have always served us well.

We've never been any place where the rate for dollars wasn't known. On the other hand, five years ago when the dollar was devalued, we had to wait three days before any bank would cash checks because of the scare. Now we buy two currencies to protect ourselves.

After we have bought our six-months' supply of travelers checks, we put six months more money in our checking account for which we have a check-cashing card. When we are low on funds we plan a stop at some city that has a yacht club and we ask a member to recommend a good bank. We present our check and card and wait the eight or ten days while the check is cleared. If we're terribly clever we can combine this with haul-out time so the wait goes quickly.

We have tried other ways; we wrote to our bank asking for a cashier's check to be forwarded to us in Acapulco. When we arrived two weeks later, there was no check at the Port Captain's office. We wrote to the bank. We waited. Finally two weeks later in desperation, we called the bank and asked for a new check. The second check arrived, and we proudly walked into a Mexican bank. "Sorry, we don't accept cashier's checks without a guarantor." After two days we met a Mexican gentleman who was a large shareholder in the same bank. He guaranteed the check for us. Two months later the real Port Captain of Acapulco returned to work from his holiday and forwarded our first check which he had locked in his desk for safe-keeping. Very much to our surprise and inconvenience, we found that Danish banks also won't cash cashier's or banker's trust checks.

There seems to be no easy way. To transfer large amounts of money you must be prepared to wait.

If you do want your bank to mail you a check for any reason, ask them to issue a banker's trust check guaranteed by a New York foreign exchange bank if you are American, a London bank if you are British, or a Syndey bank if you are Australian. Ask the bank to send your check to you in a plain hand-addressed envelope, i.e., no bank letterhead. Have the check wrapped in a piece of paper. Envelopes that obviously contain checks seem to disappear in the mail quite often.

One final note on getting your half-yearly supply of cash. Warn the bank you are dealing with how much in cash or traveler's checks you will be needing. In northern Mexico we arranged for a transfer with the small bank in a village. When the funds came through, the manager told us that the largest denomination bills he had were 10-peso notes (80 cents, U.S.). We walked out with two paper bags full of money. Had to clear a place in the linen locker to store it all.

A police chief in Colombia made a good suggestion. His town had a bad reputation for pickpockets, but what he said could apply to any big city. "Don't carry any more money in your wallet or pocket than you are willing to lose. Keep the rest stored carefully away in your boat. If you want to buy something very expensive, go back to your boat and get the extra money."

Handling foreign currencies is an interesting part of cruising in my opinion—pretty new bills, different exchange rates. Many banks in the United States, England, and Australia offer a good service that takes some of the pain out of your first days in a new country. They sell packets of $20 in foreign currency with a guide to the value of each coin and bill you will use. It's nice to arrive in Mexico with enough pesos to take a taxi to the Port Captain's office or buy an ice cream cone without that mad rush to find a bank first.

Credit cards have some use while cruising. With an American Express card you can get $100 cash and $400 in traveler's checks if you find an American Express office. On the other hand, unless you happen to stop in the right city, you'll get no help at all. My mother tried to cash a check against her Bank Americard when she was visiting us in Falmouth, England. She was told that Barclay's Bank in London, 250 miles away, or in Bristol, 100 miles away, would be glad to accept her check.

Paying bills by credit card means involving a third person to do your accounting at your mailing address. You must give someone power of attorney and hope they will recognize your legitimate signature should your card be stolen or lost.

A final thought on the financial end. Don't be surprised if foreign shipyards, marinas, and yacht clubs refuse to accept checks and demand advance cash payment for services. Transient yachtsmen have a very bad reputation in many places. We worked with a Costa Rican shipyard owner who had over $3,000 in bad checks from yachtsmen who had had work done and then disappeared. A Falmouth boat company said they had had about the same in bad checks and unpaid debts. Foreign yachtsmen had had work done, then sailed off at night.

Now what about getting your mail? There is only one way we have found that works. Arrange for a permanent mailing address—your parents, a bank manager, an accounting firm. Have all mail sent there no matter where you are. Ask for your mail agent to forward your mail on a specified date to a specified address, preferably a yacht club. Ask for all of it to be sent in one envelope or package. Then wait until the one package arrives. The mail slots of yacht clubs worldwide are full of old letters that missed the yacht they were intended for. How do you know how many letters to wait for unless all of your mail is in one package from one address?

We suggest yacht clubs as mailing posts because only yacht clubs are aware of the fact that yachts often arrive late. Poste Restante is good if you are sitting and waiting for your mail packet, but after thirty days your mail is returned to sender.

Very few people quit cruising because of storms, bad weather, or calms. It's the little hassles like getting phone calls through, cashing checks, or finding your mail and a hot shower that annoy you most. But then, if cruising were easy, everyone would be doing it.*

* See update on page 316.

40

The Case against the Well-planned Cruise

Cruising is for pleasure. Therefore, the large number of cruising people we have met who are not enjoying themselves presents a sad contradiction. Yes, over half of the yachts we met were inhabited by people who couldn't wait to finish their voyage or sell their boat.

In La Paz, Baja California, we saw deserted yachts rotting. In Costa Rica we saw the same. Singapore was a treasure chest of yachts for sale by disillusioned cruisers, and so on everywhere we've cruised.

Why? Cruising is a dream cherished by almost 80 percent of the people who build or purchase a yacht, according to recent surveys. What changes the dream to a nightmare?

Our private survey and observations have exposed three main reasons for an unsuccessful cruise: too large a vessel; financial difficulties; and overplanning.

The difficulties of too large a vessel are obvious—crew, maintenance, and expense. Financial problems are not so obvious. They happen when one finds living costs higher outside the United States and normal jobs are not readily available to the transient worker living on a boat. But overplanning is the hidden danger in cruising.

Where are you going? Are you headed around the world? How long will it take? A person leaving on a cruise is asked these questions a thousand times. If he is new to cruising, he tries to answer, in detail. But an experienced cruising man says merely, "I'm headed south. I've got six months free."

In preparing for a cruise, we and many of our successful cruising friends plan only to the extent of carrying all the charts of the area we expect to visit, with detail charts of all intermediate ports, food and supplies for the length of the cruise plus one-third for emergencies, and we invite people to join us *only* when we telephone or wire.

Breakdowns, bad weather, illness, and clearance problems are all schedule-ruiners. It's nerve-racking to try to meet a friend in La Paz, say, on Friday when there is no fuel in Cabo San Lucas on Wednesday and the fuel truck isn't due till Thursday morning. With no rigid dates, the humor of the manana spirit can turn a delay into a fiesta as you explore around that interesting bend on the way to the pueblo.

The most pleasant aspect of an unplanned cruise is the element of surprise that enters when you can say, "That island sure looks interesting. Let's stop." Our eleven years of cruising were made into a wonderful adventure by our unforeseen stops. One especially comes to mind. As we left the Panama Canal and visited Porto Bello, Isla Grande, and Nombre de Dios on our way toward Cartagena, Colombia, we sailed past the Archipelago de la Muletas. Larry said, "Shall we anchor for the night or press on?"

I answered, "If we get our hook down by nightfall, let's stay." We anchored at 1930, just as it became dark. We stayed almost two months in the now-famous San Blas Islands. We visited eleven of the 360 islands and made friends we'll have for life.

There are, of course, some people who just don't *enjoy* cruising once they start. After giving detailed plans to all the folks at home plus instructions for visits to dozens of friends along the way, it becomes impossible for them to turn back. The owner of one large cruising yacht who had guests scheduled for a week each for a four-month voyage through Mexico, told us his sad story. He hated cruising—couldn't sleep well, got seasick, didn't like fishing—but he said, "I can't disappoint all the people I've invited to join me. I'll just have to stick it out."

Even on a limited cruise of two to four weeks, a schedule ruins the purpose of a cruise. Cruising is an antidote to the pressures of modern life. Why bring your pressures with you? Set as your ultimate goal one-half the distance you think you can cover, and if you move quickly you'll have twice the time to enjoy the people and places along the way. If, on the other hand, you are delayed, no bother, because you've got lots of time.

And what about the guests who'd like to join you? The excitement of not knowing exactly where you will be going makes an adventure of a normal visitor's cruise. Establish an approximate port for your meeting and call the day you arrive in your meeting port. Make final arrangements then and then only, and wait for your guests. The expense of a phone call is minimal. The fun of a jeep ride from La Paz to Tres Cruses will add excitement to your visitor's arrival, and your calm, nonhassled greeting will prove that you are one who does enjoy your dream because you have learned the secret of proper, unplanned cruising.

Afterword

If you have read this book from start to finish, you are probably tired of the word *self-sufficient*. But in a way this term sums up our philosophy in life. We've found self-sufficiency offered many rewards as we sailed. We also found it had its pitfalls.

What surprises most people is that saving money is one of the lesser rewards of trying to be self-sufficient. When you simplify your sailing life so you can repair or rebuild almost everything you need on board, you'll end up with much more free time. It's amazing how long it takes to sail to the port where there's a good diesel mechanic, locate him, and arrange for the work to be done. Then there is the wait for parts to be shipped in because the supply house rarely has them on hand. It's not the least bit unusual to see cruising boats tied up for three months in steaming hot Singapore while mechanics swarm over the boat or worse yet don't show up at all.

Added to the time loss and cost is the frustration of putting up with service people who may not speak your language and definitely will not respect your boat like you do. Even more frustrating is the insecurity of knowing someone else is controlling your fate. If you are stuck in a foreign port because of some breakdown you can't repair yourself, any one of these frustrations can tip the load so you begin to wonder, "Who ever said cruising is fun?"

Once you decide for self-sufficiency you can learn to grab hold of these same problems and personally do something about them. You'll make mistakes, you'll get dirty, you may even lose money, but every time you attempt your repairs you'll learn something new. When we first decided to try recutting a staysail that flogged at the leach we proudly rehoisted the sail and found we'd sewn the tape back on too loosely. It looked like a ruffled skirt edge. So we had to remove each stitch. But this time we used a regular desk-type stapler, stapled the leach tape in place, hoisted the sail, adjusted the tape a few times, then stitched it in place. Our success on this job led to building our own 135 percent genoa from precut panels supplied by a sailmaking friend at half the cost of a finished sail.

It's this growing sense of self-confidence that makes successful offshore sailors. As you build your own boat or learn to repair it and outfit it yourself, you become aware of just how much work is involved. This leads to finding ways to prevent problems. You'll learn to change leads which cause chafe instead of constantly repairing chafe-related problems on woodwork, spars, or sails. Once you've repaired your own smashed toerail you'll learn to come alongside docks more carefully. I know I rarely learn a lesson when I pay to have my mistakes repaired. But when it's I who has to face up to the work of scraping away the damaged wood, then building up the varnish coats, I remember to be more careful about where the far end of my boat hook swings.

At the same time we've learned that everything on board except the radio and chronometer needed for navigation can be repaired by one or the other of us. Our confidence in each other has grown as our do-it-yourself approach taught us to work together and showed us just how far our own personal reserve of imagination, determination, or strength could stretch.

The people who take the time to learn sailing and all of the skills related to caring for their own boat become valuable additions to the cruising fleet. There is a worldwide shortage of skilled riggers, ships' carpenters, bosuns, mechanics, and sailmakers. So the self-sufficient sailor can be more confident of finding work as he cruises from country to country.

The pride you'll feel as your skills develop can't be easily described. The first time you sail your 6-tonner up to the dock so she stops within a foot of the cleats, the first hatch you build that doesn't leak a drop, the first repair job you successfully complete—each is a triumph that will bring a glow to your life. Eventually this self-sufficiency will grow to be a sport. You'll set new goals and reach them. Then some day there will be an ultimate test. I am convinced that to every person who goes to sea for long periods of time there comes at least one time self-sufficiency will save his life or his boat.

I feel that there are countless decisions made by confident, experienced sailors which seem small at the time but may be vital in the last analysis. Simple decisions such as keeping a night watch, changing a shroud because it looks weak, rebuilding a through-hull fitting as a matter of routine, making a second check on your navigation, or moving to a slightly different anchorage may never cause a ripple in your life. But had you not made these decisions with the subconscious knowledge gained by being self-sufficient, chain reactions could have led to grave consequences.

Of course self-sufficiency has its drawbacks. Friends will turn to you and say, "Why didn't you hire so and so. He would have saved you hours of work." Then as they watch you simplify your boat they'll call you backwards, prehistoric, a stick in the mud.

At times being self-sufficient is hard work. It's far easier to telephone your sailmaker and order a new genoa than it is to restitch all the seams on your tiny hand-operated sewing machine. It is easier to have the shipyard handle your haul-out while you simply write a check.

And finally, if things do go wrong, you have only yourself to blame. The other side of this coin, and the fact every sailor learns sooner or later, is that when you let other people do your work, things still go wrong. In the final analysis it's you who is going out to sea. No shoreside mechanic or tradesman cares as much about your boat, or your life as you do. So if your goal is enjoyable, trouble-free voyaging, self-sufficiency is the answer.

Index

Update to Chapter 15

Spars

The same method as described in this chapter can be used to make a round spar, one that will be hollow and square inside. To make the spar round instead of rectangular, all four sides would have to be the same thickness—i.e., the width of the pieces of wood used to make the side would be reduced from the dimensions shown in this chapter so the glued-up spar blank would be square inside and outside. When the corners are rounded off you have a spar that would be the ideal choice for a gaff-rigged vessel, as a hollow spar tends to be stiffer than a solid one. So there would be less tendency for the spar to bend between the gaff jaws and mast partners in a fresh breeze.

I would avoid the use of epoxy adhesives for spar building since they are not waterproof, UV-resistant, or heat-resistant. The last is probably the most serious problem, as it means the glue will start to soften at temperatures as low as 122°Fahrenheit (50°Celsius). The epoxy people call this creep. If there is any stress on the warm joint, it is likely to delaminate and fail. (See *Details of Classic Boat Construction* for more on adhesive choices.)*

When we were in Sydney, Australia, we met a New Zealand sailor who had cruised and raced the South Pacific for 12 years using a mast built from pressure-treated (tanalized) radiata pine (the same material used in construction of houses and decking onshore). This makes an affordable alternative that could be very practical, especially if you use resorcinol-type adhesives and then paint the spar white or light brown. The spar would be highly rotproof due to the treatment, waterproof because of the choice of adhesives, and easier to maintain than a varnished spar because it is painted. Reasonably clear treated pine can be found at local timber yards around the

---

* During our voyaging in Europe this year we were introduced to a newer-generation, more user-friendly resorcinol adhesive. Aerodux 500 and 501 come with a choice of three different resins to provide three different working speeds. It is a 1-to-1 resin-to-liquid-hardener mix, is gap filling, gives full-strength joints even if used in temperatures as low as 42°F (5°C), requires only close-contact clamping, and is government-tested as fully waterproof, fireproof, and UV-proof for extreme-exposure use (definitely what your mast will be facing). It costs about 50% less than most epoxies. You can order it from Dynochem (Duxford, Cambshire CB2 4QB, England, tel. 44-1223-837370, fax 44-1223-837231) or through Custom Pac Adhesives (11047 Lambs Lane, Newark, Ohio 43055; tel. 1-800-454-4583).

world. Because of its abundance, the merchant would probably let you sort through the piles to pick out pieces that have only a few small knots. Radiata pine is approximately 12% weaker than sitka spruce, so the wall thickness should be increased proportionately. There will be only a slight increase in weight in the finished spar.

If you do choose to use this method, the manufacturers of resorcinol adhesives recommend that any timber that has been treated with a preservative be machined or vigorously sanded on the surfaces that are to be bonded. The wood should also be checked for moisture content, as preservatives can increase this beyond the acceptable level of 25%. It would pay to consult the producer of the adhesive you are using before gluing up a spar out of treated timber.

Update to Chapter 19

The Self-Sufficient Sailor's Emergency Abandon-Ship Kit

During our cruising on *Taleisin,* we decided to add the following items to our abandon-ship kit:

> Two solar blankets
> 100 aspirins
> Emergency hand-operated watermaker
> An add-on flotation collar
> EPIRB

The solar blankets are not only for our protection from cold or heat but also serve as water catchments and reflectors to flash signals toward any ships passing during daylight hours. The aspirins can help alleviate the discomfort of sunburn.

In 1980 we tested various watermaking options for emergency use. These tests are described in our book, *The Capable Cruiser.* As a result of the research, we were asked to add the Pur reverse-osmosis miniature watermaker to our test program. It was just being developed. We were very impressed with the results and glad that our input helped bring the unit to the emergency-equipment market. Now these watermakers are easily available, and we carry one in *Taleisin.* A word of warning, though: The membrane on any RO unit can dry out and become unusable if it's not treated on an annual basis with the supplied solution. If this happens, replacement costs are very high.

The add-on flotation collar is simply a tube just like that on an inflatable tender. It wraps around the dinghy and, once inflated by the pump that is stored with it, makes the dinghy into a hard-bottom inflatable. Not only is this excellent for life-boat circumstances, but it makes the dinghy a super-buoyant dive tender. Details of this collar and other gear we use to turn *Taleisin*'s 8-foot Fatty Knees dinghy into a sailing lifeboat are shown in the video "Voyaging with Lin and Larry Pardey" (available from Paradise Cay Publications, 800-736-4509). Most of these inflating collars must be custom-made, but Henshaw Inflatables (Bennet Field Trade Estate, Wincanton, Somerset, BD 9DT, England) does produce some off-the-shelf for standard-length dinghies.

We now carry a class B EPIRB. With it we carry a set of replacement batteries to extend its usable working time to four days. We feel this unit is adequate for most cruising situations. We added this to our kit because it made friends and family more comfortable with our lifestyle. Furthermore, the possibility of one of us needing outside medical assistance does always exist. To eliminate the feelings of guilt that could haunt a surviving partner if they felt they had not everything possible in such a situation, we feel the $240 cost was justified. With the advent of 406 Mhz EPIRBs ($995), it is even easier to guarantee that your emergency call will be recorded and responded to quickly. But is the cost justified? We can't answer that for ourselves yet—but if it makes you and your crew feel more comfortable then it would be one of the additional items you should consider.

We do have some concerns about carrying an EPIRB—first, are we more likely to call for help instead of trying to save our ship because we have the EPIRB? With our skepticism we'd probably figure the unit wasn't working when we needed it. But we can't really answer that question without a trial we hope never comes. Secondly, there is no PAN PAN call on an EPIRB. When you push the button it is a MAYDAY. When people spend thousands of dollars and possibly put their own lives at risk to come out and rescue you, you will have a hard time saying "No thank you. I have the situation under control." Instead you may feel forced to abandon your boat even if time, innovation, or sheer hard work has stabilized the situation. We feel strongly that the EPIRB is an addition to, not a sub-

stitute for, a well-thought-out emergency kit and careful preparations before you sail, plus vigilance when you are under way.

   We made one final change in the emergency kit we carry on *Taleisin*.
When I (Lin) tried to lift *Seraffyn's* kit I often worried about its weight,
especially when I thought of handling it on a rolling deck in an emergency situation. *Taleisin's* kit weighed 14 pounds more. So we divided it into two kits—one in a red, water-resistant pack, the other in a
blue one. In the red pack we put items we'd need to survive for one to
three days if we had to abandon ship on coastal areas. This includes the
EPIRB, solar blankets, signal equipment, and Add-A-Buoy. The red
bag is kept easily available just inside the lazarette hatch even when
we are only gunkholing or doing local races. The blue bag has longer-
term offshore survival gear like the solar stills and food supplies. Both
bags are light and easy to handle, and as soon we head offshore on a
passage, both bags are stored inside the dinghy ready to go overboard
with it if we should have to abandon ship.

Update to Chapter 39

Business and the Long-Term Cruiser

A much more complete discussion of cash and cruising appears in *The
Care and Feeding of Sailing Crew,* second edition. The main differences
between our cruising days on *Seraffyn* and today on *Taleisin* are that
we now use a credit card for the majority of our day-to-day money
needs and that we have found a helpful new service available through
the U.S. post office.

   Cash advances can now be had through machines in an amazing
variety of ports. By keeping your credit-card account in credit (i.e.,
paying in advance) you avoid interest charges. But check to see that
you aren't paying a high service rate for each cash advance. Through
the Bank of New Zealand, we pay only $2 for each cash advance we
make. Some cards charge 2 percent of the total. Also, avoid using a
debit card while you cruise. As this is direct access to your private
accounts, your account could be emptied by someone who steals your
card. Although your bank will try to get the funds back when you prove
you didn't make the charges, your account will still be empty until the
searching is finished. On the other hand, with a credit card, once a dis-

pute over a transaction is established, your credit-card company cannot hold you responsible until they have investigated the matter.

The U.S. Post Office offers an excellent service if your postal forwarder is within 75 miles of an international airport. For $6.95 you can mail up to four pounds of post to any country in the world with delivery guaranteed to take less than a week. We have used this with great success over the past two years. When our forwarder find she needs to use more than one envelope for our monthly packet, she marks the packets 1 of 3, 2 of 3, 3 of 3. That way we know how many to wait for.

A final note of receiving post: With the advent of the fax machine, we find it usually works best if we sail to some place where we intend to stay a week or two, find a good local address—a club, a friendly hotel or business, and then fax the information to our forwarder. We then settle in to do the work we came to do, or sail away to some of the other local anchorages and come back a week later to have our post waiting for us.

Useful Addresses

Oil lamps for navigation and cabin use are available from
Den Haan - DHR lamps
Wijnhaven 81
3011 WK
Rotterdam, Holland
North American supplier of running lamps - Traditional Marine
P.O. Box 268
Annapolis Royal, Nova Scotia, Canada B0S 1A0

From U.S. call 1-800-363-2628
          or   902-532-2762
        FAX   902-532-7013

Nauticalia Oil Lamps
Ferry Lane
Shepperton on Thames
Middlesex TW17 9LQ England ph. 44-1932-244936

West Marine Supplies
500 Westridge Dr.
Watsonville, CA 95076 ph. (408)728-2700

Note—although oil running lamps are not coastguard approved, they are still definitely legal as long as they meet Col-reg requirements, i.e. they must be visible at a certain distance. Coastguard aproval means only that a certain item, and certain brand has been tested by them. Although several electrical fixture companies have submitted their gear for testing, oil lamp manufacturers have not.